Their Finest Hour

Master Therapists Share Their Greatest Success Stories

Jeffrey Kottler
California State University–Fullerton

Jon Carlson
Governors State University

Boston ■ New York ■ San Francisco
Mexico City ■ Montreal ■ Toronto ■ London ■ Madrid ■ Munich ■ Paris
Hong Kong ■ Singapore ■ Tokyo ■ Cape Town ■ Sydney

Executive Editor: *Virginia Lanigan*
Series Editorial Assistant: *Scott Blaszak*
Executive Marketing Manager: *Amy Cronin Jordan*
Editorial-Production Service: *Omegatype Typography, Inc.*
Composition and Prepress Buyer: *Linda Cox*
Manufacturing Buyer: *Andrew Turso*
Cover Administrator: *Joel Gendron*
Electronic Composition: *Omegatype Typography, Inc.*

For related titles and support materials, visit our online catalog
at www.ablongman.com.

To obtain permission(s) to use material from this work, please submit a written
request to Allyn and Bacon, Permissions Department, 75 Arlington Street, Boston,
MA 02116 or fax your request to 617-848-7320.

Library of Congress Cataloging-in-Publication Data

Kottler, Jeffrey, A.
    Their finest hour : master therapists share their greatest success stories /
Jeffrey Kottler, Jon Carlson.
        p. cm.
    ISBN 0-205-43003-1 (alk. paper)
    1. Psychotherapy—Popular works.   2. Psychotherapy—Case studies.   I.
Carlson, Jon.   II. Title.

RC480.515.K686   2005
616.89'0092'2—dc22

                                                                        2004052846

Printed in the United States of America

10 9 8 7 6 5 4 3 2 1   09 08 07 06 05 04

The authors and the publisher would like to caution readers about the graphic
subject matter and language within some of the chapters, especially within
quoted materials. Changing such subject matter and language would have
resulted in a lack of authenticity.

CONTENTS

CHAPTER

1

The Finest Hours

We have each spent our lives doing therapy and trying to make sense of how and why it works. Between us, we have written seventy-five books on the subject, covering almost every facet of this mysterious process imaginable. That is not to say that we can say with confidence that we do know what it is about therapy that is most beneficial, but we can speak with authority about its most salient features.

In our research, we have had the privilege of interviewing hundreds of the greatest therapists who have lived during the past century. We have talked to them about their careers, filmed them demonstrating their theories in action, and interviewed them extensively about what they did in these cases and why they chose those particular paths. We have also had the opportunity to interview dozens of the most famous therapists about the worst session they ever had and what they learned from it (reported in our book, *Bad Therapy*), as well as the most bizarre or unusual case they have ever seen (reported in *The Mummy at the Dining Room Table*). During these quite intimate conversations, we became hooked by the drama, the pure magic, the stunning brilliance of these stories that highlight human transformation during times of adversity. We were struck not only by the changes that took place in the clients in these seminal cases, but also how these greatest minds of our profession were also affected by these relationships.

There have been some excellent books in the past about the most interesting and seminal cases of psychotherapy, but never have the greatest successes of the most accomplished theoreticians been assembled in one volume, and told in their own words. *Their Finest Hour* brings together two dozen of the greatest living therapists, who tell the stories of their best work, however that may be defined. We chose these particular theoreticians not only because of their professional reputations and stature, but also because they are such great storytellers. We wanted to write about those "finest hours" that best lend themselves to a good read, as well as providing important lessons on living life to the fullest.

All of the therapists we interviewed faced the challenge of deciding what constitutes great therapy. If a client improves in a single session, but the therapist had little to do with the improvement, is that one's finest hour?

Likewise, there are times when a clinician engages in some masterful intervention, or builds a fabulous relationship with a client or family, but there is no discernable progress even after months or years of treatment. And then there are those times when you *know* you have done a fine piece of work that has made a huge difference in a person's life, but the changes won't be acknowledged. Another variation on this confusing theme is when a client claims that vast improvement has occurred—thank you very much for your tremendous effort—but neither you nor anyone else can see a whit of difference. This is one reason why it is so difficult for us to research the outcomes of our efforts, much less to choose what we believe are the best examples of our work.

To make matters still more complicated, we are not altogether certain how therapy works in the first place. That is one reason why there are so many schools of thought, many of them represented in the chapters of this book. Each of us has distinct notions of what is most important in a therapeutic relationship and what the ideal role is that a therapist should take in promoting changes. Cognitive therapists (such as Arnold Lazarus and Albert Ellis) believe that the main focus of our efforts should be on changing the ways people think and talk to themselves, and that this will lead to subsequent changes in feelings and behavior. Psychoanalysts (such as David Scharff) believe that the past shapes present issues and that until we resolve those underlying struggles, people are doomed to repeat their dysfunctional actions. Adlerians (such as Jon Carlson) take a more integrative approach, one that looks at family constellations and family-of-origin issues. Existentialists (such as Jeffrey Kottler and Alvin Mahrer) focus on helping people to find greater meaning in their lives. Constructivists (such as Robert Neimeyer, Stephen Madigan, and Michael Mahoney) seek to help people to re-story their lives, creating new narratives that are more self-enhancing and self-empowering. Ericksonians (such as Steve Lankton) downplay theory altogether and instead concentrate on innovative interventions that disrupt current dysfunctional plans and substitute alternatives. And this is just a sampling of the ideas represented in this book and in the profession!

In spite of the incredible diversity in approaches to therapy, there is some consensus about what tends to work best. A solid relationship needs to be developed, one that is trusting and collaborative. Clients are taught new ways of viewing their problems, especially alternatives that create more hope and possibilities. They are further offered the support and guidance they need to try new things and practice them in their lives. Most practitioners spend some amount of time working on developing greater self-awareness and insight, although this type of work takes many different forms (focusing on the past or present, thoughts or feelings, individual or family dynamics, and so on). Hope and faith play a big role in what all therapists do: instilling a strong belief that change is indeed possible. Finally, all therapists do "stuff." They have their favorite interventions and strategies, and while these may look different and have varied goals, they do essentially the same things, which are to get people to stop doing things that are not working and try other things that work much better.

This is a gross simplification, of course, but one of the things that is so amazing about the therapy profession is the different forms it appears to take and yet still produce positive effects. And make no mistake: therapy does help people most of the time. Some of these individuals might very well have improved anyway, but they would not have done so as quickly, nor would they have learned the lessons that go with this type of growth.

Although you will see many types of therapy described in this book, and cases of miraculous cures, the routes taken on these journeys are as different as the individuals. That is probably no different than the way people approach their work in your own chosen field.

In spite of the variety of approaches represented in this book, as well as the diversity of cases described, all the contributors were asked essentially the same questions, to use as a basic structure. First, we asked them which case came to mind that represents their best piece of work. We encouraged them to tell the story of what happened in this ground-breaking episode, followed by queries about their own understanding of why things unfolded the way they did. This will give you a unique window through which to view the way each prominent therapist thinks about his or her work and makes sense of the world. Finally, we asked about what could be learned from this situation that might be useful to others. We are not just speaking about other therapists, but what *anyone* can draw from this case that might help him or her to initiate more powerful and lasting changes in his or her own life.

Each of the interviews was recorded and then transcribed, then written by Jeffrey into narrative prose, including re-created dialogue that was based on case notes and recordings. We sent each chapter to the contributor to check for accuracy, and in some cases, to fill in further details. The contributors also worked to disguise further any identifying features of the clients.

We will talk to you again at the end of our journey, after you have had a chance to enjoy these therapeutic tales and the wisdom they contain. At that point, we will revisit the central themes of the stories and what they have to offer us as object lessons for how change best takes place. In the meantime, fasten your seatbelt and be prepared to alter your views of what therapy is all about and how it really works. In the stories that follow, you will have the opportunity to observe the most accomplished therapists in the world work their magic with some of their most challenging and yet rewarding cases.

2

The Ball,
the Snowflakes,
and the Wheelchair

Cases from Jeffrey Kottler

Jeffrey Kottler has been a leader in humanistic and experientially based therapies, devising an approach that is highly pragmatic and integrative, including features of a dozen other models. In his dozens of books about the therapeutic process, and the therapist's experience, he emphasizes the power of personal contact and caring. He uses creativity and humor to help clients take risks and challenge themselves in new ways. He likens the role of the therapist to that of a "travel agent," whose main jobs are to help structure and guide transformative journeys.

Some of his most highly regarded works include On Being a Therapist, The Imperfect Therapist, Compassionate Therapy, Finding Your Way as a Counselor, *and* Making Changes Last. *He has also written several highly successful books for the lay public that describe rather complex phenomena in highly accessible prose (*Beyond Blame, Travel That Can Change Your Life, Private Moments, Secret Selves, The Language of Tears, *and* The Last Victim: Inside the Minds of Serial Killers*). Jeffrey has collaborated with Jon Carlson on a number of other projects:* Bad Therapy, The Mummy at the Dining Room Table, *and* An American Shaman.

Jeffrey has been an educator for twenty-five years. He has worked as a teacher, counselor, and therapist in preschool, middle school, mental health center, crisis center, university, community college, and private practice settings. He has served as a Fulbright Scholar and Senior Lecturer in Peru (1980) and Iceland (2000), as well as worked as a Visiting Professor in New Zealand, Australia, Hong Kong, Singapore, and Nepal. Jeffrey is Chair of the Counseling Department at California State University, Fullerton.

A Dying Breath

It has been said that when people are about to take their last, dying breaths, they see their lives pass before their eyes. I imagine that such a stream of images would include snapshots of faces more than flashes of landscape or objects, but perhaps that reflects my own priorities. I would also guess that many therapists would see the faces of their clients among their loved ones as their last memories on this earth. I know that would be true for me.

Like most of the contributors to this book, I have seen and helped thousands of people over the years. If I add to this list those I reached through the media and writings, it is staggering to consider that the potential audience is well into the millions. Of course, I have never met most of these people, nor will I ever hear any indication, one way or the other, about how I was helpful to them. It was my clients, however, whom I will most remember. And if I am granted moments of reflection before I take my last breath, I'm certain some of their faces will pass before my eyes.

Breaking the Cardinal Rule

It is interesting to consider which clients we most remember and others we have long forgotten. I remember some of my finest hours, but also some of my most trying sessions and challenging cases (but that was the story of another book). Foremost, I will never forget the single session of therapy I did with a couple from India.

"How might I help you both?" I addressed the couple in my most earnest voice. The husband, an immaculately dressed physician, spoke in clipped, regal sentences, emphasizing his British accent. The wife, dressed in a traditional sari, remained quiet while he did all of the talking.

"My wife," he said, gesturing toward his wife who sat placidly, "she wants to work."

"I see," I said, not seeing at all.

"We do not do this sort of thing in my family. Women are supposed to stay home and raise a family."

"And how do you feel about this?" I addressed the wife.

Before she could answer, the husband chimed in on her behalf and said that she would like to work but he still felt this would dishonor his family. "It would tell all our people back home that I am not capable of taking care of her."

I understand that there were some complex cultural dimensions to this story. Apart from my own biases in favor of greater equality among men and women, and the cultural norms of our community, I understood that they had been raised in a very different milieu. Still, I was annoyed by his controlling behavior, and perhaps that was revealed in the impatience of my next question.

"So, what do you want from me?" I asked.

The good doctor nodded, pleased that we had gotten to the heart of the matter. He looked very busy and preoccupied, ready to get back to the hospital and continue his work. "Well," he said, "we are now living in a different country, a place where you have very different rules for this sort of thing." He said this distastefully, clearly indicating that he did not agree with these lax standards.

"That is true," I agreed with him. I was still uncomfortable that we were talking about his wife as if she was invisible. So I turned to her again: "I'd like to hear from you, Mrs. Vejay. How do you feel about this?"

She looked at her husband for permission to answer me, but he just stared straight ahead. She presumed this was a sort of tacit permission. "It is true," she said, "I would like to work. As yet, we have no children. I am so far away from my family and my parents and my friends back in India. I do not like staying at home all day. I want to do something else. I see all the women here, in this country, have jobs. I would like to work as well."

I was nodding my head in agreement all throughout her brief statement, then caught myself. "Thank you, Mrs. Vejay. So if I understand this situation, the main problem that you would like assistance with is related to whether you should be able to work or not. Doctor, you would rather she didn't, and Mrs. Vejay, you would very much like to do so."

"That is correct," the husband agreed.

"Okay," I said, still confused about what they wanted from me. "How can I help?"

The doctor looked at me as if the answer to that question was rather obvious. "Well, we would like you to tell us what to do."

"You want me to tell you whether your wife should be allowed to work or not?"

He nodded solemnly.

"So, if I tell you that your wife should work, then you'd agree to let her do so?"

Again he nodded.

"And if I say no, then she doesn't work?" This time I looked toward the wife, who also nodded her head.

I could feel the panic start to well up in me. I knew that giving such advice was absolutely the worst thing I could do. I rehearsed in my head just how I would tell them that I—or any therapist—does not give advice in this way or make decisions for people. Instead I would help them sort things out for themselves, explore the relevant issues, and negotiate a mutually acceptable solution. That's what I was thinking. But it certainly was not what I actually did. And even now I don't know whether to feel proud, or ashamed, of my intervention.

Maybe I responded as I did because people rarely listen to me, even when they do ask my advice. Perhaps I was just appalled at the doctor's sexist, controlling attitude and I wanted to annoy him. I'd like to think I was responding in a culturally appropriate way when I chose to do exactly what they asked of me: "Okay then, if what you want me to do is to tell you whether your wife should work or not, I think that decision should be left up to her. That is the way we often do things in this country. But still, I understand that in your . . . "

"So," he interrupted, "you are saying that she should work?"

I was visibly sweating now. I'd just broken a cardinal rule and I was trying to figure out how to get myself out of this advice-giving fix. "Well, I was trying. . . ." Then I just stopped. I looked him right in the eyes and nodded my head firmly, definitely. "Yes," I said, "if that is what you are asking me, then I think that is perfectly okay."

"Thank you," he answered. "Well then, I think we are done here." He looked at his wife, indicating it was now time to leave.

"That's it?"

"Yes sir," he said in a calm voice. I was pleased he didn't seem visibly angry. "That is all we wanted to know."

Indeed the couple left the office, and unless it was my imagination, they seemed quite affectionate and relieved. Because I was concerned about what damage I might have done unwittingly, giving in to my impatience rather than taking the time to help them figure out things for themselves, I followed up with the couple a few weeks later. The husband answered the phone and reported that his wife had found a job and was now working 20 hours per week. He seemed fine with that, thanked me politely for all my help, and promised to contact me again if they ever needed more help.

Well, this was hardly my finest hour of therapy, even if the outcome was so spectacularly positive from the point of view of the couple. But I cite this as one example of faces I will never forget. There are others of course—many other successful cases that turned out quite well as a direct or indirect result of my interventions. But I would rather not talk about any of these.

■   ■   ■

Successes and Failures

It is curious to me that it is a lot easier to remember the worst representatives of my work rather than the best examples. It is not that I've rarely helped anyone—just that once a case is completed, I tend to move on to the next challenge rather than dwell on what happened. For me, therapy often feels like magic, beyond my comprehension. Whenever someone makes a dramatic breakthrough, I sit in awe at what transpired yet feel reluctant to analyze what happened lest the illusion fall apart. I also wonder if whatever role I played in the transformation will desert me next time. Maybe I've lost my healing magic. Maybe what I have, or whatever I can do, won't last.

This is not good science. Everything that I've learned (or at least been trained in) has encouraged me to measure the impact of my work, assess the outcomes, analyze what happened and why, so that I might more reliably work skillfully in the future. If I don't know what I do, and what effects such actions have on others, how can I duplicate my actions next time?

Although I know that I am supposed to spend considerable reflective time deconstructing the successes of the work (notice the absence of the possessive pronoun, "my," since they don't feel like they were mine), there are always another half-dozen people around who appear to be stuck no matter what I do to try and help. There is precious little time to think about the glorious victories (and it does somehow feel like a war at times) when the battlefield is littered with failures. And make no mistake: while I am reluctant to accept much responsibility for the major breakthroughs that take place, that is certainly not the case with respect to the failures.

I should know better by now. I teach my students and supervisees to process negative outcomes in more constructive ways than I handle them. But the fact remains that I can name at least a dozen things I did wrong before I list something I did right. And this isn't at all because I'm a bumbling, ineffectual idiot, but because I seem to learn more from my mistakes than I do when things go according to plan.

It is not that I can't think of many people I helped, because I am darn good at what I do. I listen well. I hear and see and sense things that are beyond the awareness of most other folks. I am good at explaining complex things in comprehensible language. I know how to confront people sensitively, and bring their attention to things they'd rather ignore or avoid. I feel a lot of love and compassion toward others—I care a lot—and I seem to be effective at communicating this consistently. I'm a genuinely nice person and I work hard at treating others with respect. I'm a good talker (and writer)—persuasive, clear, and honest. I'm flexible, creative, inventive, curious; I'm playful too and like to have fun. For all these reasons, I help people—whether students, clients, supervisees, or colleagues—most of the time. And after each happy customer who leaves my office, I immediately turn my attention to the next dissatisfied soul who requires assistance.

The Ball

It was the giggling that hooked me. I looked up from my comfortable seat, my feet propped up on the table, and creaked up into my standing position. My muscles ached and I was almost certain I had pulled something. I could breathe only with difficulty since the altitude was well over 13,000 feet. I was trekking in the Himalayas, in the Langtang region that straddles the Tibetan border. I had already spent a week on the trail, climbing steadily higher, but this was the toughest day so far. There were vertical peaks on all sides, snowcapped mountains that were covered in spring wildflowers. I was racing to beat the monsoon, covering distances that were probably beyond what was reasonable. That's why I was winded and weary (that and the fact that I'm getting old).

I had given a lot of thought to planning this trip. I had not only plotted my itinerary but had given considerable thought to each item I had brought with me; I wanted to keep the weight down.

Having spent a lot of time in remote places, I like to bring gifts with me when I travel. I'm careful about my choices, wanting to be culturally sensitive and yet true to my own convictions. For instance, when visiting a hunting village in East Greenland, I was told to bring cigarettes to show appreciation to people who were nice to me. I couldn't quite bring myself to do that, instead bringing a few Frisbees for the children. But I wondered if I had actually changed the culture of these people by introducing this foreign flying object to their play; prior to my arrival the kids seemed to delight in throwing snowballs at one another; now they had Frisbees to fight over. So I've learned to be careful about such things.

Friends who had visited Nepal warned me not to take gifts at all. They said that the people in the mountains were gracious and hospitable without any external rewards, and it was best not to "ruin" them with material temptations that might encourage them to beg from others. This made sense, but nevertheless, I stuck one thing in my pack. More about that later.

There was something irresistible in the children's laughter. As I said, I was resting at a stop for travelers, a modest stone dwelling with thatched roof and a fire to heat up tea and yak milk. The plot of land was no bigger than a football field, and it was the only level ground for miles in any direction; the drop-offs were steep and endless. So this family of a husband, wife, and two kids had settled themselves on this habitable horizontal space in a totally vertical universe.

The kids looked to be about 4 and 6 years old and they were positively adorable. They were playing soccer with a deflated ball, their only toy, it seemed. In between kicks and giggles, they flirted shyly with me, glancing at me only when they thought I was not noticing. Their father was pounding rock into smaller stones, which he would later smash into gravel that could then be mixed into concrete. Their mother was standing over the clay oven, baking fresh bread to serve with my tea. And the kids were thoroughly entertained by their deflated ball, delighting in the idea that they had an audience to watch their play. Soon, their crowd was about to join them in the game.

I stood up on creaky legs and immediately the youngest boy, the 4-year-old, kicked it my way before falling on his butt. His brother giggled and ran over to help the little guy up; he started laughing too.

So for the next few minutes we had a little game of international soccer, Nepal against the United States. The score may have been tied, or perhaps one of us was winning—it was hard to tell since we didn't have any goals, we didn't keep score, and the little boy kept changing sides when he felt like it. Their parents watched us while baking and pounding rocks, grins on their faces. I can't recall ever having so much fun playing soccer (but then, I never liked the game much).

As things proceeded, the 4-year-old became more competitive with his older brother. He took a mighty kick at the ball, this time managing to remain on his feet. But to our collective horror, the ball took flight off to one side and sailed over the edge into the abyss. I must say the kick was quite a powerful effort, even if it was in a wayward direction.

The two boys ran to the edge of the world, staring off into the clouds below where the ball had now vanished. For all I know, it may still be falling.

We all just stared off into the edge, motionless. I don't know what we were waiting for. Maybe expecting that someone "down there" would kick the ball back up to us on the top of the world? Maybe that the ball had landed on a ledge below so that we might retrieve it? It was not to be: the ball was gone forever.

Both boys turned around in absolute dejection. This was their only toy in the world, their most cherished object. They lived in a place so remote that it took 4 days' walk just to get to a road, where a bus might take 12 hours to take them to the nearest city. The children had no friends on this mountain except one another. They had only the ball to play with, even if it had been deflated and worn.

The smallest boy looked up at me helplessly and started crying. Then his brother started in; they were both heartbroken. Even their parents looked as deflated as the ball had been.

I signaled to both boys and called them over to me. They ignored me first, lost in their own grief, but when I repeatedly gestured for them to join me, they inched a bit closer. They had been doing just fine before I arrived; maybe they held me responsible for their misfortune.

The 4-year-old came over to me cautiously, then learned against me for comfort. I pointed to my bag and gestured for him to watch what I was doing. Now curious, his brother joined us. I reached inside my bag and felt all around along the bottom, searching for something that I had stored away. I now had the kids' full attention. Then I pulled out my hand and out came a ball, the only thing that I had brought with me as a gift. I formally presented it to the youngest boy, nodded thanks to the parents for the meal, and then turned and started to walk down the mountain. When I looked back over my shoulder, I saw both boys peering over the edge of the cliff, watching me descend toward the valley floor. I waved to them, but they seemed spellbound that this stranger should appear out of nowhere, offer them the one thing they needed most, and then disappear into the clouds.

■   ■   ■

Feeling Useful

I've been doing therapy for 25 years and seen thousands of people in my office. As I mentioned, because I'm pretty good at what I do, most of them left my services far better off than when they first came in. So then: why are the examples that come most vividly to mind those that involved children on the street? In another case that follows, you will see that these children were not clients of mine, nor did I ever learn their names or see them after a single encounter. Yet I am still haunted by our interactions. And I have never felt more useful in my life.

Feeling useful is an important theme for me. I grew up feeling pretty powerless as a kid. In baseball I was always stuck in right field, bored out of my mind because nothing ever happened out there, and yet terrified that someone might hit a ball to me which I would promptly drop. It wasn't until years later that I learned that I needed glasses, that the world always looked blurry to me, but for some reason I still cannot understand, my parents never had my eyes checked. I remember memorizing the eye chart in the school nurse's office because not being able to see was just another way that I felt inadequate. It also explained why I didn't do so well in school, since I could never see what the teachers would write on the board. Whenever I was called up to point out the object of a sentence, or to balance both sides of an equation (tasks that still seem pointless to me), I would stand up there just as lost and clueless as when I had wandered right field. It was as if I was seeing those scribblings on the board for the first time—which was true!

Since I was neither a good student nor a good athlete, one would think I might find solace in some other pursuit, but truthfully, I wasn't very good at anything except building model airplanes (and even then I don't think I was so much good as persistent).

To make matters worse, my home life sucked. My mother and father hated one another, or at least they didn't like spending time together. My mother was often drunk and my father was often gone somewhere gambling, playing golf, or chasing women. Needless to say, I didn't feel very useful to anyone, least of all myself.

Ever since I can remember, I wanted to do something with my life that might be useful to others. Maybe I wouldn't feel so helpless. Maybe all the pain and anguish I went through might have been for some purpose, even if that was only to help me to understand what others live through. Anyway, I walk through life looking for opportunities to be helpful to others.

I used to have an office at the university along a hallway that became congested during class changes. My neighbors on both sides were always complaining about the interruptions when lost students would peek in the door and ask directions to a particular part of the building. They would close their doors and pretend they weren't in, so they could get their important work done. Me? I *liked* being asked directions: it made me feel useful. So much of what I do as a therapist and a teacher results in ambiguous outcomes—I'm not often sure if I've helped someone, if I was useful, if I made some kind of difference. I've learned over time that the ones I think I've helped may only be faking, or their changes may be intermittent and impermanent. And it sometimes takes so darn long to have a significant impact.

But giving directions? I loved it! I took great pride in giving precise instructions to people in need. First I would invite them into my office in the most reassuring way possible. "No problem," I would say, "that's a hard room to find. Most people have trouble locating it." Then, after validating their experience, letting them know they were not alone in their struggle, I might reflect a few of their feelings, just to let them know that I fully understood the depth of confusion. "It's pretty frustrating," I'd say in my most empathic tone, "not being able to find your way."

The students would look at me suspiciously and start to edge toward the door. They were not used to this kind of solicitude and attention—and besides, this was taking far too long.

Once I let them know they'd been heard and understood, then I would give them quite detailed directions to their destinations.

"Room 313 is a little tricky," I'd reassure them. "When you get to the end of the hall, you make a left—it's the only way you can go. By the way, you'll notice a particularly attractive bulletin board on that corner that you might want to check out—another professor on the floor designed it and it's one of the best."

The student's eyes would start to glaze over and he might begin to head off, but I'd quickly finish, being so sensitive to his needs.

"Okay then, you make a left at the end of the hall, pass the drinking fountain—very cold water by the way and excellent vertical lift of the stream of water—then you get to the tricky part because the room numbers are not actually in sequence."

And so it would go, and I would spend the better part of 5 minutes helping the student when it would have been just as easy to point impatiently to the left as my colleagues would do. But I felt so useful under these circumstances. It felt like I was really helping someone. With my clients, I can never be certain if I am getting them to their destinations, but when giving directions I can be pretty sure that I am effective in my job. I even used to like to do follow-up if I ever saw the student again. I'd yell out to him, "By the way, did you get to your room okay?" Of course, the student would tuck his head and move away from me. But that was probably because he was so grateful for my assistance. He probably didn't want to take up any more of my valuable time.

Where was I? Oh yeah, I was telling you about why it's important that I feel useful. And why the instances of helping that most stand out for me are those that took place with strangers rather than clients. As you'll see, both of these cases have similar features in that, just like giving someone directions, it was an instance of a single-session intervention that had clear, constructive outcomes—the problem was solved.

An Angel on the Curb

I was walking along the street, not far from my home, when a blur of movement caught my attention. Then I heard sounds, loud cries actually.

"Baby, baby, . . . , Baby."

It was some kind of chant. A girl's high-pitched voice. I lost the part in the middle, but she seemed to be saying "baby" in that familiar, teasing tone common to children who sense they have gotten underneath someone else's skin.

Sure enough, I looked down the block to see a taller girl standing over a smaller boy who was sitting on the curb crying. The boy's head was tucked between his knees and his hands covered the back of his neck, as if he was protecting himself from a further assault. The girl just stood over him, repeating her chant, "Baby. Baby." With no response from him, except for a few pitiful sobs, she kicked his foot in disgust and walked a few feet away.

As I hurried closer to the scene, I noticed there were papers scattered all over the sidewalk and street like huge snowflakes. There was a backpack lying open in the street; it had been run over a few times by some passing cars.

Just as I reached the boy, a bus pulled up to what I now realized was a school bus stop. The girl climbed on the bus without even a glance backward, and the vehicle pulled away. The boy still sat on the curb, his head buried in his lap. He was crying even louder now that his nemesis was no longer around.

"Hey there," I said to the boy, sitting down on the curb next to him. He jerked in a startle response, looked up at me from underneath his arm, and then continued crying.

"You had a bit of trouble, huh?" I said.

The little head nodded.

"That girl looked pretty tough," I ventured. "Big too. I guess she was giving you a hard time."

Nod of the head, more pronounced this time.

"Come on," I said in a cheerful voice, as if I came upon scenes like this all the time. "Let's pick up your papers before they blow away."

The boy looked up at me and presented the most beautiful smile I had ever seen, and perhaps ever will see again. It felt like I was an angel who had been sent to right this wrong.

We spent a few minutes retrieving his schoolwork and stuffing it back into his bag. The boy got a special kick out of our joint effort when I went out into the street and stopped traffic so he could collect the papers that were lying in harm's way.

"So, when's the next bus?" I asked him as we resettled ourselves on the curb.

"I don't know," he shrugged. "Maybe a few minutes."

"Mind if I wait with you until it comes? Just to keep you company?"

The boy looked at me shyly and smiled. So we sat on the curb together and chatted. He told me that the girl was a bully who was constantly bothering the little kids. Usually she picked on someone else, but that person must have gotten a ride that day, because the boy was the only victim available.

I never learned the boy's name, never saw him again. But I'll never forget watching the bus pull away and seeing his face through the window. He was still looking at me with awe, uncertain if I was real, or just an angel who had swooped down out of the clouds.

A Kiss on the Forehead

Now, why do I think of this as my finest hour as a helper? It was such a simple interaction. Someone in need. I was at the right place at the right time. I listened a little, offered some reassurance and support. I helped pick up his papers. I sat with him on the curb. Anyone could have done the same thing. No special training needed. But it still got me thinking a lot about why I do the work I do, and what I get out of it. It is all about that smile.

It was not too long after that, another place and another time, that I was driving down the street and caught some movement out of my peripheral vision. I don't know why I noticed the motion, perhaps it was a flash of light, or something odd that didn't seem to fit with the surroundings. For some reason, I sensed trouble even though, driving by at 45 miles per hour, I only caught the barest glance of something out of place.

I pulled over on to the gravel at the side of the road and started to back the car up to the spot where I thought I had seen the erratic movement. This was in a rural area, and there was a large field with knee-high grass or weeds or even alfalfa or something (I wouldn't know the difference). I looked out the window, and sure enough, there was someone out there, someone sitting in a chair. But it was the strangest thing—the chair seemed to be moving back and forth. I had to get out to investigate.

Once I opened the door and stood up, I could see that there was someone sitting in a wheelchair, moving back and forth, jerking sporadically. What was he or she doing in the middle of the field, I wondered? Probably none of my business, I thought and started to duck back into the car. But what if the person was in trouble? What if he or she needed help? I thought about that little boy on the curb and wondered if this was another opportunity to be of some use.

I waded through the brush to approach the person and could see immediately that it was a child, a girl actually. She was in one of those motorized wheelchairs that are operated with a toggle switch at the controls.

"Can I help you?" I called out.

"Grrrrrrr. Mnnnnnnno."

"Excuse me?" I tried again. "I was wondering if you needed any help? I was just. . . ."

"Frnnnnn. Mnnnnnnno."

Was this some kind of joke? Was she putting me on? Why was she talking in nonsense?

I approached a little closer and the girl started to make this unearthly, gutteral wail. I could see now that she was severely disabled. Her body was small for the size of her head, the feet and hands curled in. The features on her face were contorted as well, as if she had no control to direct any aspect of herself. Then I noticed that two of the fingers on her left hand seemed to be trying to work the control on the wheelchair, but it seemed bogged down in the weeds and mud.

I looked around for help but there was nobody else around. Then I looked to see where she had come from, or where she was going to, but there appeared nothing else in sight; it was as if she had dropped out of the sky.

I started to panic because the sounds the girl was making were so disturbing, so unlike a human voice. The electric wheelchair was still rocking back and forth, just like a car stuck in a snowbank. Her two fingers were moving back and forth. And she was still making that high-pitched growling sound. There was a part of me that wanted to run away.

I moved in front of the girl and kneeled down in the weeds. "I want to help you," I said in a voice louder than necessary, but it was hard to talk over the whirring of the chair's motor. "Could you stop doing that for a moment?" I gently touched her fingers with my hand and she pulled them away as if scalded. At least the noise stopped.

"Can you tell me where you came from?" I asked her. "Or where you want to go?"

The girl started making sounds but they resembled no language I could understand. Apparently she was trying to talk to me, but I had no idea what she was saying.

"Where do you live?" I said, more slowly this time. I felt like an idiot because the problem was not my making myself understood but trying to figure out what she was saying.

We just stared at one another for a minute, just looked into one another's eyes. I don't know about the girl, but it felt like we were willing ourselves to communicate. Then she started wailing again. And this time she was scared, really, really scared.

I looked around again for help. How could this girl be alone like this? How could she be stuck in the middle of a field? How the hell did she get here?

I sat down on the ground at her feet and tried to calm her down. No, that's not quite right. I was trying to calm myself down. I felt on the verge of panic. I can't recall ever feeling so helpless. This girl desperately needed help. She was in serious trouble. I wanted to do something, but we could not communicate in even the most rudimentary way—she couldn't tell me what she needed or even tell me what to do to help her.

"Is there someone I can call?" I asked her. "We need to get some help. Who can I call?" My voice was rising in panic, and I think she sensed that I was as scared as she was.

The girl started making sounds again, incomprehensible sounds that did not make any sense to me. I had been hoping that somehow, magically, I would begin to understand her if we spent enough time together. That may have been true, but it would take a lot longer than either of us wanted.

"I need to call for help," I told her, and started inching away. "I'll go call for help."

The wheelchair started to jerk back and forth again. There was no way I could leave her like this. But I had to do something.

Then I realized that she had reactivated her wheelchair in order to get my attention. I looked down at her two fingers, her only working parts, and noticed that she was moving them around. I came closer and she started to make louder noises. It was as if we were playing hot and cold and I was getting warmer. I moved over to the left side of her wheelchair so I could see what she was doing with her fingers. She seemed to be moving them in circles. I stared and stared but could make no further sense out of her movements. When she started to reactivate the wheelchair, jerking it back and forth again, I sat down on the ground at her feet and started to cry.

I have never felt more helpless in my life. And I think part of this is that somehow, some way, it was as if I was inside her. Talk about feeling someone else's pain—it was as if all her fear and frustration and anger, all of it was inside me. Maybe she couldn't cry, or even speak the same language that I do, but I could definitely feel what she was going through. Or maybe that's not it at all. Maybe I was crying for myself, not for her. This was my worst nightmare: a person who needs my help and I can do nothing to be of service. This is what it often feels like to me when I do therapy—it feels like I have so little to offer. Compared to the depth of someone's pain, the severity of their struggles, my helping efforts seem so feeble.

I think I startled the girl when I looked to be in worse shape than she was. Here I was supposed to be the rescuing angel and I had lost it. One of us had to get our sh** together, and I'm a little embarrassed to say it was her first.

I had all but given up, deciding I had no choice but to leave her and go call for emergency help when she started tapping her two fingers on the armrest of the chair. I looked up. Her head was jerking, but so was the rest of her;

it was only her two fingers that seemed to speak the same language that I do, and those fingers started making those circles again. Two circles, one above the other.

An eight, I thought. She's drawing an eight, a number! She's telling me something!

Okay, great, she's 8 years old? Gee, that's nice to know, but how does that help? Besides, she looked older than that, probably 10 or 12 at least.

Her fingers were moving again, this time up and down. They were repeatedly moving vertically in the same rhythm with which she had been making circles earlier.

"Are you making numbers?" I asked her. "Is that what you are doing?"

Her head jerks seemed to change direction and speed. Maybe that was a "yes."

"Is this a phone number you are giving me? Is this the person you want to call?"

The girl's eyes looked down at her fingers and she was forming another shape, possibly another number, maybe another 8, or a 3.

We spent the next few minutes in this way, trying to read the numbers that she was writing on the arm of her wheelchair. This wasn't like a movie where the breakthrough happens all at once, and immediately I am able to "hear" the hidden message; in fact, it took us the better part of 15 minutes—maybe longer—to agree on seven numbers. I made her send the message over and over again because her finger movements were hardly precise and consistent. Finally, we both seemed to agree that what I repeated back was the number she had in mind.

"Okay now," I said to the girl, finally calm again. "I'm just going to go away for a few minutes. I have to find a phone. Then I am going to come right back here and wait with you until someone comes to get you. Do you understand?"

I may have been imagining this—after all, I still held the image of that other little boy's smile in my head—but I'm almost positive the girl smiled at me. It could have been a smile; at the very least, I think she was reassuring me that she'd be okay until I returned. It was strange, but in this hour (or was it only a half hour?) that we'd been together, I think I was getting a lot better at reading her thoughts or feelings. Then again, maybe that was wishful thinking.

In any case, I rushed off to make the call. I dialed the numbers slowly, willing that each one was correct. Frankly, it would be a miracle if this worked, not only because I was still not sure I had "heard" the numbers correctly, but also because I wasn't sure that I remembered them.

"Hello." I heard on the other end of the line.

"Hi," I said. "I don't know if this is the right number, or if this is the right person, but I found this girl in a field. . . ." The words were rushing out of me as if I needed help as much as the girl did. I needed to tell someone about what had happened, about how hard I was trying to understand and be understood.

"Oh my God!" the voice said. "Is she okay? We've been looking everywhere for her."

"So," I interrupted, "this is the right number?"

"Oh yes, of course! Thank you so much for calling. Where is she? We'll be right there."

"Um," I hesitated. "Uh, I don't know where she is. I mean, she's in a field. It's off a street." I started to panic again. Take a deep breath.

I was eventually able to describe the location, and as it turns out, the girl had wandered away from the school grounds that were just on the other side of the field. This was a school for disabled children, many of them wheelchairbound. As best we figured out, the girl had "escaped," or perhaps gotten lost, or maybe tried to find her way home during recess.

I went back to the field, tromped through the weeds, and called out to the girl that help was on the way. She was breathing slowly now. And so was I. I reached out my hand toward her and her two fingers grabbed onto mine. I sat down next to her wheelchair and we held on to one another until help arrived. The last thing I did before I left was to plant a soft kiss on her forehead. Then I wiped away my tears.

So, why am I crying now as I write these words? Why have these three helping experiences, outside my office, had such a profound effect on my life? Why do I think of them as my finest hour?

■ ■ ■

So Hard to Choose

All three of these helping experiences had similar features. First, they were chance encounters for which I was unprepared. I seemed to delight in the serendipitous (might I say fateful?) nature of the events. Because I was not in a helping role—I was just a civilian—a pedestrian, a driver, a hiker—I felt no obligation to offer assistance; it was a choice. I reached out to someone because I felt like it. And for me, money issues have always gotten in the way. There is something about being paid for helping others that pollutes the purity of the experience. The greatest pleasure (for me) involves making a difference in someone's life when there is only intrinsic satisfaction.

Second, these were all children. Although most of my career as a therapist has been spent working primarily with adults, I have always been drawn to helping kids. My first job as a helper was as a preschool teacher. Although the subsequent opportunities led me toward working with adults (and later adolescents), I've longed to be with young children. At social gatherings and religious events, I am the first one to head to the room with the kids.

Third, as I mentioned earlier, it is important to me to feel useful. Even with my clients, I sometimes think that any other therapist could do basically the same thing—I am replaceable. But with these three fateful encounters, I was the only help available—it was me or nobody. Probably dozens of people walked right by the boy crying on the curb, dozens of cars zipped by the girl in the wheelchair. And how many trekkers in Nepal had a spare ball in their bags?

Fourth, the outcome of each of these interventions was immediate and dramatic. I did something constructive even though so much of my work involves situations where I can't necessarily see the results, or they don't last. Indeed, I hardly resolved any of the basic issues in any of these people's lives—the boy was probably bullied again the next day, the girl still had to contend with the challenges of a debilitating disease, and the other two children still had to face chronic poverty. Do any of them remember me now as I remember them? I think not, although I hope that somehow my modest gestures helped them to feel a little safer in the world.

So far, all of these explanations sound like they are part of the picture, but I'd be lying if I implied this is what they were all about. There was no ongoing commitment to any of these relationships, no hard work, no continued responsibility—just brief actions that actually required minimal effort.

So why am I diminishing my work with the thousands of clients and tens of thousands of students (or even millions of readers) I've touched over the years? I think I just find it hard to select one finest hour. I don't honestly know what my best work is. I don't trust my judgment about that, and I also don't trust reports of consumers. I'm suspicious about whether the effects will really last.

On Not Knowing and Not Understanding

Perhaps my finest hour was the last one in which I helped someone. I spend a few months each year working abroad, often in Australia, but also in South Asia. I teach and supervise doctoral students from the region. Just yesterday I spent a "finest hour" in a car with a doctoral student from Nepal. She is a physician who wants to change the health care system in her country, one of the poorest nations on Earth and with very high infant and maternal mortality. The outcome of her studies will not be just a dissertation on a shelf but real-world expertise that will allow her to shape and influence medical care to make it more responsive to the needs of sick women and children. In the hour we spent together, we talked about things like "grounded theory" and "qualitative design" and "constructivist orientation" related to exploring why Nepalese women will not seek medical services, even in life-threatening situations. But most of what I did for this doctor was offer her support. I honored her valiant efforts. I provided some degree of validation. Sure, I know stuff that she wants to know, but that was a small part of the conversation compared to the connection we shared.

So, in these days of brief therapy, miracle cures, solution-focused interventions, what is it that I am saying about what is most important in my work? Am I a dinosaur because I still value relationships over symptom resolution? Nah. Because in each of the three previous stories, I "cured" the presenting problems—the loneliness on the curb, the stuck wheelchair, the ball-less existence.

There are so many layers to the story of my finest hour that I fear readers will have a field day analyzing my deeper motives. I feel ashamed that I don't know my finest hour—I don't even know what is my best work. I'm just walking around in the world looking for opportunities to be helpful.

3 My Mama's Dead and My Daddy's in Jail

A Case from Jon Carlson

Jon Carlson holds two doctoral degrees, one in education, the other in psychology. This educational background accounts, in part, for his interest in so many different facets of human development. Jon has been working three or four different jobs for most of his adult life. He is currently a Distinguished Professor at Governors State University, University Park, Illinois, as well as an elementary school counselor. He has a large private practice, logging over fifty clients per week. He is a film producer, having developed more than two hundred professional videos featuring the world's best therapists in action. He has long been the editor of The Family Journal. *He is the author of books about family and couples counseling, and Adlerian therapy, his specialties. Finally, he is the father of five children and grandfather to four more.*

All of this is public information, of course, noted on the book jackets of his numerous scholarly works. When asked what people generally don't already know about him, Jon wondered if that might be how hard he works. After thinking about the question for a moment, he realized that this was rather obvious considering how early he leaves in the morning and how late it is when he returns at night. A more interesting question, perhaps, was how he manages to juggle all the different roles and do them so well.

"I think I would be bored if I just did one thing," Jon says. "I wouldn't feel very good about that. I guess I believe that if you are going to teach others how to do counseling, and write about it, you really ought to be doing it a lot yourself, knowing what it is like out there."

Seeing a few clients for experience is one thing, but Carlson used to see seventy to eighty clients per week (and this is in addition to his "day job"). Although now he has cut back to "only" fifty, he retains the same excitement and interest in his work that a newcomer to the profession would.

Selecting a Case

When you've seen over fifty clients per week for several decades, it is not easy to select one case that represents your best work. And then again, Jon was not sure how to focus in on one single hour as his "finest." There were times when he did see people just a few times, or for a single meeting, and produced a satisfying result. But that did not symbolize for him the kind of commitment and dedication, the day-in, day-out hard work, that represented his best work.

Jon went through the files that he's kept over the years, and there are thousands and thousands of them that he has stored. There were some that stood out because they were unusual, some he remembers because the therapy failed in some ways, and some other people he recalls because of the depth of the relationships they developed together. The cases that he quickly dismissed were the supposed "quick cures."

"I'm suspicious of cases where people improve overnight. I don't even know if that is particularly good therapy, or whether the changes last over time. Maybe there was some kind of trick involved. Or maybe it was just luck that things improved so quickly.

"I know there are therapists who claim that that they can produce cures in one or two sessions, but that has not been my experience. I think when people do change that fast, it is because they were high-functioning in the first place and very motivated. Heck, there are some people who change just by making an appointment."

In selecting the one case he wanted to talk about as some of his best work, Jon used an interesting criterion, and not the one that might have been expected. "I could narrow things down to maybe four or five families I've seen," Carlson admits, "but the one I settled on is the one that changed my life. I learned so much from these people. And I'm still learning a lot from them."

Perhaps another reason why he picked this family to talk about is that even after 12 years of treatment, he is *still* seeing them. The influence and changes that have taken place within this family parallel those that have occurred within Jon's own life and work. Maybe that is what he is most proud of about his work—that not only did he help some very dysfunctional, disturbed, and disordered people bring their lives more under control, but he allowed himself to be influenced by them in constructive ways.

When Elephants Can Fly

In choosing the story that he wanted to tell, Jon was reminded of another case that brought up a similar challenge that required dedication and commitment over a period of many years. This was a young girl who came to see him when she was in high school. "She was one of the most bizarre people I had seen," Jon recalls. "She was incredibly self-destructive and constantly suicidal. Sometimes I had to call the police to rescue her at the last moment.

"I worked with her for 8 years and during that time she ballooned from 120 pounds to over 350. Her parents disowned her. She lived in a homeless shelter, wandering the streets all day. But she would still come in and talk with me. I kept believing in her ability to turn her life around. Finally, she got herself a job in a laundromat. It was very hot in there, so she sweated off pounds to make herself more attractive. She met a guy who was wonderful. I got a card from her after they had just gotten married and were expecting a child. She said how happy she was. They had bought a house and she had reconciled with her family and was leading a normal life. She sent me a mug with the card, and on the mug was a picture of an elephant."

Jon pauses for a moment, feeling choked up as he remembers this incident. Regaining his composure, he says aloud what was written on the mug: "Only you would believe that elephants really can fly." Next to the words was a picture of a flying elephant.

"That shows what is possible when you don't give up on people," Jon explains, "when you stick with them even during the hardest of times." That is an important lesson he learned that is certainly relevant to the case he most wants to talk about.

The Long Walk

The family filed into the office as if they were part of a chain gang, each one following the other with shuffled feet and downcast eyes. They entered the room as if they had been presorted according to their height. Dad came first, leading the pack, a striking 6-footer, with long blonde hair combed straight back. He looked a little like Leonard Nimoy without the "Dr. Spock" ears. Mom followed right behind, also attractive but petite, and with an uneven gait that Jon later learned was the result of an artificial leg. The three daughters trailed just behind their mother, each with their father's striking blonde hair. There was something almost symmetrical about their evenly descending heights, moving from Dad's 6 feet to Mom's 5½ feet, and then to the three teenaged girls, aged 17, 15, and 13.

Dad sat on one side of the room and all the women located themselves on the other. This was probably not a good sign, but it is not uncommon in a conflicted family. Of more concern was that none of them seemed inclined to get the conversation going and say what had brought them in for help.

"Um," Carlson said a little awkwardly, feeling the tension in the family, "what can I do for you?"

Burt scowled and looked away, not at all happy with being here, and letting everyone in the room know that he was there under protest.

"Well," Kim, the mom, began slowly, "yah see, it's kinda complicated and all but basically he's been having trouble and all and, well. . . ." Each word was enunciated slowly, but carefully, until she just trailed off at the end. Carlson immediately noticed that speaking was not exactly her forte.

"He won't let any of us do stuff," Lisa, the eldest daughter, finished for her mother. "He says we gotta do what he wants, all the time."

"Yeah," Samantha, the youngest one, agreed in a voice that startled even her in its force.

Carlson looked to Dawn, the middle daughter, but rather than speaking, she just nodded her head. There seemed to be unanimous agreement that Burt was on all their cases, a pronouncement that he did not look all that pleased about. In fact, he looked furious.

"Burt," Jon addressed him directly, "what seems to be going on here?"

"I'll tell you what's going on, although if you got half a brain you can see it for yourself." As he said the last word, he swept his hand dismissively toward the female side of the room. "These girls have got in their minds that they should be doin' whatever the hell they want, and I won't have any part of that. They's just rebelling and all, and I've had just about enough of it." Burt crossed his arms to emphasize his point.

In talking to each of them, Carlson learned that, in addition to the parents fighting all the time, each of the girls was having problems in school. They seemed to be of average ability, even if their parents were both uneducated and of limited intelligence, yet they were flunking their classes. Dawn, the 15-year-old middle child, who had been mute up to this point, had stopped going to school altogether. This sort of behavior seemed to enrage Burt, although strangely, their mom seemed almost proud of their rebelliousness, as if Dawn and the girls were standing up to their father in a way that Kim had not found the courage to do herself.

Carlson noted that he immediately found himself disliking Burt and his controlling behavior and that he found himself firmly aligned with the women in the family. This was something he would have to watch out for if he was going to secure Dad's cooperation in the therapy. And clearly, Burt was at the center of the struggles.

Before bringing this first meeting to a close, Carlson summarized what he had heard as a common theme that had been clearly expressed by each of the children and their mother. "It sounds like a big issue for several of you," he worded as carefully as he could so as not to alienate Burt further, "has to do with rights within the family. I noticed that you, Lisa, and Samantha, and you, Mom, have all said that you feel like you don't have much say over things at home. And although you haven't said much, Dawn, you seem to agree with your sisters and mother."

Dawn nodded, then looked down, as if even that response took tremendous effort.

Before Carlson could finish, Burt jumped in. "Look," he said, "I been doing a pretty good job up until this point. And what the hell's wrong with a husband and father deciding what's best for his family anyway? I can handle things better then they can. I mean, look at em, they sure ain't getting along well now, are they?"

That was exactly the point that Carlson was going to make—that Burt's controlling behavior was not helping much—but it seemed premature to confront him on this when he felt so ganged up on.

Carlson looked toward the girls. "So what do you all think of that?"

"No way," little Samantha yelled out, the feistiest of them all. The other two girls nodded their heads in agreement. Kim looked startled, as if she was expecting an explosion of some kind. She was not to be disappointed.

Burt looked across the room at the women all siding against him. There was a blue vein that was pulsing on the side of his head, just underneath his hairline. Nobody said a word. They just sat there, Carlson included, waiting to see what would happen next.

"Can you believe this sh**?" Burt said to Carlson, as if he as a fellow man would understand the crap he had to live with. Carlson just stared back at him, waiting for him to continue.

"I've had enough of this sh**," Burt said, his voice rising. He shook his head, stood up, and started for the door.

"Where you going?" his wife said to his back. For the first time, rather than sounding fearful, she seemed relieved that he was leaving the room.

Burt stood still for a moment, with his hand poised on the doorknob. Then, without turning around, he said, "I'm walking home." Without another word, he walked out and slammed the door behind him.

Total silence for about 15 seconds. Then Dawn, the quiet one who had yet to speak, started giggling.

"What's so funny?" Carlson asked her gently. He was delighted to get some response out of her and was frankly just as relieved as the others to be free of Burt's intimidating presence. Of course, he'd have to try to get Burt back into treatment to work on issues that clearly involved him, but in the meantime the tension had been considerably reduced. This was especially the case listening to Dawn's lovely laughter, now joined by her sister.

Carlson looked around quizzically, still wondering what was so funny.

"He said . . . ," Dawn tried to explain in between her giggles. "He said . . ."

". . . that he's walking home," her older sister finished the sentence.

"Yeah?" Carlson asked again. "And what's so funny about that?" He was now a little concerned about how he was going to get Burt to come back.

"Well, you see," Lisa explained. "We live 14 miles away. We know it's exactly 14 miles because Dad was complaining the whole way about how far it was."

"So you mean your father is walking 14 miles to get home?"

They all laughed so hard that it took at least 2 minutes for them to regain their composure enough to end this first session.

The Bucket

It turned out that this family actually had very little to laugh about. During the very next session, Kim came alone rather than bringing her children. She wanted to use the time to fill her therapist in on some family background, which struck Carlson as a pretty good idea.

"So," Carlson began, "where would you like to begin?"

"There's some stuff." Pause. "There's some stuff, you know." Pause. "Stuff you need to know." Kim spoke in a halting voice, lurching forward intermittently like a car with a bad clutch.

"Sounds good," Carlson prompted her. "Why don't you fill me in on what you think might be important?" He had certainly noticed that Kim looked haunted, and it was something much more than her artificial leg and speech pattern.

"I used to spend a lot of time in the hospital, down at Emory."

"The university in Atlanta?"

"Yeah. I been there. Maybe three, four times. When I was a kid. 'Fore I was seven."

"You spent a lot of time ill when you were a child?"

"Wasn't ill. Exactly. Just broken."

"You were broken?"

"'Spect so. My mama used to take me there to see this lady too. We used to play with toys and all."

"This was, like, a play therapist?"

"Yessir. I 'member this one time she gave me these 'ole dolls to play with. I guess she figured I should dress them up and all. There was a girl doll, and a little boy doll. And a doll like a mommy and daddy." Carlson noted that her voice seemed to be regressing as she was speaking, becoming higher and more childlike. "But instead I took this little toy gun." Pause. "I picked up this toy gun." Pause. "Then I started to shoot the daddy doll. Bang. Bang. Bang." As she said this, Kim pointed her finger like a pistol.

"This worried the therapist, then," Carlson ventured. "You had a lot of anger toward your father."

Ignoring this reflection, Kim continued with her narrative of growing up in a family in which her parents functioned as an abusive "tag team." "My mama would get so mad at me and all. She'd put my head in a bucket."

"Your mother would put your head in a bucket?" Carlson felt silly just repeating what Kim had just said. But he was stalling, trying to figure out where this was going, and trying to get a handle on the various pieces of the story that Kim was putting out there.

"Yessir. She'd fill that damn bucket up with water. Then she'd put my head in the bucket. Hold it under 'till I thought I'd drown. I think a few times I probably did go unconscious and all. 'Cause I remember waking up alone on the floor."

"So your mother used to discipline you by holding your head under water? What did you do to deserve this sort of treatment?"

Kim sat silently. Just looking down. Remembering.

"When I got older. . . ."

"How old were you at this point?"

Shrug. "Maybe six. Seven. Something like that."

"Okay. Go on."

"This one time I got so mad at my mama. She was trying to hold my head in the bucket and I pushed her. Just as hard as I could. In the stomach. I didn't mean nothing. Didn't mean to do nothing."

"What happened, Kim?"

"Mama was pregnant," Kim said, tears pooling in her eyes. "I pushed her in the stomach and the baby died. My mama made me dig a grave for the baby in the backyard. She kept sayin' to me that it was my fault that baby died. That I killed that baby and I was going to pay for it."

Carlson could see the tears were starting to fall now, but he couldn't tell if Kim was crying for the baby, or for herself. "You had a lot you had to face as a child," he said. "And all this when you were so little."

Kim didn't seem to hear what Carlson said. She was nodding to herself, almost as if she was building up her strength to continue the story. "They used to lock me up in the basement."

"Your parents?"

Nod. "There was a pole down there. To hold up the house. And they'd chain me to that pole so I couldn't get loose or nothin'. They wouldn't give me food. Or water. Or nothin' else. My brothers would sometimes sneak down in the basement when they weren't watching and they'd bring me some food. But most of the time, I didn't have none."

Carlson could feel his hands clenching as he heard this story. He was trying to stay neutral and calm, so he could listen objectively to what his client had to say. He had heard a lot of terrible stories of childhood during his career, but this was just about the worst. And Kim obviously had a lot more to tell.

"At night, they'd bring me. . . ."

"When you say 'they,'" Carlson clarified, "you mean your parents?"

"Mostly my Mama," Kim explained. "He'd do other stuff."

Carlson wanted to ask about what "other stuff" but figured she'd get around to it. So he just nodded, signaling for her to continue.

"At night they'd bring me upstairs and sometimes I could sleep in a bed. But they'd tie me to the bed too. Then, in the morning, before they'd give the other kids breakfast, they'd take me back down in the basement and chain me to that pole again."

"So during this time in your life, they kept you chained in the basement all the time?" Carlson could hardly believe that any parents could do this sort of thing.

"No. Sometimes they'd let me come upstairs. But my mama, she'd put me in the corner and told me to stare at the part where the two walls come together. That's where I had to put my nose."

"I'm sorry," Carlson said, confused, trying to picture what she was talking about.

"Just when I was upstairs I had to put my nose between them two walls and stand there. But the good part is that I could hear the TV and people talking and all. 'Cause there weren't nothing to do in the basement all day. I didn't have nothing to play with."

By the time anyone figured out what they were doing to Kim, why she wasn't in school, why she was so "clumsy" that she kept having accidents, she was literally quite "broken." She was taken out of the home and placed in the care of an aunt who, while not exactly a nurturing mother type, was still stunned at the extent of the damage: Kim had several broken ribs where she had been kicked, and numerous bruises and lacerations on her body. Her fingers, nose, collarbone, and arm had obviously been broken before and not set properly—probably because her parents never took her for medical care. And all this before she was 7 years old.

The Leg

There had been one thing really puzzling Carlson, but he had been reluctant to interrupt Kim while she was recounting the story of her extensive abuse. Even though she still had a lot more to say, she seemed to realize that there was only so much of this that someone could take in.

"Kim," Carlson said gently, "I was wondering why your parents picked on you like this and left the other kids alone. Why you?"

Kim shrugged and shook her head. She'd obviously given the subject a lot of thought, especially during all that time she'd spent chained in the basement without any food, or drowning in the bucket. "I expect 'cause I got yellow hair."

"Excuse me?"

"'Cause I got me this blonde hair. Everyone else has black hair and I got yellow hair."

Carlson was obviously missing something here and didn't see the connection as to why having blonde hair would invite such horrible abuse.

"My daddy figured I must have been someone else's child. Not his at all. Mama told me that I was damn lucky because Daddy wanted her to get rid of me altogether. They used to fight about that all the time." Kim said that as if she felt guilty creating so many problems for her family, having blonde hair and all.

This was definitely not a Cinderella story, Carlson realized, in which she was rescued from the abusive home and lived happily ever after. Her adoptive home with her aunt and uncle was reasonably free of physical abuse, but hardly of neglect. Since they were a reasonably well educated couple, they seemed to have little interest in this uneducated, marginally bright child.

Kim stayed with her aunt and uncle until she was 17, until she met a boy who was on leave from the Navy. After knowing Burt for less than 2 weeks, they got married. She had been pregnant at the time with Lisa, who, as it turned out, was a previous boyfriend's child.

Carlson is still trying to digest all this history with the current family he is trying to help. The mother is a victim of terrible abuse. The father is an authoritarian control freak. The kids are all failing out of school. But before he got into all that, there was still one piece of the puzzle that was missing.

"What about your leg?" Carlson asked her. He had assumed that must have happened at the hands of her parents, who must have so mangled her that it had to be removed.

"Well, I think it was about 8 years ago. I found my husband was having an affair. He said he was going to leave me. The other woman would even call me on the phone and tell me what a worthless piece of sh** I was. I didn't know what to do and didn't know how to handle this situation."

"This was with Burt?"

"Yeah. Burt." She gave him a look like what other husband could it be.

"You were saying that you were feeling lost about how to deal with the affair."

"Right. So Burt went and bought a new motorcycle. A Harley. Big 'ole black thing that made a terrible noise. And he said to me, 'You better come ride with me on the Harley, because if you don't, I know someone else who will.' It was like a threat and all—that he was throwing in my face that his girlfriend would do things with him that I won't do. That thing just scared me to death.

"But before I'd get on that bike, he wanted us to drink a little, and that was fine by me 'cause I was really scared. So we went out drinking and riding around. It wasn't too bad, until we got in that crash. And that's where I lost my leg."

"So you agreed to go riding on Burt's Harley because you were afraid if you didn't, you'd be replaced by his girlfriend."

"Yup. Spent months and months in that damn hospital. And after all that time I spent with doctors when I was little, I sure didn't like it any better then either. I had something like eleven operations on that leg and finally they had to take it off."

"You must have suffered a lot of pain with that kind of situation."

"I still take drugs because of it. It's the only thing that makes it halfway tolerable."

Carlson noted that, among her other problems, Kim seemed to be addicted to pain medication. Probably narcotics. And what she seemed to want from the therapy was that he should fix her marriage, fix the kids so that they did better in school, and fix Burt so he would stop running around with other women and stop him from trying to control everyone at home.

"I just ain't never had much of a life when I was growing up. And I want something better for the girls. They deserve better than I got. But now I ain't so sure that they got it."

Family Secrets

Eight months later, Carlson had developed a pretty good relationship with Kim and her three daughters. Sometimes they would all come together, and sometimes Kim would come alone. One thing was certain, however, and that was that Burt would not be returning. In fact, Burt was trying to do everything he could to get his family to stop seeing this stranger who was wresting control away from him. Yet as terrified as the girls were of their father, and as subservient as Kim was to her husband, this was one line they drew in the sand: therapy was the one sanctuary in their lives, and they refused to surrender it.

Carlson had been attending a professional conference away from home when he received an emergency phone call from Kim.

"Dr. Carlson," she said on the edge of panic. "I'm so sorry to bother you and all. I didn't mean to. . . ."

"That's okay, Kim," he reassured her. "What's going on?" During these previous months he had been working very hard to develop a trusting relationship with her, perhaps the first such relationship with a man she had ever enjoyed in her life. There were limits on how fast he could help turn things around with this family, but one thing he knew for certain, his main job at this point was simply to earn their respect.

"It's Samantha," she said. "She told me something. She said something that's awful. I don't know what to do. You gotta tell me what to do."

"Okay," Carlson tried to calm her. "Slow down now and tell me what's going on. You said something was going on with Samantha." As he said this, he imagined little Samantha, now turned 14, but still the baby of the family. In many ways, she had always been his favorite because of the way she had stood up to her father at that first session, the one when he had walked home.

"It's her daddy. She told me about her daddy."

Carlson was still clueless about what Kim was talking about, but he decided to just wait and let her tell the story her own way.

"And Dawn and Lisa too. All three girls and their daddy. He's been having sex with them. All of them." And then Kim just broke down on the phone.

"Okay now," Carlson said, trying to think this through, but he was just as stunned as she had been. It was not that much of a shock that such an abusive, controlling, oversexualized, morally corrupt man would molest his children—just that he had been able to hide it so well for so long, all the while keeping his daughters quiet so they didn't report what was going on. It seemed that the abusive cycle that Kim had experienced in her own family was now repeating itself.

"What I want you to do first, Kim, is to report this to the authorities. You must do that immediately. Today. As soon as you hang up the phone with me. I'll be home in a few days and then we'll talk this through and figure out what to do next."

As soon as their conversation ended, Carlson felt awful for not having recognized the signs earlier. On one level, even as he reviewed everything he had seen and heard, he realized that there were few definitive signs that indicated sexual abuse. Of course, the children's school performance had been poor, and Burt *was* extremely controlling, but that in itself did not lead to the conclusion that they had been sexually assaulted. Apparently, this had been going on for so long that all three daughters had simply accepted the situation as normal and adjusted themselves accordingly. They managed to hide their predicament from teachers, from friends, even from their mother, who had no idea what was going on. Or, at least, that was what she had said. Carlson knew from prior experience that mothers may sometimes collude with the abusive father in such situations, but his sense was that this was not the case in this situation. Kim may not have been the brightest or most sensitive person in the world, but she would do anything to protect her children from the sort of things she had faced as a child. And the shock in her voice was real: she was totally surprised by this revelation.

Burt was arrested the next day and carted off to jail. If the family thought this would bring them some relief, however, they were certainly mistaken. Burt was the only one in the family earning any sort of money, and with him gone, they had no other source of income. They lived in a nice house, and still had some money saved from a settlement from the motorcycle accident, but otherwise they had no resources. With Kim having no education beyond elementary school, and being addicted to pain pills, she did not have much potential as a wage earner. Furthermore, with only one good leg, it was difficult for her to stand for long periods of time. The girls were all suffering from the long-term sexual abuse, and with failing grades in school, had few viable prospects as well.

The Third Generation

Although they could not afford even a token payment for therapy, Carlson redoubled his efforts to help the family stabilize themselves. He began seeing each of the girls alone, trying to help each of them come to terms with what she had suffered. Progress was slow and hardly without setbacks. About the only thing that Carlson could say with much confidence was that they all trusted him implicitly: he was the one stable person in their lives on whom they could count.

Several years passed as the therapy continued. Carlson would like to say that, through his efforts, each woman managed to stabilize herself, but that was not nearly the case. Lisa, the eldest daughter, started to gain weight, a not uncommon coping mechanism of women who have been sexually abused and want to protect themselves against further assaults. She eventually met a boy and got married, although her weight continued to balloon out of control. At last count, she weighed over 300 pounds.

Dawn, the middle child, took off as soon as she could. When she turned 17, she ran away with a guy she later married. They stayed married 8 years; she had two kids by two other men, but she never bothered to divorce her first husband.

And Samantha, the youngest, also tried to escape home as soon as possible by running off with a guy. By age 21 she had three children of her own. Soon thereafter she was diagnosed with terminal cancer, which necessitated having one of her legs amputated. Just like her mother. Again the generation repeated itself, leaving her young children without stable care.

Carlson continued to see Kim during these years, hearing regular reports about the status of her three children. She remained addicted to pain pills in massive amounts, supplemented by large quantities of bourbon. But all through her struggles, she still managed to show up for sessions on a regular basis.

Kim finally moved in with a new guy, Thomas, but that didn't seem to work out very well either. Finally, she got so sick of living with worthless men, she just packed up and moved out one day while Thomas was out hunting with this friends. Kim laughs as she tells this story.

"The stupid sumbitch was so clueless that he didn't even know I'd left. He just came home with his buddies one day and he sees how spotless the house looks. He says to his buddy, 'Look, you see, the bitch finally went and cleaned up the house. Damn if I haven't been telling her to do that.'

"'Ah Tom,' his friend says, 'I think she done left.'

'What are you talkin' about?' Thomas says to him. 'She just cleaned up the damn house. 'Bout time too. That gimp lives like a pig.'

'No,' his friend insisted, 'I'm tellin' you. She's gone. Look, your TV's missing and all.'"

This demonstration of independence didn't last long, because 2 months later Kim moved back in with Thomas. That had lasted until he was arrested for drug sales just a few months earlier. So now Kim came in to see Carlson, this time bringing Samantha's youngest child, age 2, whom she was now raising since her daughter had died. Samantha's other two children were being raised by her older sister, Dawn.

Samantha's three children, aged 2–6, were being raised by their aunt and grandmother because just after their mother died, their father was arrested for selling LSD. He had been sentenced to 10 years in prison, so he would not be getting out for some time. From what Kim had learned about the man, this was a very good thing.

As the session began, Carlson asked the two-year-old how everything was going. She smiled and said, "My mamma's dead and my daddy's in jail." Carlson is still amazed at how this third generation is repeating the same patterns that occurred before, even to the point that a daughter loses her leg just like her mother. And all the elements are in place for the grandchildren, Samantha's kids, to face the same kinds of things that their mother and grandmother faced. So far, Kim, Dawn, and Lisa have not been inclined to make choices that are any more sound than they ever had before.

■   ■   ■

Breaking the Cycle

And this case represents your greatest success? Carlson is challenged. Shouldn't this story go in our other book, the one about failures? What is it about this family that brings to mind your finest hour, given there have been so many tragedies and that this family is still not much better off than when you first met them? And also, while we are on this subject, what did you actually do for them?

Carlson thinks for a minute, trying to organize his thoughts, but it is difficult because there are so many complexities to this situation. Usually, when cases are described in books or conferences, they follow some kind of linear sequence: the client presents this sort of problem. The therapist gets to the bottom of things and heroically finds the answer that everyone has been looking for. The family leaves and goes on to do wonderful things. But here is a family in which, even after years of treatment, Carlson still can't make a dent in understanding the complexities of what is going on.

So, among all the people you have ever seen, why does this one stand out as among your best work?

"First of all," Carlson clarifies, "good or great therapy is not *my* work; it is the clients' effort that determines that. This case taught me so much about faith and resilience. It just amazes me that these people can keep on living with their situation. Sure I like to solve problems and fix things. But this case is more like when someone has diabetes or another chronic disease. The object is not to cure the problem, which is impossible, but to help people to live with it better. I have tried very hard to help them to improve the quality of their lives. During this process I've had to learn to be patient and more accepting of the limits of what I can do."

Carlson is especially proud of the relationships that he has developed with Kim, her daughters, and now her grandchildren. One of the grandchildren is now in third grade but is so disruptive in class that she is out of school more than she is there. Carlson has been the one to go to bat for the kids again and again, visiting their schools to intervene on their behalf. But it is like putting out brush fires: as soon as one is put out, another flares up.

"As much as this family has suffered," Carlson says, "most of them feel pretty good about what they have survived. They have not been as successful as they—or I—would like, but they are doing the best they can. They still have hope. Granted it has been two steps forward, two steps back, over the years, because it has been hard for them to follow through on things. But still, Lisa and Dawn both finished high school and got their diplomas, and they are really proud of that."

Carlson recognizes that after all the hardship and abuse that Kim suffered, and then having been unable to protect her daughters from their own abuse, there is a family legacy that is very hard to overcome. Somehow, some way, this cycle must be broken. That Kim and her family trust Carlson, and have done so over so many years, strikes him as truly remarkable. They have never given up, and he will not do so either. And that is what makes this case among his most important work, and his finest hours as a therapist.

4

Limits of the Past

A Case from Michael Yapko

Michael Yapko has been responsible for a number of recent innovations in treating depression through a combination of cognitive, strategic, and hypnotically based therapies. His eleven books include Breaking the Patterns of Depression, Hand Me Down Blues: How to Stop Depression from Spreading in Families, Treating Depression with Hypnosis, *and* Trancework: An Introduction to the Practice of Clinical Hypnosis. *Each of these books describes brief methods for treating depression and other debilitating conditions.*

Yapko is a psychologist in clinical practice near San Diego, California, where he works with individuals, couples, and families. He also travels throughout the world conducting workshops on brief therapy for depression and clinical applications of hypnosis.

He Doesn't Say or Do Much Any More

Mel was a huge man, large in both girth and height. He literally filled a room, spilling out in any direction that was not restrained by a belt that left a link-sausage indentation in his belly. It looked as if someone had poured him into his clothes before he expanded. That someone would have been his wife, who was sitting next to him in the waiting room.

If Mel was spectacularly obese, then his wife, Rachel, was a miniature doll by comparison. Their respective sizes seemed particularly pronounced because the little woman's tiny arm was attached to her husband's beefy appendage.

"Good morning," Yapko greeted the couple with a friendly smile. He held his hand out to the husband first, but Mel was immobile, eyes closed, breathing labored. He redirected the outstretched hand to Rachel, who lightly brushed it with her fingers. She smiled uneasily.

"I'm Rachel," she said formally. "And this is my husband." If Mel heard this introduction, he gave no indication.

Yapko stood there waiting for some response from the gentleman, but with none forthcoming, he addressed the woman. "Well, Rachel, why don't you both come in?"

Rachel immediately popped up, but Mel continued to sit immobile in the chair. For a second, Yapko wondered if the man was stuck in the chair and they'd have to figure out a way to pry him loose.

With a practiced movement, Rachel tugged on Mel's arm—this little woman who appeared to carry more strength on her frame than would seem possible. He rose out of his chair in a slow, hypnotic movement, as if the life force of his wife was providing the fuel for the action.

When he finally rose, Mel stood swaying on his feet, eyes still firmly closed. Rachel, still holding on to his hand, led him forward, shuffling along into the interior office.

Yapko, meanwhile, was keeping his eye on the proceedings. The whole strange scene reminded him of work he had done for the San Diego Wild Animal Park in their elephant breeding program. Mel reminded him of one of those reluctant beasts, slow to get going, seemingly harmless, but potentially volatile and unpredictable. He was determined to keep an eye on the guy until he could figure out what the heck was going on.

Rachel slowly pulled her husband along, as if on a leash, and directed him to the vicinity of a sturdy chair that could bear the man's weight. Using some sort of subtle nonverbal signal system (not unlike an elephant trainer, Yapko noted), Rachel indicated that Mel should fall back into the chair— which he did with a noticeable thud that could be felt throughout the room. Amazingly, his eyes remained shut the entire time.

Yapko watched the way the couple handled themselves, wondering how he was going to develop any kind of rapport with the husband if he insisted on remaining detached, in a state of intense internal focus, or whatever state he was currently in. Not yet knowing what to do or say about this already surprising encounter, he waited for the couple to begin.

It was Rachel who again took the lead. "I guess you've noticed that my husband has some problems."

Yapko nodded, encouraging her to continue.

"It was a year ago, I think, maybe a little more than a year ago." As she stated the timeline, she looked at Mel for confirmation, but Yapko could see no discernable variation in his posture or demeanor. He seemed frozen.

"Anyway," Rachel said, "Mel suffered a very serious heart attack. He almost died, as a matter of fact."

"I can see that has been very difficult for you both," Yapko said in a deliberately understated way. His main priority at this juncture was just to buy some time until he could figure out what was happening.

"Yes, it is indeed," Rachel agreed. "It's been hard on me, of course, but poor Mel—he just hasn't been the same."

"I see," Yapko said.

"He's been like this ever since."

"When you say been like this, you mean. . . ."

"Yes," she finished. "He doesn't say or do much anymore."

Lost Dreams

In gathering some history from Rachel, Yapko learned that after Mel had received a quadruple bypass, he awoke from the surgery a different man. He rarely opened his eyes and would just sit quietly in a chair. He almost never spoke, unless it was to ask for food. About the only communication he ever conveyed—and a powerful message at that—were the tears that would occasionally stream down his face.

Rachel reported that ever since the operation, Mel spent his days sitting immobile in a chair in the family room. Sometimes he would appear to be sleeping; when he was awake he would just cry silently.

"What was he like before the operation?" Yapko asked, wanting to find out about premorbid conditions but also feeling uncomfortable talking about this guy who was sitting right there in the room.

"Sir," Yapko addressed the man directly, "what can you tell me about what you're experiencing?" No reply. Another question. No reply. More questions, no answers.

There was silence until Rachel stepped in to answer the questions that Yapko posed. Mel had yet to move a muscle, although sometimes there seemed to be some effort to start to say something, but then the moment would pass and he offered nothing but silence. "Well, something very intense is going on with this guy that is keeping him stuck in pain," Yapko thought to himself.

Rachel went on to describe Mel's life as a successful factory supervisor. "He was a good man," she said. Yapko noted that she used the past tense.

Rachel talked about what a hard worker Mel had been. He was not well educated, but he'd still managed to earn regular promotions at his company because he was so dependable and competent. "In all those years he'd been with the company . . . What? . . . 26 years, wasn't it?"

Yapko quickly looked over to Mel for a response. If he gave one, Yapko couldn't see it.

"In all those years," she finished the thought, "he didn't take more than three or four sick days."

Yapko learned that part of the reason for Mel's reliability was his work ethic, but the other part had more to do with an anxiety-provoking image of himself as being easily replaced. His deepest fear, according to his wife, was that if he missed work he would find his place gone when he returned.

It seemed particularly tragic that Mel's heart attack and subsequent health problems occurred just a year before his scheduled retirement. They had been making elaborate plans for how they would spend their time together. They'd purchased a recreational vehicle to travel cross-country and talked late into the nights about all the states they would visit, places they would go they had only dreamed about. Then the heart attack changed everything.

Rather than spending their golden years on the road, Mel was now anchored to his chair, a weeping blob that no longer resembled anything he had once been.

Hypnotic Stories

After Mel had become so despondent and unresponsive in the hospital following the surgery, he had been referred to a psychiatrist, and then a half-dozen other mental health professionals in quick succession as each tried to reach him and quickly gave up. He was found to be uncooperative and hopeless. In all the sessions that had been conducted by other doctors and therapists, he had yet to speak a single word to them. And that ended Rachel's narrative.

"Do you have anything to add to this?" Yapko asked Mel directly. He didn't really expect an answer, but it was worth a shot.

No response. Just a rivulet of a single tear falling down his cheek.

Unwilling to surrender, Yapko tried again. "Mel, has Rachel told me everything you want me to know? Is there anything that she can do, or that I can do, that might give us some indication of what you are thinking and feeling right now?"

No response. Not even a flicker. Even the tear seemed to halt its journey at the juncture of where his nose flared into his lip.

"Well, then," Yapko said as cheerfully as he could. "Maybe that's enough for our first session. I'll see you both again next week."

Once Mel and Rachel left the office, Yapko found himself both intrigued and challenged by the case. But he also felt tremendous doubt about his ability to deal with this rather unusual situation. He wondered what he could possibly do to engage this mute man. He seemed skeptical that he could come up with something that hadn't yet been tried. Yet, on the other hand, with all the usual things already attempted, he felt a certain freedom to be inventive and creative in ways that he might not ordinarily consider.

"One of the things about my background and training," Yapko explained, "is that I am very drawn to and appreciative of what can be accomplished with clinical hypnosis as a vehicle of communication. So I had plenty of experience to draw on of being able to talk to somebody who happens to be sitting quietly with his eyes closed."

Yapko also took inventory of what he already knew. He thought he had a pretty good idea of what was going on inside Mel's head. "It was very clear to me that this man was deeply immersed in ruminations of hopelessness and impending death. It was especially clear to me, as well, that this was a man who had already had a quadruple bypass, who was sitting in the chair day after day, hour after hour, getting fatter, getting unhealthier, who was very likely to have another heart attack, one he'd probably not survive."

It didn't take much to figure out that Mel was extremely depressed and despondent. It was also easy to imagine the sort of ruminations that must have been taking place inside him—all the regrets he must be having, all the dreams that were dashed, all the disappointments he had faced. Further, Yapko figured that the obvious stuff had already been tried. His doctors had probably told Mel that he could lead a normal life after his heart attack, but he apparently discounted this assessment and surrendered to perceptions of hopelessness and his resulting depression. He'd also probably heard all the predictable scoldings and advice about how important it was to get his fat behind out of the chair and become active again.

So, Yapko constructed a series of metaphors—stories with therapeutic messages—that he would deliver to Mel during their next session. Heck, guiding him into hypnosis would be the easy part, since he was already three-quarters of the way there during his normal waking state.

During the next session, after Rachel escorted Mel into the office, Yapko asked her to wait outside. She looked anxious about that, but finally agreed. At this point, she was willing to try almost anything, even if she had her doubts.

After Rachel left the office, Mel still sat immobile. It either didn't bother him in the least that his wife was gone, or else he hadn't noticed.

Yapko just sat with him for a few minutes, not saying a word. Then, in his best hypnotic voice, he began to speak to Mel in a soothing, even cadence. "Basically, I just told him 'going nowhere fast' stories. I started describing to him in very detailed terms a story of a kid who was in high school getting ready to drop out because he wanted to get a job so he could buy a car to impress the other kids. I told him about a girl in a terribly abusive relationship with an older man she intended to marry just so she could get away from her alcoholic, violent father. I just told him story after story of people who didn't solve problems, but made problems worse by being so terribly short-sighted. This was a realistic inference of what I knew about him, given his apparent hopelessness and despair. All the stories carried a common theme of people making bad decisions in the short run that would make their difficult lives even worse in the long run, just as he was doing."

All throughout these detailed stories, Yapko had a strong feeling that Mel was actually listening, even though there was no discernable evidence of this. So Yapko next started to pause at regular intervals in the stories, leaving the next part of the story untold. He was building anticipation and commitment on the part of the listener. He was trying to create an active collaboration with his apparently passive client.

It was during the fourth story that a most remarkable thing took place. All of a sudden, just as Yapko was building toward the end of another sad tale, Mel sat forward, opened his eyes, and pronounced: "I'm going to die." Then he leaned back into the chair and again closed his eyes. Tears were now falling in earnest.

When Yapko reflected the intensity of Mel's pain that he felt, the man began sobbing uncontrollably. It was as if a year, a lifetime, of pain came flooding out. Rather than commenting on this, or probing further, Yapko just sat with him. He was reluctant to press an agenda at such a sensitive moment. Mel opened up with his grief, expressed his belief that his life was over and that he was "as good as dead," and described the futility of doing anything other than "sitting and waiting to die." The session eventually ended with a new bond forged, a connection made that no one else had been able to make. Yapko was both relieved and burdened anew with the dilemma of what to do to help Mel.

I'm Still Alive

During the third scheduled session, when Yapko came out to greet Mel and Rachel, both returned the greeting. Yapko was openly pleased. Yapko invited Rachel to join in on his session with Mel. When Yapko gestured to them to follow him to his office, to both of their surprise, Mel stood up of his own accord and walked into the office. Rachel looked quizzically at the back of her husband, as if unsure what this new state of affairs meant.

Once the couple was settled in their chairs, Yapko did something completely unexpected. Rather than continuing with the gentle, compassionate stance he had taken the session before, this time he began by harshly chastising Mel, in what superficially seemed to be anything other than a helpful demeanor.

"I'm very disappointed in you Mel," Yapko began the conversation. "You are a very selfish man. I listened to you talk about your feelings and your fears and I can't believe how you have everyone so worried and you don't even seem to care. You are incredibly selfish!"

Rachel gasped, taken aback at what seemed to be a very rude, insensitive way of treating such a vulnerable, sick man. Mel instantly became highly attentive, trying to figure out what was going on. Was this the same doctor who had been so sensitive and supportive the last time they met? What on earth was going on here?

"You wife here doesn't think I should be talking to you like this, as you can tell from her reaction. But I gotta tell you, somebody has to tell you the truth. You sit in your chair all day, you don't participate in your wife's life in any meaningful way, you act as if you have no responsibilities at all, even to the woman who takes such good care of you. Did you hear her describe how she has to check on you all the time? How she has to stop whatever she's doing just to come see if you're okay? How she can't even enjoy a television program without interruption because she has to get up and walk into your isolation chamber of a room to see if you're alright? You've set it up so that

Rachel has to constantly check on you. She can't even tell if you're dead or alive because you don't ever move or make a sound."

Yapko paused, watching the man intently, making sure he had not shut down. More than ever before, he sensed Mel was really hanging on every word. No one had talked to him this way before, and it was compelling, though uncomfortable.

"Rachel is the one who has to clean the house. She is the one who feeds you, and that isn't an easy task. She has to do all the errands and manage the money. And you just sit on your butt all day. Now that's just not right. Wouldn't you agree?"

Yapko didn't really expect an answer, so he continued with the plan. "It must be really hard for you, Rachel, to get much done when you have to constantly stop what you're doing and check on your husband."

Rachel started to protest that she didn't mind, but Yapko continued his polite pummeling of Mel. "If you're going to make this poor woman take care of you, the least you could do is let her know occasionally that you are okay and save her the extra burden of having to check on you all the time."

"So," Mel mumbled in a whisper, looking down like a little boy who is ashamed, "what am I supposed to do?"

Yapko nodded, knowing that they were moving in the right direction. "What I want you to do is set a kitchen timer by the chair that you sit in all day. I want you to set the timer to go off at 15-minute intervals. Every time the bell rings, I want you to call out to Rachel in your loudest, most easily heard voice that you're still alive. I want you to yell in your loudest voice: 'I'm still alive, Rachel, I'm still alive!' Think you can do that little thing to make her life a little easier?"

Mel looked at Yapko as if he wasn't sure if the therapist was kidding or not. When he saw that Yapko was totally serious, he nodded his head hesitantly, apparently agreeing that he owed Rachel that regular feedback in order to save her the trouble of having to keep checking on him.

"As you can tell, I'm serious about this, Mel. I'm concerned for Rachel's well-being, too, not just yours. So, let me hear you say it now. Say: 'I'm still alive Rachel.'"

Mel responded obediently, although with little enthusiasm.

"Come on Mel! Surely you can do better than that. What if Rachel is in another part of the house? How is she supposed to hear you? Let me hear you say it louder."

They rehearsed the call several more times, until Yapko was satisfied. When he stole a secret glance at Rachel, there was a knowing look and a smile in her eyes that let him know she both understood and approved of what he was trying to do.

By the time the couple went home, Mel had accepted the rationale for his new obligation to Rachel. He followed the assignment almost to the letter, and the transformation was remarkable. In just a few days of yelling out that he was still alive every 15 minutes, Mel began to absorb the self-suggestion and the obvious reality that he was indeed still alive! He *wasn't* dead. Instead of focusing on, "I am going to die," he was now constantly saying to himself, "I am still alive." This was the turning point both in the therapy and in Mel's life.

Wish You Were Here

Mel and Rachel returned the next week, and the difference in him was startling. Rather than shuffling in, Mel walked with sturdy confidence, at least until he seated himself in his usual chair and took on a sheepish demeanor.

"I guess I've been wasting a lot of time, huh?" Mel began in a soft voice, still unable to look Yapko in the eye for very long.

"You've discovered that you're not dead yet, haven't you?"

Mel nodded.

"Look, we can't change what happened to you, but tomorrow hasn't happened yet. What happens from here on is negotiable. Almost anything is possible. Now that you are still alive, and you recognize that you are still alive, the important questions are, how do you want to live? How do you want your marriage to be? How do you want your relationship with your kids to be? How do you want your life to be from this point on?"

Subsequent sessions focused more progressively on moving things in his life back into a positive direction. That meant reconnecting with people that he had stopped connecting with, spending fun and intimate time with Rachel, and talking about other things besides the heart attack and his fear of impending death. This future orientation made all the difference; Mel not only had a reason to live, now he was actually coming to believe he would continue to survive and he could start planning for a future that included many of the same things he had originally planned for, such as trips and time with his family.

Mel returned to a cardiac rehabilitation program, began to exercise, put himself on a diet, and lost a lot of weight. Once his health had improved, Rachel and Mel packed up their RV and headed across the country. Occasionally, they would send Yapko postcards, the first of which read: "We are currently in New Mexico. Having a great time. Wish you were here to tell us why!"

■ ■ ■

The Past Is Not the Future

One of the most important lessons for Yapko about this case was how it reinforced his belief that the past does not necessarily predict the future. He has little patience for colleagues who insist on spending a lot of time delving into the past, uncovering long-standing patterns, as if this is necessary to be effective.

"One of the main problems with depressed people," Yapko said, "is that they are already too focused on the past. They are very adept at rehashing all their previous disappointments, their past failures and rejections. Spending even more time on the past in therapy is almost always counterproductive in treating depression specifically, as the research shows. The power of the future is that it has not happened yet, it's open to creating bigger and better things than have ever existed before. So the best thing that you can do to come to terms with a crummy past is to create a really great future out of it. It means having a mission in life, because it is a sense of vision that empowers people. This is very different than just talking to someone about their feelings. Too often, people become slaves to these feelings such that they take over their lives. This is what happened to Mel."

A central theme to Yapko's work is the idea that people are far more than their histories. "It always bothers me," he said, "when therapists say to their clients, 'You are an abuse survivor.' The person is then supposed to respond by saying and thinking, 'Yes, I am a victim of abuse.' This is somehow supposed to be helpful? I don't think so. No one ever recovers from depression by declaring themselves a victim. On the contrary, they recover when they refuse to be declared a victim."

Instead, Yapko likes to challenge people in ways that encourage them to free themselves of the limitations of their past and their history. He tells them, "You are more than your history. You are more than your feelings. You are more than your body. You are more than any one dimension of your experience."

This was the message that he was able to communicate successfully to Mel. Yapko may talk to people about their losses, commiserating with their grief, dwelling on their suffering, but he is clear that a therapist has to provide more than just a shoulder to cry on. He believes it only makes things worse when people complain or get so lost in their hurt that they lose sight of what's possible for them that can make life worthwhile again. In Mel's case, he was doing nothing else except thinking about his losses and drowning in his feelings, distorted and unrealistic feelings at that. It was empowering for him to realize that he could rewrite a new future when he took action in the direction of a goal.

A Memorable Case

Among the many people Yapko has helped over the years, we wondered why this one stood out to him above the others as an example of his finest hour. He mentioned several things. First, he was able to be helpful to this man when many other therapists had previously failed. Second, the case had elements of life and death, comedy and drama, and was also intense yet playful. Third, it was a novel sort of case; he had never encountered anything quite like this before. "Finally," Yapko laughed, "you have to admit it's a hell of a story!"

This led us to a discussion of Yapko's opinion about what constitutes great therapy. He finds that the best sort of work is the kind that not only solves a problem but also promotes growth beyond the presenting complaint. He finds the best therapy is always experiential, using life experiences as teachers in ways that go well beyond just talking or philosophizing.

"I am a strong believer in people being active participants in the treatment process. We have to make demands of people that they develop different ways of thinking about their experiences as a routine part of therapy. We have to do far more than merely offer people emotional support. That is certainly important, but our main job is to provide people with new skills and abilities so they can overcome the limitations of their past and create a positive future for themselves."

5 Slaying a Dragon

A Case from Susan M. Johnson

As the developer of Emotionally Focused Therapy (EFT), Sue Johnson has a strong interest in the way attachments are formed in relationships. Her approach to therapy follows the traditions of humanistic philosophy embedded in a strong empirical foundation in which ideas are supported by scientific evidence. She has specialized in helping couples to communicate their deepest, unexpressed feelings more effectively to one another. Her goal is to help people to develop greater intimacy, mutual understanding, and a more secure bond through a structured process of revising current interactional patterns. She seeks to help couples to modify those communication patterns that maintain dysfunctional behavior.

Johnson is Professor of Psychology at the University of Ottawa in Canada and Director of the Ottawa Couple and Family Institute. She has written and edited a number of influential books in the field, including Emotionally Focused Therapy for Couples, The Practice of Emotionally Focused Marital Therapy, Perspectives on Emotion in Marital Therapy, Emotionally Focused Couple Therapy with Trauma Survivors: Strengthening Attachment Bonds, *and* Attachment Processes in Couple and Family Therapy.

"Every Case Enthralls Me"

Like most of our contributors, Sue Johnson struggled a bit before settling on which case she would focus on as representative of her best work. Over the past 25 years she has worked with a number of couples in which one or both partners suffered severe trauma, but it was still challenging to pick on just one such example that stood out from the others.

"*Every* case enthralls me," Johnson laughed. Nevertheless, in choosing the couple she wanted to talk about, she decided to focus on a case that touched her most personally, people with whom she felt especially connected. This case also stood out for her because she learned so much from the clients about attachment and how to work with people who have suffered terribly and have difficulty recovering from interpersonal traumas. In one sense, this case was instrumental in the development of her therapeutic approach applied to traumatic stress in couples therapy. Even after all these years, she still thinks about the images that emerged in their work together.

"Right now, as we speak," Johnson said in a dreamy voice, "I am looking out of the window of my office and staring at the snow outside. I see a wooden carving hanging in the window that was given to me by my students to represent the central image of this case that I had told them about."

Haunting Images

Charlene first came to see Johnson because of intimacy difficulties—she was having trouble letting her husband get close to her. "I have this image," Charlene said. "I see my husband coming close to me. He stands still with his arms out welcoming me, drawing me closer. He tells me to come closer. But behind him I can see a dragon."

Johnson found this image to be particularly haunting because of her own background as a student of English literature. In Anglo Saxon poetry there are recurrent images of life as essentially an experience of someone standing in a dark, narrow place with a dragon approaching. When Johnson shared the origins of this image, they began connecting on a deep level that surprised them both.

Johnson felt particularly relieved that some connection had been established because she had some real doubts about whether she could help this couple at all. Charlene and Ed presented themselves as very bright, open, honest people, but also severely wounded. They had been referred to Johnson from an eating disorder clinic in town because Charlene had not been responding to treatment for anorexia. She had become acutely depressed and suicidal, and she seemed to be getting worse. The staff at the clinic decided that the progress must be blocked by distress in the martial relationship and so recruited Johnson's help.

Crippled by Pain

"I'm just in constant pain," Charlene confessed with a grimace. Johnson was hardly surprised, looking at her emaciated body and haunted face. Her husband, Ed, looked no better; he seemed to carry his own burdens.

"What is wrong?" Johnson probed.

Charlene just shook her head, as if she had no idea where to begin. "My life . . . my life . . . has just fallen apart." It seemed to take so much energy just to communicate this basic expression of feeling that her body seemed to collapse; her head dropped and tears started streaming down her face. Ed reached over and awkwardly tried to comfort her. This was difficult because he was simultaneously trying to brush away his own tears.

"I can see that this is quite difficult for you," Johnson observed.

Charlene nodded. "I just want to be invisible. I just want to fade away."

As she said these words, Ed turned his head away, as if he was trying to give his wife some privacy. He just didn't seem to know what to do to give her comfort, whether to move in closer or move away.

"Maybe you could tell me what this is about?" Johnson encouraged her.

"We have two children," Charlene said.

"Becca and Randall," Ed added. "Those are their names."

"Yes," Johnson smiled at him. "Thanks." Then, turning to Charlene, she asked again what had happened.

"I had this accident a few years ago. It was a few years after we were married." Turning to Ed, she asked, "When was it? '84 or '85? I forget."

"'85," Ed said promptly, delighted to feel useful. "It was in February."

"Right. Anyway, ever since then I have been in almost constant pain."

"How are you in pain exactly?" Sue asked.

"My whole body aches. I can't eat. I think about dying a lot. I just. . . ."

"There's so much pain, you can't seem to locate it in one place," Johnson finished for her.

"Yes, that's so. And my husband, he. . . ."

Ed looked over toward his wife furtively, seeming to prepare himself for a blow, as if he knew what was coming next.

"My husband and me, we just live like roommates. We really don't have much of a relationship."

"You agree with that, Ed?" Johnson asked him.

He started to speak, but then just shrugged. Johnson couldn't tell if that represented surrender or exasperation or what.

"It just all feels so hopeless," Charlene continued.

Turning to Ed again, Johnson drew him out a bit about his perceptions of their relationship and his feelings about the state of things. It became clear that the more inadequate he felt, the more he had withdrawn over the years.

"I don't know what to do anymore," he said, shaking his head. He looked over at Charlene and said, "You're always so irritated with me. You don't seem to want to be with me any more. Then you get angry with me because I am not with you. I don't know what to do any more, so I just don't do anything at all."

Johnson checked Charlene's reaction to this, but couldn't tell if Charlene was listening or not. She was looking down at her hands.

"Look," Ed said, now pleading to his wife. "I try to talk to you. I try to help you. I try to be a good dad for Becca and Randy. I don't know what else you want me to do."

Charlene just stared at her hands.

Johnson was not sure how far to push them in this first session. She thought about asking Charlene how she was feeling right now, or inviting her to talk back to Ed, but she sensed this would be seen as intrusive. Charlene was obviously upset and angry, but she was sending strong signals that she was not ready to talk much about what she was experiencing.

Being Dead

"So then," Johnson said to change the subject, "let's talk about some of your background."

Charlene looked up from her hands to see to whom the therapist was speaking. She sighed dramatically when she saw that the focus was still on her.

Beginning with some rather basic facts related to her childhood, Charlene then poured out a story that surprised both her husband and the therapist. Ed had known that his wife's parents had died when she was very young, but he did not know the details of what had happened afterwards. Charlene had gone to live with an older cousin, who had been both abusive and neglectful. With little time to grieve for the loss of her parents, Charlene had been beaten and starved in her new home. Moreover, the male relatives present had sexually abused her as well.

As Sue listened to this tragic story, she wondered how Charlene had managed to survive at all. It was no wonder that she was having trouble with intimacy! She noticed that Ed seemed to be blown away by the story as well; he was staring out the window and crying silently.

"Until now," Johnson asked her, "have you told anyone about what you lived through?"

"You mean, like, the other therapists?"

Johnson nodded.

Charlene shrugged. "They never asked. I told them a few things, but they didn't seem to be all that interested so I didn't get into it."

"You act like it's no big deal," Johnson reflected, struck as much by Charlene's casual attitude as by the horrid details of the trauma she suffered.

"Well, lots of people have stuff they have to live through. I was no different." She paused for a moment, then looked directly at Johnson. "I should have been able to get over this. It happened a long time ago."

Charlene saw herself as toxic, hardly worthy of recovery, perhaps beyond the point where it was even possible. She believed her husband and children were better off without her, which was why she was so serious about taking her own life.

"Look," Johnson explained. "Everything you are going through, and all that you are feeling, is typical for a trauma survivor."

"I'm not a. . . ."

"Please hear me out. You've been through some things that few people could have survived, much less flourished the way you have. Yes, you are having some problems now, but your situation is far from hopeless."

Charlene vehemently disagreed. She felt she was damaged goods.

"It's no wonder you see dragons behind your husband when he tries to approach you," Johnson tried again. "It's amazing that you could ever trust anyone ever again, given what you've been through. And the courage you've shown even to come in here and talk about this is absolutely remarkable."

Charlene gave no indication whether she heard this message or not. Once in this zone of deep empathy, Johnson could feel such intense pain from this woman that she could barely breathe.

"I just feel like I'm dying," Charlene said. "No," she corrected, "I feel like I'm already dead."

Meanwhile, Ed was still caught up in his own grief and sadness. Charlene looked over at him for a moment, then said, "I just can't look him in the face anymore. I can't let him see me. I can't even look at myself. I refuse to look in the mirror. I get up in the dark so I can hold onto being invisible."

Johnson could see Ed trying to reach out to his wife, but he just didn't seem to know how to do that. He'd extend his hand, but he wasn't sure where to put it. It was obvious that he wanted to help, but he couldn't figure out how to proceed. "If you'd just let me hold you sometimes," he offered through his own tears, "maybe it would be better."

"I just can't handle that," Charlene responded. "Not now. Maybe not ever."

A Boomerang

Johnson felt captivated by this case, and totally drawn into the lives of her clients. She felt challenged by how difficult this would be, but far more than that, she found herself caring deeply for this wounded couple. "Here was this woman," she said, "who had not only faced a dragon but had been scorched again and again. There was no reason for her ever to trust anyone again."

Traditional wisdom holds that someone like this, with trust issues, would first work in individual therapy and learn to reestablish trust before attempting to work on the interactive issues in the marriage. But Charlene refused to go for individual therapy. So Johnson felt there was little choice but to proceed in working on these deep, vulnerable issues with her husband also present. She wondered if, in some ways, this might even present some advantages, since he would perhaps become part of the safe haven that would be necessary in order to heal these wounds. The question was whether he could handle the intensity: they were going to be slaying dragons and this would inevitably draw some scorching heat.

Johnson figured that she would try to help Charlene and Ed create more safety in their relationship, maybe even build a bond that would become safe enough that they could stand together to fight the dragon. Over the course of the next year, Johnson did exactly that. Together the three of them entered into a kind of existential arena where they could explore the deepest and most authentic moments. It was during such times that, predictably, Charlene would have difficulty with the level of trust that developed. The good news was that she was totally open in expressing this reluctance and fear.

"What's happening for you right now?" Johnson would cue Charlene when she noticed her pulling back. "As Ed turns to you and says that he doesn't want to leave and that he's sticking by you no matter what, what is going on?"

"I hate him. . . ."

"Talk to Ed directly," Johnson instructed.

"I hate you when you do that," Charlene said.

"What do you mean?" Ed asked her, confused and frustrated. He was doing everything he could think of, but it rarely seemed to be enough.

Ignoring Ed for the moment, Charlene looked at Johnson. "Why do you insist on zeroing in on me? Why don't you get off my case for a change?"

During these moments when Charlene felt too threatened or insecure, Johnson helped her to stay with the experience as much as possible, to give it shape and color. But at times the intensity was just too much and they had to back off and begin again.

"What do you need right now?" Johnson asked, letting Charlene guide where and how far they went. Johnson wanted to be very cautious about not doing anything that might be construed as a breach of trust or a violation of their boundaries.

When things got too dicey with Charlene, they would focus on Ed and his issues. The man needed a lot of support and reassurance. He was still so uncertain about how to get close to his wife and what he could do to show how much he loved her. Previously, other therapists had told him to give Charlene space, which meant that he backed off and she felt further abandoned and alone.

Instead, Johnson worked with Ed on ways that he could approach his wife more effectively and sensitively. As it turned out, he was a quick study and responded well to the relationship instruction. He learned to separate his sensitivities from Charlene's issues so that he didn't overpersonalize everything.

As the couple learned to become closer in measured increments, Charlene realized the difference between being a toxic person versus being exposed to toxic behavior. Although this was a useful concept, it did not stop her from alternating between wanting comfort from her husband and also pushing him away in anger.

"No, you can't be there for me," she would scold him. "I am not going to let you in. You are the enemy, just like everyone else. I will never let myself become vulnerable again, so you cannot betray me."

Throughout this barrage, Johnson would encourage Ed to stay with his wife and not back off. He was encouraged to take a stand and express himself more fully to her, asking that his own needs be met. Until this point, he had been fearful that if he ever asked for what he wanted, she would reject him completely. But paradoxically, helping her husband also made Charlene feel more useful.

"You are worth fighting for," Ed insisted one day, refusing to be chased away as he had before. "I'm not going away."

"He is my boomerang," Charlene said to Sue, as she laughed in delight. "He just keeps coming back."

Ed just beamed in pride.

Someone to Push Away

"Maybe that's what we all need," Johnson reflected. "We all need at least one person in our life whom we can push away because we are afraid and yet know that this loved one will come back anyway because we are so precious to him or her. Isn't that what we all long for on some level?"

This was certainly the case for Charlene, who began to take some real risks. She began eating with her husband and children, something she had avoided for many years during the worst of her anorexia. She had associated eating, or anything to do with her body, as so shameful it must always be done in private.

"I don't want anyone to see me," Charlene had repeatedly complained in the past. "I don't want to see myself."

"But you are so beautiful," Ed would respond. "I *love* to see you."

Charlene would start to cry. She would inadvertently lean toward her husband, drawn to his caring and support. But then, suddenly realizing what she was doing, she would pull away. "Don't lie to me like that! I'm not beautiful and you damn well know it!"

Johnson felt exasperated. At such times it felt like all the hard-won progress they had made was for nothing. It felt like they were starting over again. Johnson felt both discouraged and yet determined that she would work on managing her own impatience.

"I was concentrating so hard," Johnson recalled. "I was trying to follow Charlene's emotions, understand them, shape them, bring some order and color to them, and help her create moments of contact and engagement with her partner. This is a huge issue in working with them, and most trauma couples. I was helping them to feel safe with one another. I was helping this woman to realize that she was worth loving, that she could turn to others when the dragon came to get her. It was all about her asking for help."

Indeed, Ed rose to the challenge, agreeing to take on the responsibility as caretaker. He talked about his own family background and how this prepared him for this role: his father had died when he was young and he had helped his mother to grieve and recover. He found he liked this job, that it made him feel useful and important. Furthermore, he found he was good at it.

But even with all that practice he had logged early in life, he had been ready to give up on his wife. He had been tired of the mixed messages and found the situation to be hopeless. He could only give so much of himself to his wife and children while finding precious little support for himself. Now, however, things were beginning to turn around. Charlene and Ed were starting to express their love to one another in a way they never had before—with anyone.

Johnson recalled that this case, perhaps more than any other, showed her the power of attachment. "What we try to do in therapy with trauma couples is turn their relationship into a healing relationship. This lady showed me that even when there is a dragon looking over your relationship, the longing for human connection is so powerful that if you can tap into it, you can fight that dragon. Charlene learned to fight all the negative images of herself that she got from those dreadful relationships in her past."

Johnson still keeps in touch with Ed and Charlene, getting regular reports on their continued progress. Eventually, they were able to hold one another again, physically and metaphorically. Their trust improved to the point where they would have hot chocolate every night together at the same time. Charlene would choose whether she was ready for a "close cocoa" or a "not-close cocoa." This was a signal as to whether they would hold one another or not when they were enjoying their nightly ritual. Charlene occasionally e-mails Johnson, letting her know that their "cocoas" are getting closer and closer as they learn to trust one another more and more.

■ ■ ■

Coping Mechanisms

Looking back, Johnson still marvels about how much *she* learned from this work together. "I learned more about trusting the process, trusting people's ability to heal themselves if they have safety. That is what Carl Rogers talked about all those years ago. Trusting that you can go into the most horrible, dangerous-looking mess of emotions like fear and irritability and shame and, if you can create safety in the session, you can deal with those emotions and actually find ways of turning them into positive actions."

Reflecting on what happened in this case, Johnson was struck by Charlene's desire to be invisible. About the only time she ever felt anything at all was when she was eating (even if this feeling was shame and guilt). As she felt increasingly hobbled by recurrent flashbacks and other posttraumatic stress symptoms, Charlene attempted to cope any way she could. In such a crisis situation, she began to starve herself. This made her both desperate and vulnerable, but also reachable in a way that she had not been before.

"I think that is why I was able to connect with them in a very collaborative way," Johnson said. "All her attachment needs and fears were right at the surface. I think if I had approached this couple as a distant expert, nothing would have happened. I could have gone into the relationship and worked with all of Charlene's emotional chaos, and labeled those emotions from a distance, and nothing would have happened. I had to be willing to stand with her while she actually walked around in those emotions, and experienced them, and faced the dragon. I had to be willing to struggle with making sense of her feelings and helping her shape them and color them and deal with them in a way that she could order and make sense of them."

So, how did she do that we wondered? How does Johnson's EFT style lend itself to this type of work?

This case definitely required a little more of everything. She had to pay extra attention to safety and trust issues in the relationship. She had to be prepared to work with more intense and sustained emotions. She had to monitor her own sense of futility and frustration during the process. Mostly, she gave the couple extra space to explore and express their feelings to one another.

As one example of this, when Ed reached out to Charlene, she would become angry and withdraw. Rather than letting this go, Johnson asked, "What's happening with you right now?"

"Nothing," Charlene said.

"Nothing? Nothing at all?"

"That's right. Nothing. It's like a ping."

They would then spend the rest of the hour taking "ping" apart. What did it mean? What did it express? What *was* ping? It was rage: "He has turned away from me and I'll show him!" Ping was numbness: "I am not going to feel anything." Ping was shame: "He doesn't want to be near me because I am so unlovable." Ping was grief: "I am all alone and I can never be with anyone again." Ping was fear: "If I let him close I'll be destroyed." Each part was examined and expressed.

There was so much going on with this couple, so many issues, both individually and collectively, that Johnson felt challenged to construct a road map along the way. Yet with all the complexity and depth to this case, everything seemed to be related to focusing on fears of attachment and intimacy.

That is one reason, she mused, why other therapists gave up on the couple. Charlene was perhaps seen as too demanding, too pathological. Ed was seen as too co-dependent. Together, they were viewed as hopeless. Yet Johnson found them simply interesting. She knew it would be a challenge to work with them, but she found herself learning so much during the process that all the effort was worth it. This is one reason why some of our best work occurs with the most challenging cases.

"The bottom line," Johnson summarized, "was that I respected the hell out of Charlene. She blew me away with her courage. If I hung in there, and I worked hard enough, and struggled hard enough to understand her experience, I believed she would respond to me, and to her more accessible partner."

Johnson believes that is the secret to doing good therapy. If we can hang in there with our clients, even when they test us the most, then we earn their respect. And their trust.

What Else Is to Be Learned?

It is standard operating procedure in the field that a client's level of distress is supposed to predict therapy outcome. The more messed up someone is at the beginning of treatment, the less likely he or she is to respond favorably to the therapy and end up with a successful outcome. Yet in Johnson's own research, she has found just the opposite: that where clients start at the beginning of treatment has little, if anything, to do with where they end up. What matters is how emotionally engaged they become in the process. If Johnson is right, this is very good news. For it means that we can remain optimistic and enthusiastic about the power of our interventions no matter how disturbed someone might be. It does not depend on how dysfunctional they are when they start, but rather on how expert we are as therapists to create a safe, collaborative relationship so we then can work on things.

In order for this to occur, therapists have to get over their own fears of intimacy and emotional intensity. Our culture teaches us to be afraid of feelings, to minimize and marginalize them as distracting, irrelevant, and destructive. Everything is about staying in control. "Rule your emotions," we are told, "lest they rule you!"

This is certainly a major premise behind cognitive therapy. But Johnson doesn't believe this for a minute. "In intimate relationships, if you leave the emotion out it is like leaving the onion out of onion soup. What people want are emotional attunement, engagement, compassionate connection, and tenderness. You tell me how to make that using cognitive reason? There are no ingredients. You can't make that soup with nice thoughts and cognition and reason. It doesn't work."

Johnson believes it is her English working-class background, growing up above a pub, that taught her about the power of emotions. "There are really only about six emotions," she says, "and there is nothing irrational about any of them. I never met an emotion that didn't make sense to me. I have met all kinds of thoughts that don't make any sense to me at all. Working with the chaos of Charlene's emotional life and her relationships, there were so many twists and turns. What do I do when I am lost? I go for the most powerful emotion and I stay there with it. When I do so, it is like it comes out like the sun and just illuminates the whole landscape."

Johnson finds interesting the way theoretical approaches are so often gendered. Many male theorists worship rationality and logic and thought control but devalue women's affective experiences. She finds this unfortunate. "Emotion comes from the Latin word 'to move,'" Johnson explains. "Emotion moves us to action whether we like it or not. I think for a therapist to ignore this powerful source of movement and motivation is neglectful, if not irresponsible. Emotion is where people are most of the time in close relationships, especially when they are in trouble. That is the music that is playing, if we can only hear it, and can use it to create change."

6

The Control Freak with the Gun Collection

A Case from William Glasser

Positive addiction. Reality therapy. Choice theory. Quality schools. These are just a few of the major contributions that William Glasser has made to the fields of counseling, psychotherapy, medicine, and education.

Bill Glasser has lived several distinct careers as a theorist. His early work in psychiatry made him suspicious of the prevailing frameworks that sought to label people as mentally ill rather than as making poor choices for their behavior. Whether delving into the field of addiction, chronic illnesses such as fibromyalgia, or so-called mental illnesses and conduct disorders, Glasser has been a consistent and outspoken critic of approaches that seek to label and stigmatize people, as well as reduce control and responsibility for their behavior.

*Glasser has written a number of classic and influential books that have had significant influence in the fields of education (*Schools without Failure, The Quality School*), substance abuse (*Positive Addiction*), marital relationships (*What Is This Thing Called Love?, Getting Together and Staying Together*), psychotherapy (*Reality Therapy Counseling with Choice Theory*), and more recently,* Warning: Psychiatry Can be Hazardous to Your Mental Health.

A Maverick

William Glasser has always enjoyed the role of maverick in his profession. While completing his residency at UCLA as a young psychiatrist, he was both critical and skeptical of the usual procedures favored by other doctors to treat emotional problems. After 50 years his position has hardly changed, as he still refuses to recognize that mental illness, as a concept, actually exists in the world.

It was during the last year of his training, with a largely affluent group of patients, that Glasser began to repudiate publicly the psychoanalytic practices of the time. "The idea was that you didn't really help people," Glasser says with a laugh, "you just listened to them for a few years, and occasionally talked to them. Supposedly that would make something good happen." Glasser shakes his head, still amazed that anyone could actually believe that such a process would really make much of a difference.

Glasser not only spoke passionately about his suspicions that there was really no such thing as mental illness, and that regardless of what emotional struggles were called, there were certainly better ways to help people rather than talking about their dreams and secret desires, but he also was quite critical of any approach that only attempted to promote insight. "People already have insight," he complained to his supervisors. "The last thing they need is to spend more time thinking and talking about their symptoms and their so-called mental illnesses. What they really need to do is to figure out what to do about these problems."

It wasn't as if Glasser couldn't understand the attractions of a long-term talking cure that might run into years of practice and hundreds of sessions. He was dirt-poor at the time, scrambling to support his family by opening a private practice. His unconventional methods had already alienated most of his colleagues and teachers, so he couldn't expect many referrals. He was also experimenting with a briefer, more action-oriented, confrontive style that would require a lot more patients to earn a living.

It's All about Choices

One of the first referrals to show up in Glasser's new office was a very striking, forceful kind of guy. In the first few minutes of the meeting, Jake let it be known in no uncertain terms what he wanted, what he expected, and what he demanded. He was used to taking charge of things in life, and he intended to do the same with this young psychiatrist he consulted.

For reasons that Glasser didn't fully understand, they seemed to hit it off quite well and developed a close, respectful collaboration. Whereas Jake was inclined to control others, and quick to become angry, he always spoke politely to Glasser.

"I'm really a screenwriter," Jake announced one day. "Yeah, I know I work at the car dealer, but it's just a matter of time before one of my scripts is picked up. I told you I've got an in."

Jake had been working as a manager of a local dealership, and although he earned a good income, he felt both underpaid and unappreciated. His father was a famous actor, so he had grown up hanging around big-time Hollywood producers and directors. When he said he had an "in," he was not just blowing smoke: he was exposed to certain privileges that both raised his hopes and also frustrated him because he had not yet been able to sell one of his stories.

As Glasser got to know him better over time, Jake would express his bitter disappointments more vehemently. His festering anger began to affect his marriage, his relationships with his children, and with co-workers at the dealership. Yet somehow, he managed to maintain his composure during sessions with Glasser.

"I told you how I was raised," Jake complained. "My parents never treated me as a child, but as an equal. There was no discipline. I was totally indulged. They'd be away on location somewhere and I'd be left to do. . . ."

"We've been over this before," Glasser interrupted carefully. He was very careful not to provoke his volatile patient, knowing his tendencies to be rather explosive with this temper.

"Yeah," Jake tried to continue, "but. . . ."

"I just don't think going over this history is all that helpful to you right now. That part of your life is over. Nothing you can do about it. What we have to focus on is what you are doing right now. And what you might do instead."

Glasser was just beginning to develop his ideas about choice theory and reality therapy, a radically new approach to counseling that stays in the present rather than dredging up the past the way his psychoanalytic colleagues were so inclined. Even 50 years ago, Glasser was already experimenting with the idea that people are not predestined or subject to heredity and instincts as much as the medical establishment thought (and still thinks). People have choices, many more so than they can imagine. Glasser saw his job as helping people like Jake to make some new choices about the ways they live their lives. Jake didn't have to remain an angry, bitter, disenfranchised failure.

I'll Keep Them Safe

The work was slow-going, and eventually Jake could no longer afford weekly sessions. Glasser agreed to continue seeing him, partly because he felt committed to the relationship, but also because he had some genuine concerns about the man's potential to hurt others. Lately, Jake had been talking a lot about his fantasies of shooting people who blocked or angered him in some way.

"This was during the time of the "Texas Tower" sniper," Glasser explained, referring to the incident in which a gunman climbed into a tower at the University of Texas and began killing people at random. Glasser had serious concerns about whether Jake might be similarly dangerous. This was of special concern because the man had a collection of hunting rifles with 'scopes, which were just the sort of weapons that one would not want to have in the hands of someone who was irrational, angry, volatile, and with a grudge against others—also someone who disclosed frequent fantasies of revenge.

"Look," Glasser told him one day, taking a deep breath and steeling himself before taking a big risk, "I just don't feel comfortable talking to you anymore knowing that you have a bunch of high-powered rifles at home and that you talk so much about using them."

Jake narrowed his eyes and dipped his head aggressively. Glasser could see him grip his hands into fists and so involuntarily glanced in the direction of the door in case he had to make a quick exit. But Glasser dared to suggest, "Why don't you bring them to me for safekeeping?"

Jake nodded. "Maybe that isn't such a bad idea," he admitted.

Glasser exhaled, hoping his relief wouldn't be too obvious. He couldn't let Jake see that he was afraid.

"So, then," Jake asked, "what are you going to do with them if I bring them in? And when will you give them back to me? Some of them are quite valuable."

"Oh," Glasser said, trying to stall for time. He hadn't thought this through fully. "I'll keep them right here, right in the closet. They'll be safe and nobody will touch them." He reminded himself to slow down. Deep breath.

Jake looked at Glasser again, scrutinizing him with the same sort of intensity that he might use to sight through the 'scope of his rifle. Then he nodded.

"Well then," Glasser said, trying to keep his voice steady. "We've got that settled."

Jake seemed to recognize that his anger was indeed a dangerous thing, and that he was just asking for trouble by keeping those rifles within easy access.

Meanwhile, while confiscating the weapons made Glasser feel a little easier, this was not the end of Jake's creepy behavior.

Since his marriage ended, Jake had fallen in love with another woman, who also left him out of fear. She had since moved in with another man, bringing her children along with her.

Jake continued to feel a sense of propriety over her, especially since he believed that he was the father of one of her children. Since she would not agree to see him, and denied that the child was his, Jake began to sneak into her house late at night when everyone was sleeping. He would even tiptoe into the bedroom and watch her sleeping with her new lover, standing over them and imagining all the terrible things he would like to do to them for betraying him.

During this time, Glasser was seeing Jake only intermittently. Although it certainly appeared that his patient was continuing to engage in some rather unusual, dangerous behavior, and Glasser agonized over whether the threats were real or not. He decided, in the end, to continue to monitor progress as closely as he could.

Anger out of Control

Jake stabilized for a period of time and seemed to make good progress. Then he became involved with another woman, a farm girl from Kansas. After some time, she also decided to end the relationship, and this absolutely enraged Jake, to the point where he became murderous in his heart.

"I want to kill that bitch," he threatened. "She had no right to treat me this way. She deserves to die. And I'm the one to do the job."

Glasser's eyes flitted toward the closet where he was still storing the rifles after more than 4 years. They actually had cobwebs on them at this point.

What the heck should he do? Glasser wondered. This was before the time of the landmark Tarasoff Decision, in which a therapist had failed to notify the police about a possible violent threat against someone by a patient. Whereas nowadays there are clear guidelines for acting when there is a clear suspicion that someone may be a danger to others, during this time a professional was left to his or her own best judgment.

In spite of his efforts to discover more about the situation, Glasser didn't know very much about the woman except that she was from Kansas. He didn't know her name, what she looked like, or even where she lived. He also couldn't determine just how serious Jake was about acting on his threats. Glasser felt completely at a loss about what to do: if he called the police, he would lose his patient's trust forever; if he failed to warn authorities, there was a very real possibility that someone could be grievously injured. It would certainly have been easy enough for Jake to get hold of another rifle if that's what he wanted to do, even though he claimed he had not yet done so.

Glasser figured that as long as Jake was still willing to talk about his feelings, and disclose his fantasies, he was probably not yet ready to act on them. Yet if Glasser had been pressed at the time about his confidence level in this assessment, he would have admitted that he wasn't so sure. This was just his best clinical judgment based on the years during which he had seen the man.

This Calls for an Intervention

By this time, Glasser was tired of Jake's constant threats of violence. This was just no way to go about living one's life, becoming enraged and homicidal every time someone didn't live up to his expectations. Glasser decided finally that he had to confront this matter head-on, and an idea began to take shape about how he might do this.

Glasser's office had a number of framed pictures on the wall. Remember: this was in Los Angeles, the land of earthquakes, the place where it is almost impossible to keep pictures hanging straight on any wall because tremors were always knocking them askew.

Compulsive, controlling Jake had a habit of entering Glasser's office and scrutinizing the walls before he took his accustomed seat. If he noticed that a picture was hanging a little crooked, he would straighten it out. He seemed to do this not only because he preferred a sense of perfect order in those things he could control, but it was also a sort of caring gesture, repaying his mentor with a kindness. Glasser had always observed this ritual with amusement, since it had never particularly bothered him that the pictures were a little off-center.

Glasser was still worrying about Jake killing his latest ex-girlfriend, and he decided that he absolutely had to deal with this issue once and for all. So before Jake's next scheduled appointment, he knocked each one of the pictures on his wall off-center. They weren't just a little crooked, but so obviously in disarray that Jake would have to notice.

Sure enough, Jake walked in and immediately approached the wall. He took several minutes, not saying a word, just straightening each picture, stepping back to examine his work, and then making a few other adjustments until he was satisfied. Then he walked to his usual chair and sat down, looking up at his psychiatrist for the first time.

"Did I ask you to straighten my pictures?" Glasser asked him in a scolding voice.

"Excuse me?"

"I said," Glasser repeated, even more strongly, "did I ask you to mess with those pictures on my wall?"

"What's wrong? What did I do?" Jake looked just like a hurt little boy who had been caught passing notes in study hall.

"What did you do?" Glasser repeated, raising his voice. "You messed with my pictures."

"Yes," Jake admitted, about to defend himself. "They were crooked and. . . ."

"Did you ever consider that I might have turned them that way on purpose? Maybe I like my pictures crooked. This is, after all, my office, isn't it?"

"Well yeah," Jake sputtered, "but I just wanted. . . ."

"I don't care what you wanted," Glasser interrupted him again. "I put those pictures that way for a very good reason. If I want my pictures crooked, or upside down, or sitting on the floor, that is my right. They are my pictures and this is my office."

"Okay then," Jake said, looking down and starting to pout. "Fine."

"I knew you would walk in and do exactly what you did," Glasser said in a softer voice. "That's why I deliberately arranged them that way. Do you know why I might have done that?"

"No." Jake shook his head and looked at Glasser as if he was crazy. He couldn't imagine why anyone would do such a stupid thing.

"Because you so often mess in other people's lives when you aren't invited."

"What do you mean?" Jake answered defiantly, finally finding his voice after this weird demonstration. "All I try to do is. . . ."

"All you try to do is threaten to kill someone if she won't do what you want. You are like a little child who wants to control everyone and everything in the world. When things don't go your way, the first thing that comes to your mind is that you are going to punish that person, as if her only purpose in life is to do what you want."

Jake looked at his doctor with his menacing look, but Glasser refused to be cowed. "You say you trust me. You have been seeing me for years. You know I will tell you the truth in a way that nobody else will. Well, I am telling you that you can't go around straightening the pictures in other people's offices just because you don't like them the way they are. And you can't go around killing people just because they don't obey you."

A minute of silence. Then another. Jake stared at Glasser, without blinking. Then he nodded. "Am I really this way?"

"Yes. That is what you are like."

"Really?" Jake seemed unable to grasp the idea that he could really be so stubborn and controlling that this was the source of his difficulties.

"I've been trying to tell you this for years. This woman from Kansas doesn't want to see you any more. That is her right. And you can't kill her just because she doesn't want to be with you. And you can't go around messing with other people's things—like my pictures—just because they bother you."

"You do have a point, I guess."

"You guess?"

"Okay. You have a point."

"Well, then, you leave that woman alone. If she wants to see you, she'll let you know. Otherwise, there's nothing else you can do."

"But it's still not fair that. . . ."

"Jake," Glasser pointed out, "have you ever ended a relationship with a woman before she was ready to do so?"

"Sure."

"Do any of those women have the right to kill you for that? How would you like the idea of one of those rejected lovers coming after you with a rifle?"

"Wouldn't," Jake whispered.

"I can't hear you."

"I said I wouldn't."

"There you go." And with that admission, Jake finally gave up his violent threats of bodily harm.

■　■　■

It's about the Relationship

"That was my finest hour," Glasser said, thinking back on his storied career of half a century. "Jake thanked me when he left that session. And he was totally sincere when he said that he really heard me and that I really helped him."

Glasser continued to see Jake about once a month after that, up until the time he eventually closed that office. Jake even came to Glasser's home for sessions on occasion, not because he needed them, but to report on continued progress he was making.

Of course, it was not a single hour that cured Jake of his murderous rages, but rather a long-term relationship in which incremental progress was made one tiny step at a time. Yet among all the hours of therapy that Glasser has conducted over half a century, in psychiatric hospitals, prisons, schools, and private practice, this hour stands out as representing some of his finest work.

Glasser felt good that he stuck with Jake over so many years, even without charging him a cent. Although he had never been doing psychoanalytic treatment, going back into the past, he had sustained rather long-term relationship-oriented treatment over many years. Yet the turning point in the case occurred at the moment that Glasser decided to take action, to stop playing it safe.

"A good counselor should be active," Glasser said, "and this was the session when this became most clear to me. I felt good about the way things turned out because I probably saved Jake's life. I may have saved a woman's life. And maybe I saved my own life as well."

While Glasser is referring to saving his own life from Jake's homicidal urges, that can be taken at another level as well. It was during this formative time in Glasser's career that he was just beginning to shape the structure of what would become reality therapy. While professionals most often associate this brand of therapy with a rather structured process of asking people what they are doing, what the consequences are of these actions, and what they might do instead that would better meet their needs, this is actually a relatively small component of the theory. Cases like Jake's taught Glasser about the power of commitment to a helping relationship. It is within such an alliance that Glasser was able to help Jake, and so many others like him, to move beyond mere talk to confronting their destructive behaviors and making more constructive choices for the future.

"The relationship we develop with people is about 99 percent," Glasser explained, "the rest of what we do is about 1 percent. If you can't figure out how to make a relationship with people in a way that they allow us into their worlds, they will never listen to us. But people like Jake were in my world as well. They have been as important in my life as I have been to their lives."

Time to Swim and Stop Treading Water

Jake also taught Glasser a lot about the importance of moving far beyond his early training at the hands of psychoanalysts who operated so passively in their work. Glasser was learning about ways to become far more active, challenging, and confrontive in his sessions. For instance, when asked how he could tell the difference between his finest hours as a therapist and those that are just satisfactory, he immediately thought of another case to illustrate his point.

"I had a lot of sessions that were just sessions. We were just treading water. I was talking to people about the choices they were making and the potential control they had over their lives. I explained to them about how their symptoms were not the result of some mental illness but were part of poor relationships that could very well be improved."

This brings to mind the case of an extremely depressed woman who seemed to have everything in life that anyone could want. She was wealthy and privileged, yet spectacularly unhappy and suicidal. She didn't seem to know why she was so miserable, and neither did Glasser. One day, not unlike the way he brought things to a head with Jake, Glasser decided to become more direct and confrontive with her at a time she was complaining that she didn't have a boyfriend.

"Something is going on with you," Glasser said to her, "and I don't know what that is. This isn't something in your subconscious, but something that I sense that is very well within your awareness. You're just not telling me what's really going on. And I think we're just wasting our time."

The woman looked at Glasser, trying to decide whether to become angry or indignant or tearful. Finally, she just waited to see where he was going with this.

"Look," Glasser said, "I'm not saying that I won't keep seeing you. But I just know that there is something going on in your life that you're not telling me about. And it certainly seems to have something to do with the reason why you are so depressed. Now are you going to tell me what is really going on, or are you going to keep coming here and keep it a secret?"

It turned out that the young woman, a student at UCLA, had gotten involved with one of her professors. He was abusing her terribly—humiliating her, degrading her, treating her as if she was just a plaything, which in one sense she was to him. She had kept this a secret from her parents, and even from her friends, because otherwise the professor threatened to end the relationship.

When Glasser heard this story, he felt himself become so angry that he had a passing thought about giving Jake back one of his rifles to take care of this worm of a guy. This was an instance when he could actually imagine someone resorting to violence because of the way she was treated. Holding his own feelings in check, Glasser instead confronted her.

"You can spend the rest of your life stuck in this relationship," he told her. "You can choose to be miserable for the rest of your life. Or, you can dump this loser and move on. That is totally up to you. So, what's it going to be?"

Glasser didn't delude himself that this single confrontation totally turned things around. For one thing, he seemed to have caught her at a ripe moment, when she was so sick of herself she really couldn't see another alternative. He is also clear about what he didn't do with her—no dream interpretation, no digging up the past, no endless talk about why she was so screwed up and how it resulted from her childhood. Glasser just told her essentially to stop complaining and to take back control of her life.

This story, like Jake's case, had a happy ending. The woman soon ended things with her professor, became involved in a much healthier relationship with a man she eventually married. Like so many of Glasser's memorable cases, he stayed in touch with her over the rest of her life.

"Most of my ex-patients are all retired now," Glasser says with a laugh. "And yet here I am still working."

Working indeed. Now almost 80 years old, Glasser still maintains an active schedule, traveling all over the world to give workshops and training seminars at the various William Glasser Institutes, consulting with the several Glasser Quality Schools, and writing several new books that focus on mental health rather than mental illness.

7

An Immovable Object

A Case from Pat Love

Pat Love was trained originally as a counselor educator and family therapist, before moving into the realm of consultation and public speaking. She operates from an approach that combines systems and attachment theory with a biological basis for behavior.

Love has written several best-selling books, including The Emotional Incest Syndrome *and* Hot Monogamy. *In her latest book,* The Truth about Love, *she tackled her most challenging subject by combining the latest theory and research on the nature of love in a way that empowers people in their relationships.*

Love also likes to sit in the backyard while listening to birds and fantasize about how she could possibly improve the landscape design.

Too Little, Too Late

From an early age, Milt was bound and determined to become rich and successful. Through hard work, single-minded determination, and neglect of his wife and family, he managed to achieve his life-long goal.

It was only after his wife, Cassandra, announced to him that she was leaving the marriage that he realized how desperate things had become. Until that point he had just tuned out his wife's nagging; after all, what right did she have to complain? He was an excellent provider who had built them a mansion, not to mention a sizable fortune.

While Cassandra had raised their three children (who were now grown and had children of their own), Milt spent all his time at the office. He felt this was a fine division of labor, at least until his wife told him she'd had enough and he could keep the damn warehouse they called a house.

Milt immediately consulted a therapist; for the first time in his life, he felt a complete loss of control and went into a tailspin; he became severely depressed. Not only had Cassandra told him that she was out the door, she had found another man—someone who showed her the attention she had always yearned for.

The therapy proceeded well, and Milt made steady progress. He finally accepted the reality that he had wasted a good part of his life on work while neglecting those who loved him the most.

In spite of these insights, Cassandra informed him in no uncertain terms that it was far too little, too late. "I love you," she told him, "but I'm not in love with you any more. I have someone else in my life right now and he makes me feel like I've never felt before. I've given the first half of my life to you and the kids; now it's my turn."

Milt was remorseful and penitent, yet he accepted that he could not change the past and would have to move forward as best he could.

The Referral

The colleague who had been seeing Milt and Cassandra referred the case to Love for treatment. It seems that in the few sessions Cassandra had attended, she had been adamant that nothing that either the therapist or her husband had to say was worth listening to. This colleague hoped that a fresh start with someone new might be helpful to her.

Love's style of therapy, or at least the structure she uses, is somewhat different from the norm. Her practice consists primarily of couples she sees in intensive sessions that last 1, 2, or even 3 days. She had found that seeing people for an hour or two was far too limiting; by the time things got warmed up, it was time to quit. So she developed a model that was more congruent with her therapeutic approach, as well as her personality and travel schedule.

"Couples really need to spend time focusing on their relationship and developing skills," Love explained, "but also giving themselves the time and attention that they need to build some sort of connection and intimacy. It has been my experience that many couples, and most that are in trouble, don't spend enough quality time together to create the relationship they say they want. In order to orchestrate any type of breakthrough, I've found that 50 minutes just doesn't do the job."

When Love's colleague called her about the new referral, he described Cassandra as an "immovable object." "I've been working with this couple for a while. The husband has spared no time and effort to make up for lost time and has been really working hard. But the wife—that's something else."

"What do you mean?" Love asked.

"This guy has agreed to do anything it will take. He has cut back his business involvement and is willing to turn the whole thing over to his sons. He's had a complete change of heart, backed up by his behavior, but. . . ."

"But the wife has had enough," Love finished.

"Yeah. That's about it. Her heart has grown cold."

Love wondered why this other therapist was referring the case. What did he imagine that she could do that he had not been able to accomplish? She thought maybe because she was a woman, that might make some difference, but also because she was nationally recognized and that could have some influence. Also, the whole idea of the couple traveling across the country to work with Pat for 3 days seemed kind of interesting to them.

"So," the colleague asked, "will you take the case?"

Love agreed. When Cassandra called to make the appointment, Love talked to her about the structure of their work together, how they would spend 8–10 hours per day for 3 days in a row. She has found that often one such intensive is enough to break through impasses, but sometimes she schedules a follow-up some months later.

"I have to be honest with you," Cassandra said before the phone call ended. "I'm not coming to save the marriage; that's over. Milt may believe that's why I'm coming to see you, but the reason is for me to work on myself. That's where I am at this point in my life. I've spent almost 50 years, and especially the last 30, taking care of other people, and now it's my turn."

"That's fine," Love told her. "Thanks for being honest about your expectations." They agreed on the time and the terms and said goodbye.

Day One

When Cassandra walked in, Love was struck by her natural beauty. She was a striking, fiftyish woman. No makeup. No jewelry. Very healthy. Very fit. As it turned out, she had a fitness expert who worked hard on her body, so it looked like it belonged to a dancer.

Cassandra crawled into one of the overstuffed chairs in the office and folded herself like a pretzel, legs crossed. She then spent the first several hours talking about her romance with her new lover and how wonderful it was. Love got the impression that she was trying not only to convince her therapist how amazing the relationship was, but also to convince herself.

It is indeed a fortunate accident that Pat Love's name reflects her chosen expertise in the field of romantic love. She has spent the last two decades researching and writing about the cultural, personal, and biological nature of this phenomenon. So she has a fair degree of understanding of the ways that people experience love, and the ways people report these experiences. Although she felt that Cassandra already trusted her, Pat didn't want to push her too hard in the beginning, nor contradict her idealized (and distorted) image of what her new relationship could offer.

Cassandra went on at length about how great her new lover was and how perfect their relationship was, not realizing that what seemed so special and unique to her was pretty typical of the infatuation stage of a new relationship, when neurophysiological processes are firing at their peak.

"I don't even think of him as my lover," Cassandra said a little defensively. "I just like being with him."

"I see," Love said neutrally, again recognizing a fairly classic description of infatuation that is common in this honeymoon phase. She then asked a series of leading questions designed to build a closer bond from which to challenge some misconceptions that were evident.

"So then, you must be having interesting conversations with him?"

Cassandra nodded with a smile.

"Do you especially like the way you feel with him?"

"Yes," she agreed and nodded.

"And you find that just thinking about him gives you good feelings."

Again a vigorous nod.

"I imagine, as well, that the most mundane tasks in your life now seem to take on new meaning since this relationship began."

Cassandra looked at Pat quizzically, as if to say, "How did you know that?"

"And I bet you find your sexuality awakened in ways that you haven't felt in years."

"Maybe ever!"

And so the conversation proceeded, in which Love was careful not to upstage or contradict her client. Cassandra went on to talk about how she and her lover had started out as friends, but that he saw things in her that nobody had recognized before. It felt like what had been missing in her marriage all along. "Even Milt admitted that he's taken me for granted. He just thought I'd always be there."

Day Two

The second day of their intensive session continued much like the first. Cassandra talked about how her lover didn't see her as a mother, or a grandmother, or helpmate, but as a talented, creative woman. All the while that Love nodded her understanding, she thought about how often people get into affairs because of positive mirroring, in which the lover reflects back those qualities that have long been ignored. This guy saw her as sensual, interesting, competent, vibrant, all the qualities she'd always wanted to have; and as long as she was with him it seemed to her that she *was* this amazing person.

As the story unfolded, Love learned that things were not what they seemed. Cassandra admitted that Milt had hired a detective to investigate his wife's lover and turned over the report to her, a report that described this man as an illegal immigrant who was still married back home but had abandoned his family. "But this isn't true," Cassandra protested. "It's not like it seems! I even brought the report to show you."

Cassandra had indeed brought the investigation summary, which she handed to Love to scrutinize. In the margins next to each piece of damning evidence she had scribbled notes to refute the key points.

"Not true!" one note said in careful script. "Marriage already over when he left."

"Doesn't need my money," another note said next to the item about the lover's excessive debt. "Has his own income."

"Besides," she added, while following Love's scrutiny of the report, "money isn't important to me. And I never intend to marry again so it's a moot point."

Cassandra had an answer for everything, a rebuttal to each of the detective's discoveries about the man's irresponsibility and deceit.

In spite of her skepticism, Love kept herself in a fairly compassionate position, reflecting Cassandra's excitement and enthusiasm over her relationship. She did not want to polarize her client even further. Up to this point no one had listened to or supported Cassandra's position, which left only her to defend her actions. Plus, Love knew that Cassandra's system was flooded with the chemicals associated with infatuation and it would be difficult to hear any type of negative reality check. Cassandra had boundless energy and felt that, at age 56, she had been reborn by this relationship. She needed to tell someone about her experience, so Love listened as empathically as she could and resisted the temptation to do reality testing too quickly, choosing instead to be strategic in her approach.

As sessions progressed, Cassandra carefully structured their time together. She brought in notes and photographs and diary entries to illustrate her stories. She had taken this therapeutic journey very seriously and had invested considerable preparation into how she wanted to spend her time.

Day Three

If the first two days had focused mainly on the past and to some extent the present, the third day began with talk about the future. By this time, Love felt attuned to her client, sensitive to her rhythms and pace and her unique way of communication. Cassandra talked about her plans for the future and what she'd like her life to look like in the years ahead. One interesting feature of her narrative was that for the first time she was talking more kindly and generously about her husband. Whereas the first day, everything she had to say about Milt was highly critical, and the second day she had softened just a bit in complaining about his constant neglect of her, by the third day she actually had some positive things to say about him. Moreover, she also acknowledged that her lover was not nearly as perfect as she had first portrayed him.

It was while talking about how successful a team Cassandra and Milt had been in building their fortune that Love saw the first real opportunity to paint a more balanced picture of their marriage. She also realized why the previous therapist had been so committed to helping the couple to salvage their relationship rather than letting them go their separate ways; there seemed to be more investment than at first appeared.

"So you're saying that Milt trusts you in a lot of ways," Love reflected at one point.

"What do you mean?" Cassandra asked.

"Well, for the past hour you've been talking about how Milt has always treated you as an equal partner. He may not have met all your needs for intimacy, nor invested enough time and energy into your relationship, but it sounds like he has relied on you in a lot of ways."

"I guess so," she said thoughtfully.

"For instance, you were saying how he valued your input on decisions he made in the business. And for all practical purposes, he deferred to you completely about the way the home was run."

"That's true."

"And you also talked about how your sex life together was quite satisfying, even after all these years."

She nodded.

"It might not rival the excitement of your new relationship, but then what partner could compete with the novelty of a new lover?" This was a key point, so Love waited to gauge its effect.

"Yeah, I guess you're right," Cassandra agreed. "I kind of feel guilty about some of this, you know."

"Guilty how?" Love pressed.

"Well, like, I'm sort of a one-man woman. And now. . . ."

"Go on."

"It's just that I don't really like having to decide between two men. I know I said that I don't want to be married again, but I like being in just one relationship at a time."

"So commitment and exclusivity is important to you," Love summarized.

Cassandra nodded.

One reason why Love so likes the intensive therapy format is that, once momentum is begun, it is easier to follow through with things. In taking inventory of what they'd accomplished thus far, Love noted that they'd developed a solid alliance. Second, by remaining neutral and carefully nonjudgmental, she'd created the space for her client to consider the consequences of her behavior at her own pace. Once Cassandra indicated a readiness to look at her situation more objectively and critically, it became possible to introduce more direct interventions.

Love asked Cassandra if she'd like to come back for one more intensive session in a few weeks. She agreed to do so, and surprisingly, even seemed amenable to bringing along her husband for one of the two days they scheduled.

Second Chance

"How are things going since I've seen you last?" Pat asked Cassandra.

"Pretty interesting, actually."

"Interesting?"

"Yeah. My husband has made some changes in the last few weeks."

"Changes? What sort of changes?"

"Well, he turned over more of the responsibilities of the business to his board of directors."

"That *is* interesting."

"And he gave the boys—our sons—more work as well, the kind of stuff he used to insist on doing himself."

"I see," Love answered, trying not to grin too obviously.

"But the really strange thing is that he planned a trip for us. He wants us to go away somewhere and he already made all the arrangements and everything."

"That's . . . " Love started, then hesitated, wanting to choose a carefully neutral word.

"Interesting," Cassandra finished with a smile.

"Yeah," Love smiled back. "That's just what I was going to say."

"But the thing is, I'm not sure if that would be a good idea. I mean, considering that we're going our separate ways and all."

"What would it be like for you if you did go on a trip with Milt?" Love asked, changing the direction of the conversation back to a focus on a more optimistic future for the marriage. She then followed this with questions about other trips they'd taken together, and other times they'd shared.

Cassandra found herself reminiscing about some of the sweet experiences they'd shared and exotic places they'd visited. Almost against her will, she started telling stories about some of the funny things that had happened, as well as some of the intimate moments they had experienced.

Love looked at Cassandra and cocked her head.

"What?"

"I was just thinking," Love said.

"Thinking what?"

"I was just thinking that you seem so different than the last time I saw you just a few weeks ago."

"Different how?"

"Let me ask you the same question," Love turned the question around. "How do *you* think you're different?"

Cassandra struggled a bit, but eventually articulated that last time she had been unwilling to see anything good and worthwhile in her marriage and her husband's behavior. Now she felt differently. She acknowledged that he had been a good father and was a very attentive grandfather. Although she had said he couldn't change, he had proved in the intervening weeks that he *could* make dramatic alterations in his patterns.

What Love had been attempting to do as their first sessions together had ended was to invite Cassandra to complete an exercise called "searching for goodness." The result had been that Cassandra was spending more and more time looking at the positive features of her marriage and her husband's behavior. To her, it had appeared as if only her husband had changed; in fact, her transformed attitude made changes visible.

Love doesn't believe these dramatic changes could have taken place nearly as fast in traditional, weekly therapy. Cassandra had traveled to another state to spend three straight days as a captive audience, removed from her normal environment and usual influences. She had been free to explore possibilities that would have been otherwise impossible.

Sharing Souls

"In some ways," Love summarized, "you don't really miss something until you risk losing it. Just at the point that you are considering leaving your family and ending your marriage you are realizing that you would feel some real losses."

Cassandra looked intently at Love, but didn't answer. She was thinking about this, thinking hard.

"You have been reveling in your freedom these past months," Love continued. "You have been feeling appreciated in ways that you have not in a long time. Yet in spite of how exciting this feels, you also realize that there are some real sacrifices you will make in order to take the chance that this euphoria will persist beyond the usual 6 to 12 months that is typical for an affair."

Cassandra was a very bright woman. She understood immediately the logical, scientific explanations for the biochemical mechanisms of romantic love. In some ways, this knowledge was as helpful to her as any compassion she felt from her therapist.

"I do feel a lot of affection for Milt," Cassandra admitted. "I love him, I do. He is a good friend and we'll always be close. We have our three children and our grandchildren. But I just don't know if I'll ever desire him sexually again the way I once did. It seems to have lost the intensity."

"I'm curious," Love responded. "You mentioned before that you and Milt had once had an outstanding sex life but now you're saying that things tapered off. What happened?"

"At first, we used to have sex several times a day." Cassandra smiled mischievously as she said this. "But lately it's tapered off to maybe three or four times per week."

Love was struck by how sexually active the couple had been, but she kept this thought to herself for now. "You mentioned the frequency of sex, but what about quality?" she asked.

"Well, you know. It started out kind of conservative because we were both young. But over the years we've experimented a lot. We've done a lot of things." Cassandra smiled again, not because she was embarrassed, but something about this struck her as funny. "We've done a lot of fantasies. We've tried all kinds of positions. I've studied yoga and read a lot of books about sex. And Milt's always been willing to do whatever I wanted."

"So," Love said, "you are saying that in the beginning of your relationship with Milt things were as intense and interesting as your current relationship. But over time, that intensity slipped a bit, just as it does with any couple that has been together for more than 18 months."

This point was not lost on Cassandra, who understood that Love was telling her that no relationship can sustain the sort of euphoria that is first experienced with a new lover, especially one who is seen only occasionally.

"But I don't think this is just about sex for you," Love continued. "You have wanted not only to be closer to Milt physically, but also in other ways. You've wanted him to see your soul."

Cassandra nodded, looking down. Tears were falling onto her lap and she was starting at the dark indentations they made on her blouse.

"What's going on for you right now?" Love prompted.

"I suppose you're right that I've wanted to be closer to Milt. But. . . ."

"But what?"

"But I think I'm afraid for him to see my soul. I'm afraid for anyone to get that close to me."

"The vulnerability is what frightens you. The trust that would take, especially with someone who has known you as long as Milt and been through so many of life's finest moments by your side."

Cassandra nodded, wiping her eyes. "But I think before I would ever share my body with him again we'd have to share our souls."

■   ■   ■

Epilogue

The next day, Milt and Cassandra came to the session together. But by then, most of the groundwork had already been laid. Love found it remarkably easy to negotiate the terms of their new relationship, and the couple agreed to reconcile and begin again.

We were surprised how briefly Love went over this last, culminating session, considering the detail she had supplied for the others. But it turned out that most of the difficult therapeutic work had taken place earlier, when she taught Cassandra about the nature of romantic love and the context for this experience.

Love thinks about this case, perhaps more than others, because it was so clearly a time when she helped to "save" a marriage. Cassandra had abandoned all hope. Even the previous therapist didn't think there was a chance but only wanted Love to see if she could budge this "immovable object."

Perhaps another reason this particular couple came to mind was because they contacted Love again recently. They've stayed in touch over the years. Not only did they continue to make great gains in their intimacy, they got involved as mentors for other troubled relationships in a structured program.

Love hopes that what others might learn from this case is how important information giving can be in therapy. Certainly the relationship she developed with Cassandra was critical—the empathy, the compassion, the trust that was forged between them. But more than anything else, Love believes that it was teaching her client about the nature of love and its life cycle that made the most difference.

"Students ask me all the time," Love said, "when are we going to get to the techniques in therapy? But information *is* technique, and I think this case is a good example of that."

A second critical lesson has to do with timing. Love recognized that Cassandra first needed to tell the story of her infatuation, without feeling ashamed, criticized, or as if she needed to defend her actions. Love didn't challenge her client; if anything, she communicated consistently how clearly she understood what Cassandra was going through. She waited patiently, which is something you can do when you have three 8-hour days ahead of you. "That's like 24 weeks of therapy," Love remarked. "That's a long time. If I had been seeing Cassandra once a week, I couldn't have used this same strategic approach and effected change within the short critical time frame that was available."

However, the success in this case involved far more than patience, and even information giving about the neurobiology of sex: Cassandra's soul was touched by Love. Literally and figuratively.

CHAPTER

8

Extreme Therapy

A Case from Nick Cummings

Most people know Nicholas (Nick) Cummings as the past President of the American Psychological Association who has been predicting the future of psychology for the past 40 years, and founding organizations to meet the emerging challenges. He founded the professional school movement with the California School of Professional Psychology, wrote the nation's first prepaid psychotherapy insurance benefit (in the mid-1950s), and did the research demonstrating its efficacy, designed the freedom-of-choice legislation that obligated insurers to reimburse psychologists if they reimbursed psychiatrists, and a host of other accomplishments.

The other and less known side of Nick Cummings is his vast experience with, and devotion to, the practice of psychology. For 55 years, whatever other full-time jobs he had, he saw forty to fifty patients a week. He saw his patients from 3:00 a.m. Monday to midnight Tuesday by needing only 3 hours of sleep, and with 45-minute back-to-back sessions, enabling him to see four patients in a 3-hour period for two stretches of 21 hours each. He also became the therapist of last resort in San Francisco, successfully treating everyone's failures and impossible cases. His skill in this regard became nationally recognized, and patients from as far away as Chicago, New York, Miami, and other distant cities commuted to San Francisco for their sessions with him. This case is illustrative of just one form of what he termed Extreme Therapy that he employed in over half a century of independent practice. He was emboldened in these unusual techniques by the conviction that patients always know when you are conscientiously taking chances with your own career in their own best interests. It might be helpful to other psychologists to know that with hundreds of such patients, he has never been sued or been the subject of a patient complaint.

Help with Dying

"I'm dying," the young man said to begin the session. With his bald head, and devoid of any body hair, Dan looked even younger than his 21 years. Indeed he was suffering from advanced lymphatic cancer. He had relocated across the country specifically for experimental chemotherapy and radiation treatments at a teaching hospital.

Cummings's first thought was that this guy was far too young to die. He was tall and strikingly handsome, even with the toll the treatments had been taking on his body.

"I see," he said. "And what brought you here to see me?"

"I came to this city originally because my oncologist said he could help me. He had been very optimistic and said that I had an excellent prognosis." Dan shrugged.

"It hasn't turned out that way, I presume."

Dan shook his head. "No, things just haven't turned out the way we— the way I hoped. I haven't been responding to the treatments. The doctors, they told me to get my affairs in order."

Cummings nodded, although he couldn't begin to imagine what it must be like to be told that you've only got a few weeks to live. "And so the doctors sent you to me to help you do that, to get your affairs in order?"

"Yes, they did. I'm here so you can help me to die."

Playing a Hunch

Dan had been living in a small apartment on a hillside. On the first floor, next to the front-door vestibule, was a large mound that was part of the hill. The landlord was always talking about how some day he wanted to have that area excavated so he could build a storeroom for the tenants. Dan decided that he would help the landlord out, so every morning on his way out he would take a small sandwich bag, fill it with dirt, and deposit the tiny load in the nearest trashcan. He was following a magical belief, common to those who are terminal, that he couldn't die until he finished the job and removed the whole hillside. At the rate of progress he was making, Dan was hoping to have a very long life.

Cummings noticed other manifestations of denial that were evident. Dan was driving a very old car that was giving him lots of trouble and was totally unreliable. He had been trying to purchase a new car but was having trouble getting the loan approved because he insisted on a 7-year loan. Banks don't give auto loans for that length of time, but Dan was determined to find an institution that would make such a long-term commitment. Again, he believed that this lengthier contract would keep him alive longer.

In spite of his attempts to keep death as much at a distance as possible, Dan's oncologist had urged him to seek counseling. He needed to talk about the things that were left undone, the things that he wished to take care of, and come to terms with his impending death.

Cummings learned that Dan's parents had died when he was 8 years old, leaving him and his 3-year-old sister as orphans. Although raised by grandparents, Dan regretted that he never had the opportunity to know his parents, who were supposed to have been wonderful people. Although well meaning, his grandparents were elderly and not at all like the parents of his friends. He and his sister were so grateful to have a home at all, they never dreamed of rebelling in ways that would have been typical for adolescents. But rather than dwelling on the restricted way he had been raised as a child, Dan focused on idealized features that are typical for those who are saying goodbye to the world.

During one session, when they were talking about a number of things, Dan casually mentioned how unusual it was for someone his young age to be dying of lymphatic cancer. "It's almost like I made a pact with the Devil," he said with a laugh.

"What was that you said?" Cummings asked. It struck him as a curious remark.

"Nothing really. I was just thinking that there were so many things I wished I would get the chance. . . ."

"No, wait a minute," Cummings interrupted him before he could change the subject. "I'm struck by what you just said. It's kind of a defining statement."

"Not really."

"Well, what do you think it could mean?"

"No idea."

"This is just a hunch on my part, so it might not fit, but I have this sense that, somehow, it has something to do with your parents. Maybe you could say more about how they died."

A Deal with the Devil

Dan's parents had died in a tragic automobile accident while on vacation—a head-on collision with a truck. He and his sister had been staying with his grandparents when it happened. They were supposed to be joining their parents, but at the last minute, their parents decided to leave them behind.

"That's very interesting," Cummings observed.

"I still don't see what this has to do with anything."

"You don't see any connection between what happened. . . ."

"No, I don't! And what the hell difference does it make anyway? I'm dead. History. Toast. Get off my case, willya?"

In subsequent sessions, Cummings kept coming back to these early memories, and each time, Dan would change the subject or become downright hostile. Some interesting details emerged. Dan had been awakened in the middle of the night to be told that his parents had been killed. Extended family—aunts, uncles, cousins, grandparents—all sat around weeping and wailing. Dan would never forget what his grandmother said to him when she came in the room to tell him the news.

"I wish God had taken me instead of your parents," she said. "I've already lived my life, but your mother and your father. . . ." She broke down crying. "God should have taken me and spared your parents. That way we wouldn't have two orphaned children."

"Wow," Cummings responded after he heard the story.

"Wow? That's all the f*** you can think of to say? Wow?" Dan was totally enraged. He got up out of his chair and started pacing the room, absolutely furious. He lashed out and knocked over a lamp. He kicked over a chair.

"What's going on?" Cummings whispered in the most gentle voice he could.

Dan stopped moving for a moment, looked around, stunned at the damage he had done. He seemed surprised. "I know what you want to know!" he screamed again. "Do you want me to say it? Okay, I remember thinking to myself that I was glad God didn't take me either. I was glad I hadn't gone with my parents on that trip."

Dan stopped, suddenly exhausted. Cummings worried that he might keel over. He was already so weak, and this outburst had taken a lot out of him.

"You know," he said in his softest voice, barely above a whisper, "I don't know if this happened or not."

Whatever actually occurred, Cummings knew that his job was to help Dan come to terms with it. He thought about using hypnosis to help uncover the memories but knew that this shortcut sometimes led to recollections that were neither accurate nor useful. He decided that because of Dan's magical thinking, he would avoid the use of a shortcut and instead continue working within the context of their relationship.

During a subsequent session, things were becoming especially volatile. Dan kept swearing over and over in response to any intervention that Cummings tried, yet he kept pushing. For one thing, Cummings didn't know how much time they had left, with Dan's condition worsening; and for another, he sensed that Dan's will to live was so strong that he would not give up. Nevertheless, this already angry man became more and more enraged as things proceeded.

Finally, in the midst of one especially virulent temper tantrum, as he was about to start attacking furniture again, Dan blurted out, "I made a deal with the Devil. I promised him I would go at 21." As he said this, he collapsed into a chair.

There was an assortment of things that Cummings wanted to say by way of a response, but he thought it best just to wait. He wanted to give Dan a chance to calm down and realize the full significance of what he had just confessed. So he waited.

In a soft, tearful voice, Dan now remembered what had really happened immediately after his parents had died. That same night that his grandmother came in the room to tell him what had happened, when she told him that she wished God had taken her instead of his parents, Dan did indeed think to himself that he was glad that God had not taken him as well. But that was not all of it.

In the middle of the night, perhaps in a dream (although it seemed as if he had been awake), Dan had been visited by the Devil. He wasn't sure if it was a hallucination, a vivid dream, or what, but he was an 8-year-old boy who had just cried himself to sleep after learning his parents had been killed.

"So," Cummings asked, "what did the Devil say to you?"

Dan started to sob. "He told me that I was an ungrateful son. He said I didn't deserve to have parents as good as mine had been. Because I had not been willing to give up my life for them the way my grandmother would."

"And then what did you say to the Devil in return?"

"I told him I was only a little boy. I didn't mean it. I begged him and told him that I didn't mean it. I said I was just 8 and please could he give me a break." Dan paused, breathing in great gulps of air.

"And then what happened?" Cummings asked gently, knowing the answer already.

"The Devil said he'd let me live for now, but when he came for me when I was 21, I'd have to go willingly." Dan looked up at Cummings for a moment, to gauge his reaction, and then continued. "The Devil said, fine, he'd be back for me. But I'd better be ready. But I guess I'm not, huh?"

Both Cummings and Dan sat in their chairs staring at one another in silence. Each was drained and exhausted, unsure where to take this next.

"Look Dan," Cummings finally said, "I can't promise you anything, but this is a bum rap. An 8-year-old kid is not responsible enough to take this kind of burden and promise to die at 21. That is what the lymphoma is all about."

When Dan began sobbing, Cummings was surprised that his own tears started flowing spontaneously. The two of them sat quietly for the rest of the session, each lost in his own tears.

Expressing Anger

"So," Dan said to start the next session, "What do we do now?"

"I'm not sure," Cummings admitted, still struck by the depth of his own empathic grief. "But I'm pretty sure that this whole thing is not as simple as it seems. I'm curious about your relationship with your parents before they died."

Little by little, it began to emerge that Dan's parents were not quite as wonderful as they had originally been portrayed. In fact, they were rather cold, aloof people. Dan remembers one incident that seemed to capture the extent of his mother's self-centeredness. "I remember one day I was home in my room, trying to do my homework. I heard the horn honking, so that meant I was supposed to drop whatever I was doing, run downstairs, and open the garage doors so my mom wouldn't have to get out of the car. Even when I was a little kid, I thought this was rather odd, that my mother refused to do anything for herself if she could get someone else to do it for her."

As Cummings heard some of the stories Dan told about both his parents, it became clearer just how angry he felt toward them. But because of their sudden death, he never allowed himself the luxury of dealing with these feelings. When Cummings tried to draw these feelings out, their already stormy relationship became even more emotionally charged: Dan would frequently yell at Cummings, who, in turn, would yell back. Cummings eventually realized that they had slipped into the roles of child and parent. He noticed, for instance, that Dan would sometimes respond, or rather *over*-respond, to the slightest provocation. This gave Cummings an idea that he decided to try out during their next session.

Usually, Cummings would greet his patients in the waiting room, escort them into the office, and then close the door behind them and take his own seat. On this one occasion, instead Cummings just opened the door for Dan and then immediately started to walk back to his accustomed chair. He looked back over his shoulder and said in a carefully modulated voice, "Hey Dan, would you mind shutting the door?"

Dan looked startled. This was exactly what his mother would say to him, and even with the identical intonation she would use. "I thought you were supposed to close the door?" he said, with both confusion and irritation in his voice.

Remaining seated, Cummings again said, this time in a firmer voice, "Shut the door." No please. No request. Just an order.

Dan just shook his head, got up, walked over to the door, and slammed it shut. He had no idea they were enacting the prototypical scenario he had experienced with his mother over and over again.

"I notice that you don't talk much about your father," Cummings observed once they were seated.

"He wasn't around much," Dan responded, still a bit piqued.

Once calmed down, Dan talked about how his father was always playing golf or hanging out with his friends. If his mother had been emotionally distant and, at times, abusive, then his father had been negligent and largely absent from the home. Dan remembered one time in particular, when he was in a school play and his father never even bothered to show up. In fact, he could hardly remember doing anything with his father.

It was a few sessions later, when Dan said he didn't want to talk about his parents any more, that Cummings stood up and walked to the window. It was a stormy day outside and he was watching the rain falling.

"What are you doing?" Dan asked him. Lately, he had noticed that his usually predictable therapist was acting pretty strange in sessions. Like that thing with the door. Now he was standing up and staring out the window. He'd never done that before, even after all these months.

"Oh," Cummings said casually, "I was just thinking that I have a golf engagement after lunch today. I'm wondering if this damn rain is going to let up."

"You're not even listening to me, are you?"

"Oh," Cummings replied, still apparently distracted. "I'm sorry. What was that you said, Dan?"

Cummings was deliberatively and provocatively mirroring what he knew Dan's parents were like. He was trying to be as cold, distant, and self-centered as he could, knowing that this would bring out the anger that Dan had been holding in for so long.

"How can you call yourself a psychologist?" Dan screamed at Cummings back. "You are a sadist with a P at the beginning." That was Dan's favorite thing to call Cummings when he was mad at him—a sadistic psychologist. "You're just like my goddamn mother. Worse than that, you are like both my damn parents rolled into one. You're just a sadistic asshole."

This was one time when Cummings did not fight back. He just let Dan give vent to his rage. He noticed an interesting phenomenon unfolding, in that Dan had appeared to be getting healthier physically just as he was becoming more emotional in sessions. Over the previous few months he had started to gain weight again and to regain color in his face.

"You know," Dan's oncologist said in a phone consultation soon after this, "I can't figure out what is going on, but this young man appears to be going into remission. It seems impossible, and I can't account for the improvement, but against all odds he seems to be improving."

"Really?" Cummings responded, trying to control his own excitement.

"Yeah. Really. I keep trying to get him to come down here for testing, but he refuses. Maybe you can do something to encourage him. Somehow, we've got to figure out what's going on. This is most curious."

During the next session, Cummings did urge Dan to keep working with his doctors. He soon learned that the cancer cells had retreated and no more evidence of the disease could be found. He seemed to have been cured even if there was no medical explanation for how it happened.

Soon thereafter, Dan ended the therapy. Although Cummings was ecstatic that Dan had recovered and would not die after all, he was also puzzled by the way the relationship ended. Dan just announced that he wouldn't be coming back anymore, that he didn't need to see any sadistic f***ing psychologist anymore, and took his leave. There was no thank you or even much expression of warmth.

Before they said goodbye, Cummings explained his belief in brief, intermittent therapy throughout the life cycle. "Any time you want to come back and chat, or talk things over, I want you to call me. Dan, for you, it is particularly important that if you ever feel a swollen node in your neck while you are shaving, then call me right away. Will you promise to do that?"

Dan agreed and they said their goodbyes in a remarkably restrained, cool manner. Cummings was confused by this, but felt he had to honor not only that his patient wanted to move on, but also *how* he wished to do so.

Unfinished Business

Three years later, Dan had been shaving and, sure enough, felt a small lump in his neck. During the intervening time, he had married and had an infant daughter of his own. Dan and his wife were now going through a very painful divorce.

Dan and Nick resumed their therapy sessions for another half-dozen sessions. They concentrated on working out visitation rights to see his daughter, adjusting to the divorce, and dealing with his residual anger about the way things turned out. Interestingly, the node in his neck disappeared about as suddenly as it had appeared, and again the oncologist gave him a clean bill of health.

Fairly recently, Dan called Cummings again for an appointment. By now, over 20 years had elapsed, during which time the cancer had never returned.

Now in his forties, Dan had aged well. When he entered the office and shook Cummings's hand, the first thing he said was, "No cancerous nodes. Everything is great."

Cummings let out a visible sigh of relief.

Dan brought his therapist up to date on the last few decades of his life. He had remarried. When his daughter reached age 12, she had elected to live with him and her stepmother, and she had been with them ever since. He had three more children with his second wife and was extremely happy.

"That's all great," Cummings said. "But I'm curious. If everything is going well with you, what brought you back to see me?" He paused, then added, "Don't get me wrong. I am absolutely delighted to see you! But what brought you back?"

"Well, I saw this profile about you in a local magazine. The article talked about your life and I suddenly realized how old you were."

Cummings laughed.

"No, don't get me wrong," Dan continued. "I wish you many, many more years. But once I realized you were getting up there in age, it got me thinking that I never got to say goodbye to my parents. I started to feel terrible that I might read somewhere you had died, and I never got to. . . . Well, I just realized that I had not treated you right."

"Sure you did. . . ."

"No, let me finish. There's something I always wanted to tell you. I never thanked you for saving my life."

"It's all in a day's work," Cummings responded, uncomfortable with the sudden outpouring of affection and gratitude. "But I wonder, how do you remember that?"

It had actually always bothered Cummings that he had given so much to this man when he was young, had become so emotionally invested in their relationship, so determined to save his life even though it was a futile mission. And then when the seeming miracle had occurred, Dan had just left like it was no big deal.

"Come on," Dan said. "You must know that our work together was the most significant thing in my life. How could I ever forget that?"

"I just wondered. . . ."

"I learned from you that it was time to move on, to form a new life, to love, and to be loved. And that's what I have been doing ever since. I just wanted you to know that."

"Well, that feels really good to hear that," Cummings responded warmly.

"I have followed your career all these years. I actually have every one of your books. I have a psychologist friend who would always cue me in when one of your books was coming out. He would get it for me. I followed your career and I have admired the way you have innovated all your life. I wanted to come in and tell you that maybe a little bit of that rubbed off on me."

"How is that?" Cummings prompted.

Dan went on to tell him, just like he must have wanted to tell his own parents if they had still been living, how well he had been doing. He had started a new company from scratch, patented a revolutionary new manufacturing process, and had been successful beyond his dreams.

The therapist and patient, surrogate father and son, hugged warmly. And that is the last time that they met.

▩   ▩   ▩

Mobilizing Rage

We didn't really have to ask Cummings why he thought of this case as his best work. After all, he had probably literally saved a man's life. But we wondered how he reflected on what he had done.

Given the provocative and rather extreme way he had structured their relationship, Cummings had had some real misgivings about the treatment. As with so many of the people we see, he always wondered what happened to the young man. He wondered if he was even still alive.

"It felt so good to hear the end of the story," he said. "I felt grateful for two things—first, that I had the courage to bust all the rules and do extreme therapy with this young man. Second, I am grateful that somewhere along the line I have achieved such a profound respect for what we can do with psychotherapy to really put our skills and beliefs to work. I think the results can be more profound than most therapists realize."

"How, then, did you ever come up with the idea to proceed as you did?"

In order to understand his rationale, Cummings went back 60 years to when he was a combat officer for the 82nd Airborne during World War II. Forty percent of the casualties that were suffered were psychological in nature, what we would now call posttraumatic stress.

The paratroopers in this unit had a superstition that was somewhat constructive. The average life span for a soldier in this unit was three jumps. It was during the fourth jump that most people died. So when a trooper reached that particular jump, he would get what was called "jump-door fever"—he would remain frozen at the door and would not go out. This would hold up the whole operation and present huge difficulties. These were brave men, who had already risked their lives many times, so it was humiliating to have to kick them out of the door physically. In fact, when this happened, and they were pushed out against their will, they would be sitting ducks when they reached the ground; they were so terrified they would not defend themselves.

Along with a select number of paratroop officers, Cummings was removed from the battlefield long enough to attend a 6-week course to learn how to talk panicked paratroopers out the door willingly in less than the 10 seconds allotted. The course had been conceived by then-General William Menninger, who along with his brother Karl had founded the Menninger Clinic. It turned out that Cummings's teacher in this experimental program was the famous psychoanalyst Freida Fromm-Reichmann. She had a theory that mobilizing rage can be in the interest of one's health. In fact, she felt that although love is the strongest human emotion, anger is more immediately accessible. Love takes a while to get started, but rage can be ignited in seconds. Therefore, if you want to save a life, you've got to find the anger. So that's what Cummings learned to do.

After studying the men in the unit, learning their soft spots and sensitive areas, Cummings learned to use "extreme therapy" to tease, cajole, insult, or enrage the paratroopers out the door. Sure enough, it worked so well that Cummings never lost another trooper to jump-door fever. And to his relief, once battle was over, the troopers not only forgave his crude and rude remarks, they realized why he had done this and were actually grateful to him. They understood that being angered into jumping willingly prevented the inevitable panic and subsequent death of jump-door fever, thus saving their lives. So that's how he learned that sometimes it is necessary to resort to extreme solutions to mobilize people's anger. He also learned that there are absolutely no limits to the power of what therapy can do to help people, if the clinician has faith in the process.

CHAPTER

9

Put Caring at the Top of the List

A Case from Michael Mahoney

Although he was originally an influential cognitive theorist, Michael Mahoney has become a leading voice of constructivist therapy. This approach explores the ways that people create meaning from their experiences through the use of metaphors, cognitive reflection, and a collaborative relationship.

Mahoney has written a number of books, including Cognition and Behavior Modification, Human Change Processes, Cognitive and Constructive Psychotherapies, *and* Constructivism in Psychotherapy. *He is Professor of Psychology at the University of North Texas.*

The Voice

"I understand you do weight-loss therapy," Karen said over the phone when she called to make an appointment.

"Actually," Mahoney replied, "I really don't do that sort of thing anymore." Like most therapists, Michael's career has evolved over the years. Before identifying as a constructivist theorist, he was cognitive behavioral, and before that, a behavior therapist. It was during the time of transition that he was seeing this new client.

"You don't," she said, surprised and disappointed. "You mean you can't help me?" There was such despair in her voice as she said this that Mahoney agreed to see her for free, just to make an appropriate referral.

"I'm kind of curious," he said to her when she finally showed up a few days later. "How would your life change if you did lose 30 pounds?"

Karen seemed shocked by the question, as if such a thing must be obvious. But when Mahoney continued to wait patiently for an answer, she started to weep. "I was afraid you might ask me that," she said, trying to control the flow of tears that were now running her makeup.

"What's going on for you right now?" Mahoney followed up. "That question seems to have some special significance to you."

The story came out that it was really her husband who wanted to her to lose weight and who insisted that she get help. He believed that might make his wife more sexually responsive.

They ended up working together after all, but not dealing with weight-loss issues as much as her depression and low self-esteem. Karen also made reference to her relationship with her husband. Ever since their children had been born, they had not been sexually active. She was feeling guilty about this, but the truth of the matter was that she just was not interested in sex any more.

Just the previous week her husband had been flirting with her, showing every sign that he wanted to have sex, but instead of responding, Karen gave him a clear look that he'd better watch himself.

"Watch himself or what?" Mahoney asked.

"My husband knows that if he pushes too hard, I'll bring out the voice."

"The voice?" Now what was she talking about? There were some pieces of the puzzle falling into place with regard to her poor body image, but it had been tough going to get into the sexual area, where Karen was obviously quite uncomfortable.

"Yeah," she said with embarrassment. "I've got this special voice I use sometimes, kind of like the way the Hulk sounds—you know, deep and gravely?"

Mahoney was now quite intrigued. "I'd like to hear that voice."

Karen giggled. "Oh no, you wouldn't like the voice at all."

"I'm not so sure about that. It sounds to me like this voice has been taking care of you a lot all these years, protecting you. I'd certainly like to be in alliance with this voice of yours."

A Funny Smell

At this time, Mahoney was just beginning to experiment with techniques and methods that went beyond his previous behavioral approach. He had been experimenting with a stream-of-consciousness technique, once he got over its initial negative associations with Freudian theory. It was one way that he found he could access aspects of a client's life that might otherwise be difficult to explore.

During one pivotal session Karen was curled up on the couch, apparently regressed to an earlier stage of life, and talking in a childlike voice. She was rubbing her hands together as if she was trying to clean them, or rub something sticky off of them. It reminded Mahoney of a scene from *Macbeth*.

"Yucky," Karen whispered like a child. "Bad . . . Yucky . . . Ughhhhh."

Mahoney was transfixed by the intensity and the power of the scene. His client was in a fetal position, knees drawn up to her chest, hands rubbing back and forth, back and forth, whimpering, saying "Yucky" over and over again in a little girl's voice.

Once they resumed their normal conversation to process the experience, Karen was not able to offer much in the way of an explanation. All she could do was shrug.

It was in the next session that Karen came in with an idea of what might be going on. "Mike, there was something that happened last week that just couldn't have happened. I've been thinking about it all week."

"What's that?" Mahoney asked, intensely curious about what this whole thing was about.

"I smelled something last time."

"You smelled something?"

"Yeah. I felt like I was a little girl. But I smelled something that I couldn't have smelled as a little girl."

"Like what?"

Karen was genuinely uncomfortable, unconsciously rubbing her hands together again. When she saw what she doing, she immediately stopped and turned red.

"What's going on?" Mahoney asked again. He could see that Karen wanted to tell him but was also quite uneasy.

"Well, it was the smell of a man's stuff."

"Stuff?"

"You know, his sperm."

This confession might not particularly surprise the reader, but remember, this was in the days before there was much known or understood about child abuse and very little about repressed memories. Mahoney was sitting there, bemoaning why he ever left the comfort of behavior therapy to delve into this mysterious Pandora's box of stream of consciousness.

"So," Mahoney said, just as surprised as Karen seemed to be, "what do you make of that?"

"I don't know. It just makes no sense at all."

Which Group Are You In?

Over the course of the next 6 to 8 weeks, Karen began talking more about what might have occurred when she was younger. She began to suspect that she might have suffered sexual abuse, which puzzled her because she was an only child and had enjoyed wonderful relationships with both of her parents.

While talking to her mother one day, Karen asked if anything funny had taken place when she was a child.

"What do you mean by funny?" her mother asked.

"You know, like, I don't know, maybe something sexual."

"Sexual?"

"I've just been having these funny thoughts lately and . . . ."

"Oh my God!" her mother gasped.

"Mom, what's wrong?"

"It's just. . . . Well, we thought you had forgotten all about that."

"About what?" Karen demanded with increasing panic. "What the hell are you talking about?"

And so it came out that Karen had been sexually abused by her father, not just once, but repeatedly. And not just by her father alone, but by several of his friends. They'd even filmed the molestations.

Karen took a turn for the worse. She became severely depressed and suicidal. She just could not imagine that her father would do this sort of thing. She'd always believed they had a good relationship and thought she'd felt safe with him. Now it was all a lie. She felt so disoriented she didn't know what to believe, especially after learning that her mother and other family members had covered this up and pretended that it had never even happened!

During one session in which Karen was feeling particularly hopeless, she wondered if she could ask Mahoney a question.

"Why, of course!"

"How much do you think that people can change?"

"I'm not sure what you mean," he answered, mostly to buy some time as to how best to respond.

"How much can *I* change?"

Mahoney looked at Karen, weighing what to say next. He just didn't know what to say to her. She *had* been severely traumatized, and was now so extremely depressed, that he had his own doubts about how much his client could ever recover.

"My daddy," Karen continued, "I worshipped that man my whole life—until just a little while ago. He was supposed to be the person who kept me safe but he did the most horrible things to me. Now I don't know who I can ever trust again."

Karen was also thinking about her husband. After informing him of what she had just learned about her past, his response had been, "Well, so what? It doesn't have anything to do with me. So, what's the problem?" If anything, he was now pressuring her more than ever to have sex.

"So," she continued to press her therapist, "I'm wondering if I'll ever be normal. Will I ever have a normal sex life after what has happened to me? Can I change that much?"

Mahoney wanted to run. He wasn't sure how to answer the question. He could see Karen looking for the slightest glimmer of hope, the smallest bit of encouragement, but he wondered what he could say that would truly be honest. He seriously wondered how Karen, or how anyone, could really re-cover from such a thing and if she could ever have a satisfying sex life.

It was then that he heard a sound that still haunts him to this day. It was the tiniest sound of a tear drop hitting the carpet. Mahoney was startled. He was going over in his own head what he knew and understood about recov-ery from sexual abuse and the scars that such a trauma can leave. He was re-viewing what experts at the time said about such things (and it was not very encouraging). Then he thought about the human capacity for resiliency. He re-called others who had suffered terrible things in their lives but had somehow managed to lead normal, satisfying lives.

Mahoney reviewed both sides of the argument, that there were some ex-perts who shared Karen's worst fears, that she would never be able to fully put this behind her. Then he told her that others held an opposite view, that anything was possible with sufficient will and determination.

"And which side are you on?" Karen asked him. By this time, she was crying in earnest.

"Well, uh . . . that's hard to say. I mean, there's evidence to support ei-ther . . . ."

"Mike," she said again, this time in a firmer voice. "I asked you a ques-tion. Which side are you on?"

"Look," he said uneasily, "I don't want to do you a disservice. I . . . ."

"Mike, which group?"

Mahoney looked at his client. He saw the tears still trickling down her face. He saw the wounded, vulnerable look on her face. He saw the intensity in her eyes, the flash of anger, and of hope.

He nodded. "I refuse to foreclose on resilience."

Karen smiled. "That's what I thought."

Top of the List

Soon after this breakthrough session, Mahoney relocated to another state and their sessions came to an end. Every year thereafter, though, he received a Christmas card with a brief report on progress that Karen was making. She gave updates on her children. She mentioned divorcing her husband. She went back to school to prepare for another career. Then, one year, there was a "P.S." at the end of the card: "Remember that time when I asked you how much people can change? Well, you were right! Thanks for keeping the faith."

Mahoney remarked that it is so rare that we ever get to find out what happens to our clients after they move on, especially that kind of affirming feedback. "As I look back, I realize how Karen had confronted me in that ses-sion. She stretched me tremendously."

Saying this reminded Mahoney of another, related incident. He had been preparing to speak at a conference and had been making notes for his pre-sentation on a sheet of paper that was sitting on his desk. It had been Karen's custom to walk around the office a little before she'd settle into her chair. While doing so one day she saw the paper sitting on the desk.

"What's that?" she asked.

"Oh, just some notes to myself for a paper I'm giving in New York."

"Oh yeah? What about?"

"It's about the most important ingredients of psychotherapy."

Karen looked down curiously at the paper and saw Roman numerals along the left margin, next to which there was a list of main points that included such things as "modeling," "reinforcement," "cognitive restructuring," and so forth.

"Where is the caring?" Karen asked with a smile.

"Excuse me?" Mahoney answered.

"I was wondering where the caring is?"

"I'm not sure what you mean."

Karen nodded. "Well, I was thinking that the most important thing you have done for me is to care. I don't see that on the list."

Mahoney grinned back. He walked over to the desk, grabbed a pen, and wrote "caring" at the top of his list.

■ ■ ■

Wrestling Hope from Hell

One theme that is especially important to Mahoney about this case is the power of resilience. Although he had been waffling about where he stood, on which side of the prognostic fence, Karen had forced him to declare his own beliefs. As he heard himself tell his client that there was indeed hope for her future, he found this to be a turning point in the development of his own ideas.

"That is both the good news and bad news about constructivism," Mahoney said. "The good news is that there is always an alternate interpretation or possibility to the worst you may be experiencing. The flip side of that is that at any moment of joy there is another way to recast it or to say that this is fleeting."

That is what made Mahoney's interventions in this case somewhat risky. He felt he was delving into new territory, experimenting with strategies that had not been tested. Yet their relationship felt solid enough that he felt the freedom to try new things.

"I think really fine therapy is fundamentally an authentic encounter between therapist and client. That often means that it touches on existential issues, especially hope. The word 'hope' comes from the English 'hoppe,' which we think of as 'hop,' a small jump. Hope is an existential leap. It is engagement with life. Not the better life that you expect, or feel is warranted tomorrow, but just continuing engagement with life."

Mahoney believes that one of the paradoxes of our work is that we are supposed to be the sanctioned purveyors of hope, the ones who preach all the reasons why life is worth living. Yet we are constantly exposed to such cruelty, injustice, abuse, and pain. In Mahoney's words, "We are supposed to wrestle hope from hell."

CHAPTER

10 I Accept Myself, and Others: Therefore I Am

A Case from Albert Ellis

Albert Ellis is certainly one of the most influential theoreticians of the last century. He has worked tirelessly and relentlessly throughout his life promoting the benefits of rational emotive behavior therapy (REBT), producing seven hundred articles and seventy books on the subject. Some of his best-known works include Reason and Emotion in Psychotherapy, A Guide to Rational Living, Sex without Guilt, How to Control Your Anger before It Controls You, How to Stubbornly Refuse to Make Yourself Miserable about Anything—Yes, Anything, *and* Feeling Better, Getting Better, Staying Better.

Never one to mince words, and now 90 and even more forthright and opinionated than ever, Ellis equates great therapy with his therapy—the sort that actively and directly attacks people's tendencies to avoid accepting themselves and others. At the time he developed his ideas, little attention was devoted by practitioners to the influence of thinking processes on subsequent reactions to predicaments. By focusing on the irrational belief systems that lead people to exaggerate, distort, and overreact to situations they face, Ellis devised a method to counteract these counterproductive patterns. This was one of the first "brief" therapies in the field, designed to help people quickly and efficiently change the ways they think and act.

Based at the center in New York that bears his name—the Albert Ellis Institute—Ellis still maintains an active schedule writing, lecturing, and doing workshops.

Parallel Processes in the Client and Therapist

Nobody would ever mistake Albert Ellis's speaking style for anyone else's voice. In his distinctive New York accent, colorful language, and unusual speech rhythm that rises in tone and volume whenever he wishes to emphasize the key words in a sentence, Ellis recites the main features of his case with vivid detail. He may now be a little hard of hearing, but he has lost nothing of his fluent, expressive manner, which allows him to speak with absolute

93

passion, precision, and clarity about what constitutes his finest work. In addition, just as we would expect from the most outspoken voice of the profession, Ellis holds nothing back in his criticism of colleagues who fail to practice the standards that he considers highly preferable in order to help people.

We spoke to Ellis not just about his finest hour as a therapist, but also retrospectively looking back on his life and career. This particular case involved far more than helping a client deal with some rather chronic, intractable symptoms. One reason Ellis considers this story to be among the most memorable of his finest sessions is that a parallel process also took place. The work completed by the client had a reciprocal effect on his therapist, who made continued progress on his own life-long struggles to deal with unrealistic expectations for himself and others. This, after all, is one of the supreme benefits for *any* therapist doing this type of work: that the things we do to help our clients often have unintended but powerful effects on our own lives. Although these side effects can be for better or worse (in the form of burnout or secondary posttraumatic stress), this case illustrates the importance of applying to our own lives that which we teach to our clients. This has long been one of Ellis's most often repeated lessons to other therapists.

The Perfectionist

Marvin was a dreamer in every sense of the word. He dreamed of being rich. He dreamed of being a prize-winning author. But most of all, he dreamed of women. And this is what brought him into therapy with Albert Ellis about 20 years ago.

Marvin had a most active fantasy life, one dominated by obsessive thoughts about various women whom he wished to lure into bed. Because he worked as a college teacher, there was no shortage of subjects for him to think about. Nevertheless, most often he would center his attention on a particular woman who was completely inaccessible if not out of his league. This could be a gorgeous woman who was happily married but now occupied much of his waking thoughts. Or he might focus on a woman who was so narcissistically self-involved that there was no way she could love anyone other than herself. All of the subjects of his recurrent fantasies had one thing in common: they would so captivate Marvin that he thought about them continuously, interrupting his work, invading his sleep, and keeping him enslaved.

"I'm going to run away with her," Marvin insisted in session one day. "We're going to run away. Just the two of us. I've been thinking about where we're going to go. Maybe the Bahamas. I think that would be nice."

"But you're married," Ellis reminded him patiently. This is what he usually said to the man when he would come in with the latest plan to lure the subject of his fantasy into romantic bliss. "And besides, she doesn't love you. In fact, she doesn't even know who you are."

These sorts of remarks never seemed to dissuade Marvin from continuing his fantasy. No matter how much Ellis disputed, challenged, or confronted him, Marvin kept insisting that, given time, the current woman of his dreams would come around.

As further evidence of how disturbed and obsessive-compulsive he was, Marvin was constantly upset with the students he taught. "They never study," he complained. "All they care about is sports and girls."

Ellis thought about reminding his patient that he must have something in common with these students, considering Marvin's own obsession with women. Instead he turned attention to Marvin's writing projects.

"Well," Marvin said thoughtfully, "I'm on to this new novel. I told you about it. It's going to be one of the finest pieces of literature ever written. I wouldn't be surprised if it gets me a Pulitzer. I'll finally have the recognition that I deserve. I'll make millions of dollars. And *then* the women will come running for sure."

"You certainly may be a talented writer," Ellis agreed. "But I'm not sure I see the connection between finally finishing your first novel and winning a national prize. And second, I'm unclear what that has to do with all these fantasy women of yours falling into your lap. Where's the evidence for this?"

"Evidence? What evidence do you need? I am indeed writing the great American novel, and that's all that needs to be said on the matter. My colleagues will then afford me the respect that they have withheld. And the girls: Oh my! There will be more than I can ever handle."

"Well," Ellis tried again, "maybe it would be a good idea your first time to just try to get a novel published, rather than setting yourself up for disappointment. From what you've said, you've yet to find a publisher who will take any of your previous ideas."

Marvin pouted and crossed his arms.

"Look Marvin, I'm not disagreeing with you that you don't have talent. It's great to have these goals. But you have standards for yourself that you— or anyone—could not possibly live up to."

"You're just jealous," Marvin said. "When all the women come flocking to me, they'll be none left for you, or anyone else!"

I See It. I Hear It. But I Don't Feel It.

Ellis recognized that his patient was not only obsessive but delusional and personality-disordered. Marvin would attach himself to fantasy objects and remain so fixated on them he could think about little else. While this was certainly a problem, Ellis noticed as well that his patient was constantly self-downing: he would beat himself up for the slightest infraction and would be particularly merciless when he failed to attain the women of his dreams. He saw himself as a complete and total failure because of a few disappointments that resulted primarily from ridiculously unrealistic expectations.

Ellis decided to concentrate primarily on helping Marvin to increase his level of unconditional self-acceptance regardless of his less than perfect behavior.

"I see your point, Dr. Ellis," Marvin would say. "I know I do stupid things. I set myself up to fail. But I still can't forgive myself."

"So, what you're saying is that you really are a worm. You're no damn good because you don't behave perfectly 100 percent of the time. It isn't enough for you that *occasionally* you help your students, or that *sometimes* people respond well to you. In order for you to be acceptable as a person, you expect that you will get what you want *all* the time."

Marvin nodded in agreement. He looked up at Ellis as if he recognized this was the wrong answer, but it was the way he genuinely felt. "I see your point, but I do these stupid things and I just can't forgive myself for doing them. On one level, I see that they are just behaviors and they are just stupid and foolish behaviors. . . ."

"But that doesn't make you stupid and insane," Ellis pointed out again, "just because you sometimes do stupid things. And I would certainly agree that spending hours each day thinking about women who have no interest in you whatsoever is rather stupid behavior. But that still doesn't make you a stupid person. Do you see the difference?"

Marvin nodded "yes" but it was clear that what he meant was "no."

"These aren't failures," Ellis explained again. "You are exaggerating the extent. . . ."

"Yes," Marvin acknowledged. "I hear what you are saying. But I just don't feel it."

"You don't feel it because you believe devoutly that you are no good. I agree that it is not good that you are doing these foolish things. But that does not make you a no-goodnik."

Although this term usually elicited a smile, Marvin just looked pained. And Ellis felt himself becoming impatient and frustrated with their relative lack of progress. They had been working together for several months and yet this patient had made only the most modest progress. Ellis could feel himself slipping back into his own self-defeating patterns of doing essentially the same thing that he was cautioning his patient against: "shoulding" on himself or others. ("Shoulding" is Ellis's own label for the demands people make of others.) In this case, he could hear himself demanding that Marvin work faster, make more progress, respond more effectively to interventions that, thus far, had limited success.

Ellis realized that he was winning the arguments with Marvin, bludgeoning him with logic and rational thinking, but without lasting effects.

"I'm just a worthless piece of crap," Marvin complained again.

"But where is the evidence of this?" Ellis challenged him. "Just because you might do some things that I admit are rather misguided and a waste of time, how does that make you a worthless piece of crap? It just makes you human."

Marvin just shrugged, as if to say he didn't feel like arguing about it any more. Because he couldn't attract the women he wanted, or get the recognition he felt he deserved, that meant he was worthless. End of story.

"Look," Ellis tried again, "if you don't get over this insistence that your self-worth is related to what you do, you're going to be miserable for the rest of your life."

"I just think that's the way it's gonna be."

"You may not write the great American novel," Ellis agreed. "You may not win a Pulitzer or Nobel Prize. You most certainly are not going to have all these women you dream about come flocking to your bed—and that's a good thing too, or your wife would be very upset. But that doesn't make you a bad person."

One Brown Shoe, One Black Shoe

The sessions continued over the course of several years, during which time Marvin's wife eventually divorced him. Even though her husband had not once acted on his sexual obsessions and fantasies, it was not for lack of trying. She had had quite enough of his sniveling, complaining, self-blaming, and pitiful attempts to seduce other women.

For the first 6 months, Marvin attended weekly sessions, then spaced them out to monthly meetings. As is often typical for someone with severe personality and obsessive disorders, progress was slow. Then one day, Marvin announced a breakthrough of sorts: "I'm finally beginning to get what you've been saying. I told you all along that I can hear and see what you're saying but I just don't feel it."

"So what made the difference?" Ellis asked.

"Well this kid came in to see me, one of my students. This was a bright guy who should have been doing well in school, but he was barely passing. All he cared about was playing football and chasing girls. He didn't concentrate on his studies at all."

"Some of this sounds familiar," Ellis observed.

"Yeah, well anyway, I just lost it with this kid. I started yelling at him and this just isn't like me. He must have thought I was nuts or something."

"It sounds like you were trying to help him as best you could."

"Yeah, well, that's still no excuse. I felt like a failure as a teacher. I let the student down, and I let myself down too. Then, I could hear your voice inside my head, except it sounded like my voice, and it was saying to me that just because I didn't handle myself perfectly in this situation, doesn't mean I'm a lousy teacher."

This became a real breakthrough for Marvin. Once he saw the power of being more forgiving of his lapses, he was able to become more self-accepting.

Ellis sees this as simplification of a process that was far more complex. Marvin applied himself to doing daily homework with the same zeal that he had previously devoted to his sexual fantasies. He was determined that he was going to rid himself of his self-downing behavior and do whatever it took to conquer this life-long pattern.

More than anything else, Ellis believes that that the daily practice of self-acceptance and shame-attacking exercises was what made the difference. Marvin agreed to stand on busy street corners and sing songs from popular musicals, all the while ignoring the stares of passers-by (this *was* New York). Another time, he deliberately mis-dressed himself, wearing one brown shoe and one black shoe to school, and was amazed that nobody noticed. These sorts of experiences helped him to lighten up on himself and to reduce his demands that he behave perfectly in every situation.

■   ■   ■

Speaking His Mind

We were intrigued about what it was about this particular case that stood out to Ellis among the thousands of patients he has seen over 60 years of practice. We wondered why Marvin made such an impression on him and why the breakthrough session described above represents his finest hour as a therapist. Before he answered the question, Ellis stated with his usual candor what he considered good therapy to be about.

"I think that most therapy is very ineffective," Ellis said. "It does very little good and much harm because it stops people from seeing their fundamental demands for perfection and working against them. I think all therapy had better include a strong dose of self-acceptance. This is something that most good therapists agree with."

"You sound like Carl Rogers," we observed.

"Rogers was right about that," Ellis agreed, "but he didn't go far enough."

Ellis went on to explain that rational emotive behavior therapy (REBT) has several basic points that are emphasized repeatedly. The first is *unconditional self-acceptance* (USA). "You always, *always* accept yourself," Ellis said, "no matter what you do and how stupid you feel. Because you are alive and human, you don't have to *prove* your worth, as the vast majority of people are trying so hard to do. If you make a mistake, you try to do better, but you don't put yourself down because of the errors."

Second, Ellis emphasizes *unconditional other acceptance* (UOA). Just as it is important to accept yourself as worthy and a good person, no matter what you do, and how poorly you do it, so too can you accept others unconditionally, no matter what they do. This does not mean accepting others' behavior, especially actions that deny all people deserve to be treated as worthy individuals in spite of their deficiencies; just because they are alive and unique. It also means that you try to help people to change their behavior but not insist that they must do so.

Third, Ellis mentions *unconditional life acceptance* (ULA), which gets at the heart of frustration tolerance. People often demand that others behave in certain ways (Marvin's belief that all women should love him), or that the world be structured in a certain way (Marvin's belief that he should win a Nobel Prize). This leads to irrational beliefs such as "The world is unfair," and "I can't stand it when I'm not getting what I want."

"Good therapy addresses these points," Ellis summarized. "And bad therapy is the kind that mainly helps people to feel better because the therapist accepts them; but it does not help them to make a deeper change. Most therapy is ineffective, and most therapists got into this game because of their own nuttiness. They have to do well and be loved by their clients—or else they will feel worthless. That's why they help their clients to feel better but not really get better."

The Parallel Process

We asked Ellis again what it was that made the case of Marvin so satisfying to him, given that the man did not appear to manifest symptoms that were all that unusual, even if he was a bit challenging to work with. Ellis admitted he was a "difficult customer," but that is not what made this so memorable to him. At the same time that he was helping Marvin to be more self-accepting, he was also working through his own frustration tolerance.

"I noticed that I felt irritable and angry with him at times," Ellis confessed. "I said to myself that I had to stop demanding that he stop his lousy behavior and that he was no damn good to be that way. It was okay to be mad at his behavior, but I was angry with *him*."

"So what did you do?" we asked him, knowing that inevitably the answer would involve the same sort of self-talk he teaches his patients.

"I was telling myself to accept him, but it wasn't working because I was working my ass off to help him and it hadn't been working. I was saying to myself that he shouldn't resist that way and he better respond more successfully."

"You were 'shoulding' on yourself," we said.

"That's right," Ellis said, the teacher proud of his pupils who remembered their lessons. "I thought about that a lot and began doing my own homework. At one point, I even told Marvin that I had been feeling angry toward him for being so uncooperative and that I had used REBT to counteract these beliefs. I thanked him for being such a difficult customer because it gave me very good practice in dealing with my own irritability and low frustration tolerance."

"What did he say to that?"

"He appreciated it a lot."

Indeed, although Ellis does not talk much about the relationships he develops with those he helped, both authors have had personal experiences with him in which it was his essential caring that made at least as much difference as his REBT interventions. It has been over 25 years since Jeffrey Kottler volunteered to come up on stage as a client during an Ellis workshop. He brought up an issue dealing with his dying mother, and predictably, Ellis countered Kottler's residual guilt about his mother in Ellis's own trademark fashion. Yet it was Ellis's support, caring, and total acceptance that provided as much comfort and guidance as anything else that took place during that session. Likewise, Jon Carlson recently found himself engaged in an intimate conversation with Ellis at a conference when Ellis leaned over and whispered in Carlson's ear: "You know, most of these therapists are full of sh** and don't know what the hell they're talking about. But you, Jon, you're okay." This is about as close as Ellis gets to offering a warm, fuzzy endorsement of support, yet his warmth and compassion are powerful accompaniments to the method that he has spent his life developing.

It is one of the peculiarities of our work that the therapist and client often have different explanations to account for changes that take place during sessions. Ellis believes that it was the REBT interventions that made the most difference with his client, and certainly they were a powerful influence. But Marvin might also have mentioned the same things that struck us about Ellis's presence—that is, practicing self-acceptance and acceptance of others in a way that inspires us to do the same.

About That Other Acceptance

Ellis might not judge other people, but that certainly does not restrain him from being critical of others' behavior, especially that of his colleagues. "Most other therapists are severely disturbed," Ellis said, returning to our previous subject. "They got into therapy in the first place because they have major emotional problems. Others are just nice neurotics who, because they are very neurotic, blame themselves and other people in the world when they don't help their clients very much."

Ellis is speaking mostly about psychoanalysts, for whom he still holds very little respect. A practicing analyst himself for 6 years, Ellis eventually became disillusioned, if not downright frustrated, with the passive, indirect stance taken in this approach. "They don't push and encourage people, and if you don't do that, people don't get better. Psychoanalysts and many other therapists just sit there and assume that people get insight into their problems and they are going to do whatever is needed to save themselves." Ellis snorted for emphasis at the end of that sentence, leaving no doubt about his feelings.

Ellis talked more about the sorry state of the field, in which he believes that therapists don't push or direct their clients nearly enough. "I think people can change, but it is really hard to do. They want to get better magically and hope that therapists will do that for them. Many therapists go along with this nonsense and think they can cure people without the clients doing the work."

"But this isn't the case?"

"Hell no! People have to see how crazy they are and how they have to work their asses off for the rest of their lives to change their thinking."

Ellis believes that what made the most difference for Marvin was the man's commitment and determination to overcome his difficulties. He completed his homework assignments regularly. He finally learned to accept himself, and to accept others, by constantly challenging his assumptions that somehow the world should be different. And that is exactly the struggle that Ellis has been working on much of his own life.

A Composer Rather than a Therapist

There was time for one last question, so we decided to take a long shot. Knowing that Ellis looks at regret with the same disdain as he has for any sort of self-downing behavior, we asked him to look back on his life and consider what he wished he had done differently. For the first time in the conversation, Ellis paused before answering. He has answered so many questions in his life, most of them variations of the same themes, that he has canned answers already prepared. This time there was some hesitance.

"I probably should have been a composer of music," Ellis said.

"A composer?"

"Yeah. I think I have a rare talent for composing music."

We both start to giggle, recalling Ellis's penchant for setting the lessons of REBT to the tunes of popular songs and then having audiences sing them in chorus. The clever lyrics never fail to get people laughing.

"Unfortunately, when I was a kid I took music lessons. My teacher was pretty rotten and that turned me away. But now I create music all the time. I don't really know music and never learned it properly, so I can't write it the way I'd like. But I think I would have been a better composer even though I am a pretty good therapist. I would be even better at composing and I would enjoy it even more in some respects. I am very regretful, but I don't beat myself for not studying music and at least finding out whether I am an outstanding composer or not."

In one sense, Ellis *is* a composer and always has been. It may sometimes sound like he is playing a piece of music by rote with a client, repeating the well-worn lines he has used for over 60 years, but this is not at all the case. Ellis feels most misunderstood in one sense (not that he cares much about that): "People may think that I don't have any feeling, but I enjoy very much what I do helping people. Sure, I have strong goals and values which, in a sense, run my life. I like what I am doing and keep after my clients over and over again. I propagate my theory and the gospel according to St. Albert throughout the world. I am devoted to this because I very much like to see people think, behave, and act differently."

"And where does this drive come from, for you to work so hard?"

"First of all, I get bored easily. I don't understand how people take the one life that they have and p * * * it away doing practically nothing fascinating. I get bored unless I am very active. I have a life-absorbing interest in REBT and I like to spread the word. It is against my nature and inclination to be passive and inactive, so I keep working. Anything is better than sitting at home and watching television."

At 90 years of age, Ellis still feels he has a lot to learn and a lot to do. Every moment is precious to him, and he intends to use whatever time he has left to keep spreading the word, to keep teaching people about the power of hard work to change one's life.

Epilogue

Soon after we interviewed Ellis, he was admitted to a hospital to have surgery to remove his colon. The morning after the procedure, while in the intensive care unit, he was laboring with respiratory difficulties (as one might expect from a 90-year-old man who had just undergone major surgery). Debbie, one of his colleagues at the Institute, came to visit him.

"Ask me some questions," Ellis said to Debbie as soon as she seated herself next to his bed. He looked pretty awful after the ordeal, and his voice was barely a whisper.

"What sort of questions?" Debbie responded. She was puzzled by this unusual request and had expected only to make small talk.

"You know, questions that people might want to ask me," Ellis said, as if it was obvious that this is what she would want to do.

"Okay, then," Debbie said cheerfully, taking out a notebook and pen. "What would you like to say to people who are concerned about you and afraid about your condition?"

"Just tell them that it doesn't do them any good to be afraid. Just say: 'I hope to hell he's well, but if he isn't—he isn't. Screw it.'"

"Right," Debbie responded, noting that Ellis waited patiently for her to get that down. "Well, then, what was your experience like when you were told that you needed to have surgery?"

"I thought to myself that it's too damn bad but I'll have to do it anyway. I did feel concerned because anything could happen. I wished they had said no surgery was needed, but they didn't. So I accepted what I can't change and thought about things to do now."

Debbie nodded. This was all making perfect sense to her because it is exactly the sort of thing that Ellis would say. She thought for a moment, then framed another question. "What do you want your friends, colleagues, students, and clients to know about this situation?"

"Know the truth, and nothing but the truth. I've had serious surgery, but I'll be returning to the Institute to work for another 90 years in probability!"

Debbie laughed, knowing he would do his best to try to make this happen even if it was irrational. "What was the predominant emotion that you felt after the operation?"

"Concern," Ellis answered. "But not too much. I was mostly thinking about all the work I'll have to do when I get back."

"Did you adopt any humor to help you through this time?"

Ellis nodded. "Yeah, I thought of a few things, but I can't remember them all right now." He paused for a moment, then added: "I did think to myself that they may have taken my colon out, but at least they're not taking my balls."

11 Recovery from Therapy Abuse

A Case from Laura Brown

Laura Brown is known as one of the originators and leading proponents of Feminist Therapy. This approach looks at the negative impact and restrictive roles that gender places on one's life. She deals with issues of oppression, power, ethics, sexual harassment, gender roles, sexual orientation, and body image. She has also been a leader in social justice issues, especially related to gays and lesbians.

Brown has written a number of books, including Subversive Dialogues: Theory in Feminist Therapy, Recovered Memories of Abuse, Fat Oppression and Psychotherapy: A Feminist Perspective, Personality and Psychopathology, *and* Diversity and Complexity in Feminist Therapy.

Brown is Professor at the Washington School of Professional Psychology at Argosy University Seattle. She also maintains a private practice, specializing in work with survivors of severe and repetitive trauma.

Group Therapy

Alice came from an educated, professional family. She was quite bright, with great artistic talent, but she had been subjected to considerable abuse as a young girl. Her mother was quite unstable and tortured her daughter with verbal abuse and neglect. Her father abused her sexually. Not surprisingly, this led her into therapy when she was a young adult. Then the *real* abuse began.

The first therapist she saw, in the 1970s, was a psychiatrist who was experimenting with hallucinogenic drugs in group therapy. The psychiatrist was trying to circumvent the laws that prohibited the use of LSD, so he had decided to try other substances as shortcuts to lengthy therapy. His theory was that these drugs would open wider the doors of perception, or some such thing. What these drugs actually did was reduce self-control and undermine the capacity for free will.

Alice was given a rather high dose of this drug, put in a therapy group, and encouraged to have sex with other members of the group. At the time, she had no conscious recollection of her own experience of incest; she knew only that sex was extraordinarily frightening and aversive to her.

Although Alice resisted the pressure to enter into a sexual relationship with a group member designated by the therapist, he eventually wore her down. He told her she was blocking a genuine part of herself and that in order to heal she would have to let go of her inhibitions.

Alice had foggy memories of what transpired during this "therapy." She was both heavily drugged and absolutely terrified at the time. Let's just say that this treatment was not particularly helpful to her and left her with the feeling that therapists were "rapists" and not to be trusted.

The Workshop

A decade or so later, Alice attended a course on sexuality that Laura Brown was teaching. It was a general introduction to women and their experiences, with a special emphasis on feeling more comfortable with their bodies and their needs.

"I have a question for you," Alice said to Brown during a break.

"Sure, what's on your mind?"

"Well, I was wondering, is it necessary for people to be sexually active in order to be well-functioning human beings?"

Brown studied the woman for a moment. She saw an attractive woman in her late twenties whose form was hidden under layers of baggy clothing. Although Alice was trying to look as poised and casual as possible, Brown could tell she was anxious even talking about the subject.

"Well," Brown said to Alice, "it isn't necessary if the person does not want it." She paused momentarily to gauge the woman's reaction, then she continued. "Being sexually active is a highly individual and personal thing. Even being sexual with yourself."

"I see," Alice answered slowly. "So then, if you were seeing someone in therapy, you wouldn't pressure her to have sex?"

Brown thought this a rather unusual question, but she tried to give the woman the courtesy of an honest response. "No, of course not. First of all, I don't pressure people into anything. And second, making the decision to be sexual is very much about choice."

"Choice?"

"Yes, if you are choosing not to be sexual for some reason," Brown said, changing the subject from the general to the far more personal, "then I would want to support you in your choice and not pressure you to do anything that you didn't feel comfortable doing."

"Okay then," Alice answered. "Thanks." And she turned and walked away.

Sex Therapy

Five years elapsed before Alice actually called Brown for an appointment. "Several years ago," she said on the phone, "I approached you at a workshop and asked you a question about pressuring clients to have sex. I don't suppose you remember but. . . ."

"Actually, I do remember." It did seem amazing, but this woman was so nervous, and her question so unusual, that Brown did recall the conversation. In fact, she had been surprised that the woman had ever followed up with an appointment. At that time Brown was just starting her practice, and she had been doing the workshops to get her name known in the community and, hopefully, generate some referrals. But she never dreamed this woman would call for therapy. She had seemed skittish and angry in the workshop.

"Well," Alice said, "I was wondering if I could come to see you and discuss some problems I've been having, you know, about sex and things."

"Sure. Sounds good."

During their first meetings, Alice reported that she had not had sex with anyone for many years. She wasn't missing being sexual, she said. But she thought that there was something wrong with this.

"I'm just curious," Brown pressed. "Where did you get an idea like that?"

"I used to see a therapist a long time ago. And he told me that a person who isn't having sex is not living up to her full potential. He told me it was pathological. He tried to help me work on it."

Brown wondered what Alice meant by that, just by the discomfort she exhibited, but she encouraged her to talk about the previous therapy. That's when she learned about the drugs and the orgies masquerading as group therapy.

Brown was absolutely furious when she heard what had happened. She was so outraged she could barely contain herself that a colleague and professional would take advantage of such a vulnerable woman in this way. This wasn't the first story of sexual abuse in therapy that she'd heard; it was becoming a horrible specialty of hers. So she knew to keep herself in check and asked, "I'm curious how you felt about that?"

"Mostly shame," Alice confided. "I felt horrible and I hated it. But I wanted to be accepted by these people. I just did what they told me to and hoped they knew what they were doing. I was terribly depressed and anxious all the time then, and I just wanted to feel better. I sure didn't have a clue what was good for myself at the time."

Alice went on to say that it was soon after this so-called therapy that she fell apart completely. Even after the intervening years she had never regained her previous level of functioning. She kept trying to have relationships with various men that she met, but she could never bring herself to have sex with them; it was just too terrifying. The last time she had even tried, once the man got into bed with her she started to freak out and tried to beat him; she wanted to kill him. She'd been too frightened to try again after that.

"What is it that you'd like for yourself now?" Brown asked.

"Well, I've been doing some research on you and I heard that you do sex therapy for . . . for women like me. And I want to learn to be more comfortable being sexual."

"I see," Brown said, seeing all too clearly that this woman presented a goal that did not seem to be truly her own. "I think before we get into the whole issue of your sexuality we need first to find out more about what you want as a person. I'm not prepared to share your judgment that there is something wrong with you sexually."

"I'm not sure what you mean," Alice said, genuinely confused. "I mean I can't have sex. I don't feel comfortable. . . ."

"I heard you. But what I'm saying to you in return is that even if you choose never to have sex with another human being again, I would totally support you in that decision. And just at this moment it's not clear whether you want to do sex therapy to please this last therapist, or whether you, Alice, truly want to have sex."

Brown wanted to establish a contract that was clearly predicated on reducing the pressure that Alice was already feeling to become more supposedly "normal" and sexually responsive. Over the next several months they took their time developing a relationship and covering every aspect of Alice's life, except sex. That is not to say, by any stretch of the imagination, that things proceeded smoothly. In fact, Alice was volatile, unpredictable, and often furious at her therapist. Therapy was a scary place for her, and she showed it in her relationship with Brown. What she wanted, most of all, was for Brown to agree with her own self-assessment that she was irrevocably damaged and would never be normal until she could force herself to start having sex.

"I'm not willing to make an agreement to work with someone based on the premise that they're flawed," Brown responded. "Wounded, yes. Flawed, no."

Alice even went through a period during her therapy when she tried to be a lesbian, but she found she had little sexual interest in women either. She was not interested in sex. Period.

It took several years of frequent arguments over the process of therapy itself before the early history of abuse came out. Alice had begun to believe that nothing sexual would happen in Brown's therapy office; that even talking about sex would be entirely her own choice, and that if she chose not to talk about it, Brown wouldn't steer the conversation in that direction. In this context of something resembling safety, Alice began to know consciously what her body had always known.

To Brown, this emerging information about early incest explained a lot about why Alice had been so compliant at the hands of her previous therapist.

She offered to Alice the concept that her father's abuse had trained her from an early age to do whatever a man asked of her.

"Oh yeah?" Alice challenged. "Why the hell should I listen to you in the first place? You are just some crazy f***ing lesbian feminist. I bet you hate me."

Brown just smiled placidly, refusing to take the bait. "Yep, that's what I am. A lesbian. A feminist therapist. And you, Alice, are in charge of what you do with that fact."

"So you say."

"Listen. You don't have to believe me. You don't have to agree with me. I am simply telling you what I am willing and not willing to do, and what I think might be going on. I don't care if you ever believe me. The only person you have to believe is yourself, not me. You are right, all these things are true about me. But I still refuse to believe that you are some psycho basket case."

Brown offered to refer Alice to someone else for sex therapy, if that's what she wanted. Brown herself was even less willing than at the first session to use therapy to coerce Alice into being sexual.

Alice firmly declined the offer of a referral. It eventually became clear that another reason she had sought out Brown in the first place was because in that first workshop Brown had said that it wasn't necessary to be sexually active in order to be a healthy human being. Although Alice wanted to believe this, she found it difficult to let go of her own indoctrination at the hands of masters who had taught her something quite different. In fighting with Brown about this, she was fighting with her own inner oppressors. By not fighting back, Brown allowed Alice's own voice to surface—and that voice said that Alice didn't want to be sexual with anyone, thank you very much.

Alice began to have more and more difficulty once her past history emerged. She became suicidal and even more depressed. Her work began to suffer. In desperation, she began to seek other healing modalities—guided imagery, meditation, community workshops. As a feminist therapist, Brown supported all her explorations, believing that clients should trust their expertise about their own conditions.

■ ■ ■

What It Means to Be a Feminist Theorist

We interrupted the story at this point to ask Brown what it meant to her to be feminist therapist. She summarized that there are a few core ideas that she holds sacred. The first is that gender is an organizing variable in people's lives. The second is that developing an egalitarian relationship, in which both participants are seen as experts and collaborators in the process, is crucial to therapy.

In Alice's case, when she came in and said, "I've been trying out something that has been helpful to me and I want to incorporate it into our work,"

Brown considered that an important contribution. This was especially true because Alice had been turning her artistic talents to the illustration of a women's health book. She was drawing picture after picture of women's genitals, observing pelvic exams, almost forcing herself to know about women's bodies, although her own remained *terra incognita*.

Brown remarked, "It was clearly her attempt to get back her power around her own genitals and her own body, which became much more clear as the memories of the incest began to emerge. Alice was trying to know women's bodies, her own body, in a safe way, via her artistic talent which had never deserted her."

This was actually the very first case, and in fact the only case, in which Brown had used guided imagery and meditation as a way to help a client go back into the past and recover memories that had been buried. Brown herself is wary of such strategies. If Alice had not come into session announcing that this was what she wanted to do, Brown is certain that she would not have pursued this course.

When the first images of abuse came into focus, Brown was stunned. "My first impulse was to run," she said. "This was the early 1980s and I hadn't gone to graduate school to learn about this stuff. No one had talked about incest in graduate school. It was still a completely hidden topic. Alice began to have recollections, and a lot of the therapy became about that. She started looking for psychological shovels to dig more things out of herself."

Since this recovered memories stuff was so new for Brown, she wanted to proceed as cautiously as possible. Alice, on the other hand, wanted to dig deeper and deeper. She asked Brown to hypnotize her, believing that this would allow her fuller recall.

"Look," Brown told her, "we are not here as part of some archeological dig and I am not an archeologist. I am not going to do hypnosis with you and I am not going to do anything to bring more of this stuff up."

Feminist therapy is about empowering people, especially if they have been violated. Brown was reluctant to do anything that might result in a loss of personal control. Alice wanted her to use hypnosis and more guided imagery to get back into the past. But Brown refused and insisted they move more cautiously. "I don't believe that we can recover from violation by violating ourselves," she told Alice. "Trust yourself to know what you need to know. Don't push—that's what the people who wounded you did."

By this time, Alice was having terrible posttraumatic stress symptoms and increasingly intrusive recollections. The work in therapy involved integrating these bits and pieces of her past into a coherent story. Her biggest struggle was with the fact that she so deeply loved her father; he had been the "good" parent on whom she could depend, compared to her mother, who was totally out of control. She would often become angry at Brown because therapy was the place where this painful contradiction became unavoidable.

Brown mentioned that this is a classic scenario that she has seen many times, in which the incest-perpetrating fathers are the more emotionally healthy parents and have the more stable or even loving relationships with their children. In some ways, this makes the problem even more challenging for the victims, because they have to deal with the additional loss of their supposedly beloved daddy who had betrayed them. Alice knew that her mother had been a creep, but it was the image of her loving and supportive father that had helped her to hold things together. The effect of losing that image was profound.

All through their work together, Brown had been struggling to make sense of what they were uncovering. Very little had been written about recovered memories at this time, so she was inventing things with her client as the therapy proceeded. One thing about which Brown was certain in structuring a treatment plan is that she knew Alice had to remain in control of what they did and how they did it.

The Finest Hour

"I don't want you to talk today," Alice announced to begin the session. "I just want you to listen."

"Okay," Brown agreed, pleased by the take-charge attitude that Alice displayed.

There had been times when Alice just sat in the corner and didn't say a single word throughout the whole session. It had been a test of sorts, to make sure that Brown would respect her boundary and not violate it. This was especially difficult for Brown, who by her own description likes to talk a lot.

As that session came to an end, Alice said, "I think what I am doing is that I want to make sure you know what it feels like to have someone else control you."

Brown nodded. "Yeah, I think you're right about that."

Alice nodded in the corner.

"So," Brown prompted, "what does it feel like to be so in control?"

She shrugged. "Actually, it doesn't feel nearly as good as I thought it would. I don't think I like controlling someone else. But then, it sure doesn't feel very good to be controlled either."

Brown was never surprised by Alice's capacity for insight. She was a brilliant woman who had always been smart as a kid. She was like that kid you used to know in school who was your age but who was two or three grades ahead of you. Although she was intellectually and creatively gifted, this only isolated her further. She was very lonely as a child, and this stayed with her as an adult. The shame of her abuse isolated her further.

It was during this one session, when Brown felt Alice's pain so deeply, and felt such a strong empathic connection, that her eyes started to tear up. She just felt so sad for this lonely wounded person that she could not hide her reaction. Brown recalled feeling "all warm and fuzzy." So what happened next was a bit of a shock.

Rather than responding with appreciation, Alice became furious. "How dare you be sad for me! Who the hell are you to have feelings for me? Stop it right now!"

Brown was stunned. This had been a moment of true intimacy between them and yet Alice was so threatened by these emotional feelings that she fled, pushing Brown away, hard, as she ran. She had felt violated by her therapist's own expression of caring for her. Brown knew that she had no other choice but to back off and give Alice the room to express her anger.

"You weren't there," Alice railed. "How could you possibly know what it was like to have your mother beat you and your father f*** you? And what the hell can you do for me now, huh? Are you going to just make this all go away? This is all such a f***ing waste of time. And you can be damn well sure that I don't want your pity!"

Alice was constantly waiting for her therapist to step over the line and betray her, just like everyone else she had ever trusted had done. She saw this deep emotional connection as evidence of what she had been watching for.

Brown just accepted the anger and reflected it back. She tried to stay connected empathically, but the work was so emotionally charged and complex that there was precious little room to maneuver. All it would take would be the slightest error or misjudgment and Alice's anger would become activated. Brown can't recall ever working so hard to figure out what was going on and what to do next. Empathic connection was necessary—empathic connection was traumatizing. Finding the balance was a challenge at every moment.

It wasn't as if Brown could reassure her client that therapy is a safe place and that Alice should trust her. Given her past abuse at the hands of therapists, Alice had quite the opposite impression. It was only a testimony to her courage, persistence, desperation, and overpowering desire to heal that she had stuck with the sessions as long as she had.

About 6 months later, Alice said in a session, "Remember that day that I got mad at you because you cried?"

"How could I forget?" Brown laughed.

"Well, I just want you to know that I'm really glad you cried. I wasn't ready for that yet. I am still mad at you that you did it then, but I really needed to know that you genuinely felt sad for what happened to me and that made a difference."

Looking back, Brown could now see that what she had believed was a terrible lapse of her own countertransference feelings actually turned out to be a breakthrough for them. This had apparently been the first time that Alice really understood that it was possible for someone to love her but not abuse her, to connect with her and know her deeply without wanting to violate her. She was so well defended against any kind of intimacy that it took a long time for her to let anything through. But she finally got it. She understood at last that she could let people care about her, and care back in return, and not be used and devastated in the process. She had the room and time to know this on her own terms.

It is also interesting that it wasn't until 6 months after the session that Brown even realized that they had done a fine piece of work together in that one session. In other words, you can't often tell what is your finest hour while it is going on, or even immediately afterwards. Sometimes it takes many months, or even years, to realize the significance of our work.

■ ■ ■

Surprising Lessons

One of the things to be learned from this case is that our supposed clinical mistakes can actually advance the therapy in unanticipated ways. In fact, it is really hard to tell what is a mistake and what is a "good" intervention based on the client's response at the time. Sometimes we don't read accurately how the client is feeling. At other times, the client reacts in one way during the session but quite another way later. The client's experience of empathy and connection is often nothing like what the therapist imagines.

If Brown had not made the "mistake" of crying during the session, then the next piece would not have fallen into place, and the one after that. "It was something that I had to do wrong," Brown said, "in order to make amends for, and take responsibility for, so that we could do the next piece. Alice needed for me to make the mistake in timing and own up to it without making her reaction a problem. It was the whole transaction. I was with her and I was also perfectly willing to be with her boundaries."

Brown believes that sometimes the best thing that can happen in therapy is for clients to become angry with us. They need to experience this anger *and* the attachment at the same time. Here Brown is not referring to "borderline rage" or some other form of acting out in the relationship, but the kind of anger that a child feels toward a parent, in which he or she is validated and held while also being given space for anger. That is how genuine intimacy evolves.

"Sometimes we need to make the space to not interpret the anger, not defend against it, not feel like we have done something wrong, and not feel guilt that we messed up. We have to simply sit with the anger. With Alice, I didn't go away when she was angry with me. I didn't get distant. I was there with her through this work."

Brown laughed as she mentioned the last point, because she recalled how hard she worked at keeping her own composure. She consulted with many colleagues during these years she worked with Alice. Lest the reader get the impression that everything fell neatly into place, it is important to realize that this work was messy, chaotic, unpredictable, and that most of the time, Brown felt she was stumbling around in the dark.

Brown cannot recall ever having such complicated, intense, and deep countertransference feelings toward anyone before that, although she often has since. There were times when she wanted to yell at Alice, when she hoped the woman would just go away and not come back. Alice, in the beginning and middle stages of the work, was prickly and opinionated and demanding, not at all someone whom anyone would feel warm and attracted to. Alice had done a good job of making herself safe from violation that way. There were times when Brown feared her, and hated her, and felt her own anger toward her. There were times when she wanted to lash out at her client, fight back, but she recalled that this is exactly what had happened before with her previous therapist. Even if she never helped this woman, she vowed she would at least keep the boundaries intact.

"I think the other piece is that when we genuinely feel something of care and warmth toward a client, we should be transparent about that. I think our clients need to know about our human connections to them. Certainly, there are the issues of professionalism and payment, but I still think the authentic relationship is real. I could have told Alice in an unemotional way I felt sad for that lonely hurt little girl, and it might have p***ed her off just as much, but it wouldn't have moved her to the extent my tears did. It would have been formal, not real."

The other lesson from this case, which may seem rather obvious, is that therapists shouldn't violate people who need help recovering from previous violations. This might seem obvious, but Brown issued this as a warning about what you agree to do with clients. "If I had agreed to do sex therapy with Alice, and teach her to desensitize and all this stuff one would do with someone who is phobic, I would have violated her all over again. I encounter this repeatedly in my work as a consultant. Therapists need to think about what a therapeutic strategy is conveying at the meta-level."

Just because the coping strategies a client has been using are not working very well, or have certain side effects, does not mean that they don't have enormous value. Brown believes we must honor and respect the old strategies in order to discover what they are trying to accomplish. That is what guides what we should do next. And that is what prevents us from retraumatizing someone.

Another key point from this case is how important it is to keep learning from our clients, and truly listening to them. "What they bring to therapy is at least as important, and sometimes more important, than my skill, and my training, and my experience. As long as I remain open to what clients offer, the work usually goes pretty well. When I forget that, and become 'Dr. Brown, the Expert,' that is when I get into trouble. Therapy is usually more effective when there are two experts in the room, especially if they can work together cooperatively."

12 Brought Back from the Dead

A Case from Arnold Lazarus

Arnold Lazarus is known primarily for his early work in behavior therapy, and later, for his efforts to synthesize behavior therapy with cognitive methods into one of the first systematic, integrative therapeutic models. Multimodal Therapy provides a structured means of assessing and treating problems across every aspect of human functioning, including emotional, cognitive, sensory, behavioral, interpersonal, and physiological dimensions.

From his early years as a psychologist in South Africa, and then later at Stanford, Yale, and Temple University Medical School before he went to Rutgers University for most of his career, Lazarus published a series of books that were designed to take behavior and cognitive therapies to the next level. His multimodal model remains one of the most popular approaches to integrative therapy still in practice.

In addition to his many books for practitioners, Lazarus has written several books for a popular audience: I Can If I Want to, Marital Myths Revisited: A Fresh Look at Two Dozen Mistaken Beliefs about Marriage, *and* The 60 Second Shrink: 101 Strategies for Staying Sane in a Crazy World.

All of this is part of his standard biography. What is not known by many people, however, is his childhood background as a pianist from the age of 5, and his brief career as a boxer during his teenage years. This paradox of reconciling two such disparate interests—one in music and one involving battles with opponents—is typical of the ways that Lazarus has managed to bring together discrepant parts into a synthesized whole throughout much of his life. Now 72, he still likens his job to that of a trainer—whether of boxers or pianists—in which he uses supportive relationships to teach people to function more effectively "on stage" or "in the ring." His finest hours as a therapist seem to take place not during those times when he follows his own model, but when he transcends it in order to move beyond what he has already done and known.

A Broken Spirit

When Clive first walked in the door, he looked like the walking dead who had just arisen from the grave. He shuffled into the office, posture stooped, each step painfully executed, as if the act of walking itself was a chore that was beyond his capability. His eyes were half-closed, half-focused on his shoes. He exuded such an aura of gloom that his therapist could already feel himself being pulled into the despair.

Lazarus examined his new patient with a fair degree of trepidation. He had seen depressed people in his life—in fact, he specialized in working with depression—but he couldn't ever recall seeing someone who looked so despondent that he literally appeared dead on his feet.

Clive was a couple of years older than Lazarus, but age could not be easily determined in someone who had so withdrawn into himself. His hands hung listlessly at his side; when he finally managed to settle himself in a chair, he seemed to collapse with a sigh. For a minute or two, he just sat silently, not saying a word, looking down at his hands. Each breath he took seemed labored and forced.

At first, Lazarus couldn't even hear the man speak, because his voice was so soft and devoid of inflection that it didn't sound quite human. "What's that you said?" Lazarus prompted him. "Sorry, but I couldn't quite make it out."

"Sorry," Clive mumbled, looking even more pitiful because he had somehow already let his new therapist down. "I said that I deserved what I'm getting."

"You deserve to be in this bad shape?"

Clive nodded and studied his hands some more.

Lazarus waited another minute to see if Clive would continue, but it seemed to occupy all the old man's energy just to keep his sunken chest moving in and out. Lazarus had a frightening thought that at any moment he might be expected to administer cardiopulmonary resuscitation. This guy looked like he was just one tiny step from the other side of the grave.

After waiting patiently, Lazarus prompted Clive again: "You were saying that you deserved what has happened to you."

Clive looked up, startled for a moment, as if he had just realized where he was but was unsure how he had arrived there. "Yeah," he nodded. "All of this is my own fault. I've got nobody to blame but myself for this fix I'm in."

Now this was something that Lazarus could sink his teeth into. Already in the first minute of the session he'd heard evidence of some pretty extreme self-blaming and exaggerations, distorted thinking patterns that he could address. He was also struck by how much he immediately liked Clive. There was something about him that seemed so essentially kind and caring. In spite of the depression that seemed to be literally eating him alive, the man's gentle and warm nature peeked out from underneath his broken spirit.

Self-Blame

"So," Lazarus pressed him, "what is it that you did that is supposedly so horrific that you deserve to be punished in such a profound way?"

Clive nodded, not because he understood where Lazarus was going with him, but because he agreed with this assessment that he had done something so completely horrible. "It's my wife," he croaked in a hoarse voice. "I just couldn't take care of her the way she needed to be. I'm just so selfish that I couldn't make her happy."

Out poured Clive's miserable tale of being such a terrible, worthless, incompetent, unfeeling husband that he not only deserved to have his wife leave him but he should burn in hell ever after because of his marital sins.

"And what is it exactly that you did to your wife?" Lazarus questioned him further. "Did you beat her?"

Clive shook his head.

"Marital affairs then? You've been sleeping with other women?"

Clive looked horrified at the very thought. "Of course not!" he said indignantly.

"Well, then, you abandoned her? You didn't spend time with her and cherish her when you were together?"

"Oh no, no," Clive protested. "I spent every spare minute with my wife. I did everything I could think of to make her happy." He hung his head for a moment and watched his hands washing themselves, as if they were dirty. "But it just wasn't enough."

During ensuing sessions, Lazarus heard the full story of Clive's marriage, and it did not come across at all as his patient had first presented things. He found Clive to be a totally endearing fellow—charming, respectful, and considerate in every way. He just couldn't imagine that the story Clive had been telling about being a neglectful, inattentive husband could possibly fit with the image of someone who exuded such basic decency.

"I wonder," Lazarus ventured, "if your wife might consent to join us for a session or two? That way I could hear her version of things." What Lazarus really had in mind was an opportunity to assess their interactions and reconcile Clive's perception of things with those of his wife. He had a very strong suspicion that the wife was hell on wheels—a demanding, self-centered, controlling person who kept her husband firmly under her thumb. She had apparently dumped him because she'd found a more obedient slave.

Lazarus knew that this initial impression was hardly fair; each of the partners in most relationships train one another to behave in a mutually antagonistic fashion. But unless he could get the wife to come in for couples work, or at least to tell her version of the story, Lazarus did not see how he could easily help his patient to move on.

"No," Clive insisted. "She will absolutely refuse to come in. She says she's done with me." As he said these last words, he tucked his head down in the most pitiful manner. He looked so shrunken and miserable it made Lazarus's own heart ache in sympathy.

Yet there were also times, now and then, when Clive would flash a most radiant smile. These glimmers of his inner warmth were rare and fleeting, but nevertheless powerful signs of what a lovely person he had once been—before he was dead inside.

Dial Tone

Finally, one day Lazarus did manage to reach the wife on the phone at her place of work. "Mrs. Donahue," he addressed her formally in his South African accent, "might I have a few words with you about your husband?"

"If you're calling me to come in there, I told him, and I'm telling you that. . . ."

"No, no, Mrs. Donahue. May I call you Grace?"

She hesitated for a moment, as if this was some sort of trick question or psychologist's ploy. "Yes, I suppose," she conceded.

"Well, Grace, I'm not calling you to invite you in. I certainly respect your wishes on that score." This was hardly the case, but Lazarus could see no point in aggravating her further through increased pressure. He needed her cooperation in some way just to get a better handle on what was going on. Clive was still insisting that all their marital woes, and all of his debilitating depression, were the result of his own ineptitude.

"I've got nothing to say," she insisted. "I'm done with the man. I told him that. And I'm telling you. I just wish you'd all leave me alone so I can get on with my life."

"Yes Grace, but. . . ."

"Why don't you just talk to his other doctor, that psychiatrist fellow? He'll fill you in. Then you can stop pestering me."

Grace was referring to the psychiatrist who had been treating Clive previous to his consultation with Lazarus. Apparently, he had also met with Grace a few times, and when Lazarus did make contact with him, he refused to say much about the case except to mutter, "She's some piece of work. I'll tell you that."

"Well," Lazarus tried to interrupt Grace, "I'll certainly do that. But I was still wondering if you might fill me in a little more on what's been going on. According to your husband, it is all his fault that your relationship fell apart. I know that can't possibly be the case but I was hoping. . . ."

"Look. I don't give a sh**. Is that clear? I'm done with the guy. And good riddance to him! And to you! Can I be any more clear than that?"

Lazarus found himself listening to the dial tone. She had hung up on him.

Unloved and Betrayed

During their next session together, Lazarus decided it was time to go back and find out more about Clive's background since it was clear he was not going to be getting any help from his wife. Sure enough, once they began to talk about the safer past rather than the tumultuous present, Clive proved to be an articulate, charming, animated guy. He had been a successful corporate executive and had once been married previously.

"So, this is your second marriage then?"

"Yes," Clive admitted sadly, losing a bit of his earlier enthusiasm.

"May I ask what happened?"

"We were together about 9 years when. . . ." Clive hesitated for a moment, feeling awkward about the subject. ". . . when, well, she was involved with someone else."

"Your wife had been having an affair?"

Clive nodded. "We had . . . we *have* a daughter together. And I was awarded custody of her when she was 8. My ex-wife and I—we've always been on good terms and all—we still keep in touch."

Clive went on to explain that he married Grace a number of years after this and became the stepfather to her children, who were about the same age as his own daughter. Grace's previous husband had died in a tragic accident, and Clive soon realized that she had never really recovered from this loss because she was always comparing him unfavorably to her departed spouse. Nevertheless, Clive worked as hard as he possibly could to be the best husband and parent he could be, even if his efforts always seemed to fall short. Clive encouraged Grace to enroll in a graduate program, and with his support and help—financially and emotionally—she completed her degree and embarked on a new career.

As Grace became more and more involved in her own profession, the marriage seemed to deteriorate further, to the point where Clive felt like he was a guest living in his own home—and a guest on probation who might be evicted at any time. Whenever he broached the subject of their disputes, or complained about the status of things, Grace unfailingly threatened: "If you don't like it around there, then why don't you get the hell out?"

It was at this point that Clive felt so distraught that he consulted a psychiatrist, who prescribed antidepressants and saw him in therapy once a week. Grace also accompanied him to sessions on occasion, but that just seemed to make things worse: she became even more antagonistic and abusive toward him. Finally, she'd had enough of his sniveling and sued him for divorce.

"I felt like I'd been hit by a stun gun," Clive recalled, still immobilized by what he perceived as an ambush.

"Okay," Lazarus urged him to continue the narrative. "Then what?"

"Well, she just moved out one day. She wouldn't tell me where she moved. I still don't know where she lives." He seemed almost more ashamed of this last feature, that he didn't know where his wife resided, than about anything else about the sad story.

Since the separation, Grace had forbidden any of her children to have any contact with Clive whatsoever, and this wounded him deeply. It was as if he had lost not only his wife but his whole family and support system. On top of this, Grace threatened their mutual friends that if they continued their relationships with him she would no longer have anything to do with them. Finally, on the verge of suicide, and at the urging of a friend, he had decided to see Lazarus.

"Can you see now why I deserve what I've gotten?" Clive asked, feeling like he had made a strong case.

"Actually," Lazarus said with all seriousness, "no I can't. What I see is a man who is profoundly depressed, lonely, isolated, and is recovering from long-term emotional abuse that he never deserved. What I see is someone who has been unloved and betrayed. What I see is someone who is beating himself up over crimes he never committed."

Clive went on to explain that the divorce with Grace was becoming quite messy. She was demanding virtually all of their assets, most of his pension, nearly all the furniture in their home including pieces that had been in Clive's family for years, and even his old Jaguar that he loved to tinker with.

Common Sense

By this time, Lazarus had completely abandoned any plan to conduct a systematic multimodal assessment and follow his trademark therapeutic strategies. What this guy needed more than anything else, Lazarus reasoned, was some common sense. Somebody had to talk straight to him. Someone had to challenge his crazy ideas that he was 100 percent at fault for all his marital problems and that he deserved to suffer as a result.

"Are you aware," Lazarus observed, "that you are entitled to at least half the assets in your estate, including your pension fund?"

"Not according to my lawyer," Clive answered.

"Yeah?" Lazarus said to him in a challenging tone, no longer playing the musician but the boxer. "Whose side is your lawyer on?"

Thus activated, Clive went back to his attorney and relayed the conversation he had had with Lazarus. The lawyer was absolutely enraged by what he perceived as meddling by someone who had no understanding or training in the law. He told Clive in no uncertain terms that this psychologist fellow should mind his own business and stop getting into areas he knows nothing about.

Now firmly entrenched in his position as the battling advocate for his patient, Lazarus refused to back down. "Do you want me to talk to your lawyer? He's right that I'm no attorney, but I do know enough about the law in this state to realize that you are entitled to more—a lot more—than you are willing to settle for. Including your Jaguar!"

Clive's magical smile lit up at the mention of his beloved car. He then mentioned that his wife had been earning substantial sums of money, that she had never repaid him for all the money he had spent to send her to graduate school, and she never chipped in a dime toward household expenses but squirreled all her funds away for herself.

"Does your lawyer know these facts?" Lazarus asked him.

"I don't think so," Clive replied.

"Well then, TELL HIM!" Lazarus exclaimed.

Clive promised to go back to his attorney and insist that they take a more aggressive rather than surrendering stand.

No Angel and No Rogue

Soon after this conversation, Lazarus received a call from Clive's first wife. Lazarus was delighted to talk with her, to finally get some corroboration that this was a decent man who had been mistreated.

"He's just about the nicest man I've ever known," she said with genuine affection. "I can't tell you how many times I've regretted cheating on him."

"So," Lazarus asked her, "he's never been abusive or neglectful or anything like that?" He was trying to reconcile his own impressions with those of Clive's wife, who claimed he was such an unfeeling monster.

"No," she laughed. "Quite the contrary. He's just a sweetheart. Surely you know that about him if you've been talking to him?"

"Well, sure," Lazarus answered, "it's just that. . . ."

"You've been talking to that vicious witch, haven't you?"

"Excuse me?"

"His wife. Grace. The bitch. Have you met her?"

"Ah no," Lazarus said, smiling to himself, "I haven't yet had that pleasure."

"Well, then, consider yourself lucky and leave it at that."

Now more clear about the nature of the conflict between Grace and Clive, Lazarus was more convinced than ever that he had to keep attacking the man's insistent self-blame. Each session Clive would come in with a new list of things he could have done better and things he should have done differently. "I just don't deserve anything better," he continually insisted.

"On the contrary," Lazarus argued back in a blunt manner, "you married a woman who never loved you, who never even *liked* you. She never got over the death of her previous husband and married you out of convenience and desperation. She used you, Clive, in every way possible. You put her through school. You took care of her children. You gave her all the love you could—she took the money but never let you get close to her. Then, once she could support herself, she didn't need you any more and so moved on with her life. And now, after it's all over, she still wants to take you for every penny you've got."

Lazarus waited a second to see how his patient was taking this confrontation before he proceeded further. So far, he knew that it took some pretty strong blows to get Clive's attention, much less make anything stick. "You'll just have to excuse me if I am being too presumptuous," Lazarus said, "but this lady you married is no angel and you are no rogue."

Clive closed his eyes and shrugged his shoulders. Then he nodded his head. He wouldn't say it aloud, but Lazarus could almost hear him thinking:

"That could very well be. Maybe there *is* some need in me to punish myself needlessly and to glorify my wife. And maybe it's perfectly true that I am not this awful person."

It was clear to Lazarus, even if it had not yet sunk into Clive, that his wife had brainwashed him over the years into thinking of himself as pretty reprehensible. He had been poisoned, almost to death, actually believing that he was worthless and not worthy to be alive. Lazarus saw his job as providing an antidote to the poison, and that's why he kept administering measured doses again and again.

Clive left the session determined to start taking charge of his life instead of remaining so apathetic and dead inside. He presented his lawyer with facts and figures and he announced that he intended to fight this divorce by negotiating for his fair share of assets. To his surprise, the attorney responded to the facts he had been given and this newly found assertiveness and resolved to take a firmer stance.

Straight Talk

Clive was almost cheerful as he reported the progress that had been made with his attorney. For the first time, he actually seemed open to the arguments that Lazarus presented to him about the distorted ways that he had been looking at the situation.

"Look, Clive," Lazarus continued the conversation, "it isn't your fault, and it isn't Grace's fault either. She's been trying to do the best she can, but she never really recovered from the tragedy of her first husband's death. She was bitter and twisted. There was no way that you could rewrite that script because it was etched in steel, granite, and tungsten."

The words finally seemed to get through to him, to the point where Clive no longer saw himself as a villain and victim. Unfortunately, the effects would not last long, and Clive would slip back into old patterns of self-blame. That was when Lazarus decided to try the use of paradox, since direct action was having only a temporary impact.

"All right," Lazarus agreed. "You've convinced me. You really are a worthless piece of crap, just as your wife claims."

Clive seemed stunned for a moment, although Lazarus was not clear if that was because he had taken him by surprise by this reversal or it was his rather strong language. Clive was a pretty conservative guy by and large.

"And furthermore," Lazarus continued the lament, "I also agree that you aren't entitled to be happy, or even anything other than half-dead. Here you married this perfect person, this goddess who never makes mistakes and is so totally accepting, and you've absolutely screwed up all by yourself."

Clive had the most delicious, hearty laugh, and when he launched into a contagious bout, Lazarus couldn't help but join him.

"Okay, okay," Clive agreed in between his giggles. "I get your point."

Lazarus may have gotten through to him on this one point, but he was still concerned that Clive needed to be weaned off the antidepressant drugs (which his physician agreed to take charge of). But most important, Clive didn't have a single friend with whom he could share pleasant time, let alone confidences. Clearly, building a support system was where they would have to go next.

"Have you thought about going to one of those support groups in your area?" Lazarus asked him. "There are several such organizations nearby that are designed for those going through divorce or loss."

"Yeah, I went to one of those meetings once," Clive countered. "They were just a bunch of losers."

Lazarus smiled at Clive's feistiness. A few months earlier he had been so compliant it would have been inconceivable that he could have disagreed about anything. "The purpose is not for you to meet dozens of scintillating and fascinating people who would become your lifelong friends. You could go to a few meetings just to get out of the house and get together with a few people."

Somehow, Lazarus had to break the cycle of Clive's isolation and loneliness. He decided to use a rather advanced strategy called "nagging." There was really nothing complicated about this, nor was it even remotely related to Lazarus's preferred theory. But his patient needed some straight talk from his "trainer," so he was determined that he would keep pressing him to get back into the ring.

Just to get the persistent therapist off his back, Clive agreed to attend several meetings. As luck would have it, he met Kathy, a woman with whom he formed a rapid bond because of their shared interests. Then, on a roll, he made another friend in a man who shared his love of tinkering with old cars.

At this juncture, Clive announced that he no longer needed therapy. "Thanks to you—well, you and Kathy and Viagra," he said with a warm and radiant smile. "You've brought me back from the dead. I feel like a young man again!"

Several months later, when his divorce was final, Lazarus received an invitation from Clive to attend a "Feeling Better Party." This was a catered affair, complete with a piano player. Lazarus had the chance to meet Kathy, Clive's new friends, his physician, his lawyer, and even his first wife and their daughter. There were even some friends there who had chosen to ignore the edict from Grace and wanted to remain friends with Clive.

As Lazarus made the rounds at the festivities, it truly felt this was his finest hour. He knew that he was only one small part of Clive's recovery and resurrection from the dead—all in a day's work for someone with a name like Lazarus, he chuckled to himself. Clive's daughter solemnly thanked Lazarus for helping her dad so much and for sticking with him.

It now strikes Lazarus as ironic that he actually did so little to make a difference. "Clive is such a lovely human being," Lazarus admits, "that all I had to do was offer him a little common sense."

13

The Queen of Shock

A Case from Bradford Keeney

After a career as a cybernetic epistomologist (someone who examines the way that knowledge is circularly organized), Bradford Keeney pursued more serious study of family systems while working with Gregory Bateson and Carl Whitaker, grandparents of the field. Next, he became an academic psychologist, creating theories of resource-focused therapy, improvisational therapy, and the aesthetics of change. New interests in cultural anthropology and indigenous healing led Keeney to abandon psychology and psychotherapy as professions, traveling the world to work with the most powerful medicine men, witchdoctors, shamans, healers, and tribal elders. Keeney's devotion to performing jazz piano and improvisational theatre only added greater flexibility to his unique style of practice, which builds on people's resources and strengths. He now takes pride in being a "nontherapist," impatient with conventional approaches that promote understanding, and focusing on problems and solutions instead of working at a deeper level, to help people promote their own healing. He has moved away from seeking knowledge from great intellectual traditions and now spends his time seeking the holders of practical wisdom, many of whom are illiterate.

Keeney is Vice President of Ringing Rocks Foundation, an organization formed to advance knowledge about alternative healing practices in diverse cultures. He is also a cultural anthropologist for the Mental Research Institute in Palo Alto, California. Keeney's books include Aesthetics of Change, Resource Focused Therapy, Improvisational Therapy, Mind in Therapy, Everyday Soul, *and the* Profiles in Healing Series, *which includes ethnographies of great healers around the world. More recently, he has co-authored (with Jeffrey Kottler and Jon Carlson)* American Shaman, *the story of his adventures working with indigenous healers around the world.*

One Session as Good as Another

While selecting this particular case, Brad Keeney is not at all sure what it means to pick a "finest hour" of his work. Nowadays, he operates in many different professional capacities—as a therapist occasionally, but much more often in the role of healer like that of indigenous shamans throughout the world. Keeney may use so-called talk therapy, but it is far more likely that he will exhort an audience to get up and move, use music and drumming to awaken the inner spirit, shake with the Bushmen of the African Kalahari, perform Gospel songs on the piano, or prescribe ritualistic tasks. Keeney, you see, is not a big fan of talk therapy unless it includes processes that involve a person's whole being.

Keeney is not certain how to make a judgment about what might be his best therapy. He might find himself one week conducting a session with an Ojibway medicine man who has lost his visions, the next week with a Zulu chief in a depressive funk or a !Kung bushman who feels blocked with this spirit world, and the next week doing a spiritual healing in Brazil. As such, he has not done much traditional psychotherapy in a long time, so the following case stands out to him for a number of reasons: (1) it does show the variety of methods Keeney likes to employ that emphasize accessing a person's inner resources, (2) he was able to establish a solid relationship and build trust with the woman in a remarkably brief period of time, and (3) it is a recent case, so it is easier to recall the details. Is this, however, his finest hour?

Keeney shrugged. "That's hard to say. I don't even make evaluations like that about my work."

Keeney selected this case because it was conducted on videotape and it was already conveniently transcribed. That allowed us to work with an accurate representation of what took place, although we have edited and rewritten the dialogue a bit to make for a more coherent story.

Looking for Resources

"My husband is an alcoholic," Melanie began the conversation. "We've been married three years and we have a baby at home. We've had problems and I just moved out of the house. Now I'm kind of confused. My husband plays emotional games with me: one minute he tells me he wants the marriage to work, and the next minute he backs off."

Keeney nodded in understanding, gesturing for her to continue. It is typical of him not to speak very much in the beginning. Not only does he want to give the client a chance to tell her story, her own way, but be moved himself into a trance state during this initial phase. "It's a zen-like place," he explained. "I move myself into a state of being nonreactive and nonjudgmental to any of her complaints and suffering. I do not feel her pain, nor do I have any naïve sense of compassion. On the contrary, I see that life has arranged a situation that is perfect for Melanie, or anyone else, to face challenges and learn from them."

According to Keeney, this is a far more spiritual way of practicing empathy and compassion, quite different from the ways that therapists ordinarily conceive of their job to feel the other's pain.

"I left," Melanie continued, "because of Sam's alcoholism, but also because he abuses me verbally. I can only take so much of this. I have a baby at home and that's a lot of responsibility."

Keeney nodded again.

"Well, about two weeks ago, I just about lost my mind. I asked my mom if I could come home. From that point on my husband has been even more unpredictable. I don't know what he wants from me. I don't even know what I want for myself. Sometimes I think that I married him for better or worse. But then I think that maybe we'd be better off on our own. I just don't know."

Whereas another therapist might reflect Melanie's feelings of despair and confusion at this point, Keeney was more interested in focusing on her strengths and resources rather than dwelling on her suffering. He is watching and listening carefully, looking for the slightest evidence of positive resources in her life. Keeney avoids talk about problems, symptoms, and psychopathology. He does not react to her narrative related to feeling trapped; instead, he is waiting to react as soon as she talks about the resources in her life. Since his work with indigenous healers emphasizes the power of intuition, he is also quite trusting of his own felt sense about what others might be experiencing. In this case, he senses immediately that Melanie is quite proud of being a mother. This is clearly a strength that he wants to draw upon. He has identified this in the first 2 minutes of the interview.

"Tell me about your daughter," Keeney prompted. "How old is she?"

Expectantly, Melanie smiles broadly. "She's 20 months old. She'll be 2 in just a few months!"

"You've got your hands full," Brad says, matching her smile.

"You've got that right!" Melanie's whole demeanor lights up. Gone is the dour, depressed, helpless exterior; now she is grinning and leaning forward. "She's such a talkative little thing. She's just the joy of my life, so active, so alive. But it's so much work too. I haven't felt comfortable leaving her with anyone else besides my mom and my sisters, so I try to do as much as I can. I don't really trust leaving her with Sam because of his alcohol."

Ignoring the comment about the problem, Keeney noticed the resourceful side of her statement and wants to contextualize this in a more positive frame. "So," he reflects, "you really want to be a good mother and do the right thing for your daughter."

"Yeah. My husband thinks that I want to be a mother more than I want to be his wife, but I don't think that's true. I don't think he realizes how much work it involves taking care of her. She just needs more attention than he does right now and he's used to being the center of attention—not just with me but everyone."

Keeney noticed that Melanie was talking about her husband as if he is a child. But rather than labeling this in a psychopathological way, he again preferred to see her mothering as a strength, extended beyond her infant daughter to her husband. Next he wanted to move things away from talk about Sam's drinking problem. He wondered just how serious this alcohol abuse was and how it interfered with other aspects of their lives.

"When you say that your husband is an alcoholic, what does this mean to you? How does his drinking affect his work, for instance?"

"Well, he has a good job."

"So," Keeney said to stress the point, "he has been able to keep things together well enough to keep his job."

"Yeah," Melanie said with a sigh, "Sam's had this job as long as we've been married. He drinks one or two six-packs of beer every night, but he still manages to show up at work the next morning."

"How is your husband different when he drinks?" Keeney asked. "And how do you change when he's been drinking?" Keeney wanted to emphasize the interactive nature of the ways they respond to one another.

"Basically, I kind of ignore him. I have my routine when I come home. I fix dinner for the baby and get her bath. I read to her and then get her off to bed so I can have a little time for myself. But I just can't take care of my daughter the way I want. I can't do it the right way. I can never seem to do anything right." As she says this, Melanie shakes her head in disgust.

Keeney heard the strong perfectionistic theme, that Melanie needed to be not only a good mother, but a *perfect* mother. He resisted any temptation to pathologize either her behavior, or that of her husband, and instead wanted to draw out more about the family interactions. "You seem to be facing some real challenges," he offered.

"You can sure say that! I try to be the best mom I can. I put Kim's interests and safety before anything else. But I sure could use some help. I mean, I can't even take a phone call at night without telling my husband to help change a diaper or clean up a mess. He just sits there sucking down his beers. Then he'll say to me, 'You stupid bitch, you take care of it.' He tells me I'm fat and worthless. I don't think I should have to put up with that."

There was a question implicit in that statement, as if Melanie was asking Keeney's permission, whether it is all right for her to stand up for herself. Putting aside that issue for a moment, he instead redirected her attention in another area.

"Let me ask you something, Melanie. What would your husband say about all this? What is his take on things?"

"He doesn't think there is a problem. As far as he's concerned, about the only problem is that I don't obey him. He's just angry that I walked out on him."

"So he feels that you abandoned him."

"Right. He'd say that I don't touch him enough, that our sex life is bad because I'm too fat. And I tell him it's because he's always too drunk to get it together."

"So you each blame one another for the problems," Keeney ventured.

Melanie ignores this interpretation of things, looks off into the distance for a minute. "On the way in here today my husband called me on my beeper. I called him back and I told him that I loved him and I wanted things to work out. Then he says to me that the marriage is over. So I walked around in tears all day thinking I'd better get used to things. Then later he calls me again to say that he changed his mind and he does want us to be together. And now I don't know what he'll say next."

Keeney now felt he had a sense of the pattern that had been taking place between Melanie and Sam. He wanted to move toward helping her in some constructive way. He had developed a therapeutic style during the previous decade that borrows heavily on the ideas of his original mentors—Gregory Bateson, Milton Erickson, and Carl Whitaker—combined with influences from a number of Native American medicine men, South American and African shamans, and Japanese sensei. His work is organized around therapeutic rituals, action-oriented assignments that evolve from his intuition and his sense of what a person needs. If pressed to explain how and why he came up with a particular course of action, Keeney might very well make up some reason or explanation, but you'd have a sense that sometimes he doesn't really know himself.

From Talk to Action

At this point in the session, Keeney felt ready (and sensed his client was ready) to do something about her predicament. "There are so many things going on for you," he said by way of transition. "What do you think would be most useful to you right now? What would help you to sort things out and make things clearer for you?"

"I don't know," Melanie answered predictably. "I just have so much on my plate right now. I'm worried about Sam for sure. His drinking started after his brother died, just a few weeks after we got married. His brother was his best friend. They shared everything together. They were so close."

Keeney immediately sensed something was different as soon as Melanie mentioned her brother-in-law's death. He was struck by a way that he could reframe Sam's drinking as something other than the pathological label of being an alcoholic. "So your husband has been conducting a three-year wake for his brother."

Melanie nodded her head right away, jumping on this idea that the drinking represented a coping mechanism. "He was abused a lot when he was a kid. I've seen the way his father treats him. His father doesn't know how to respect people. He doesn't know how to talk to people. That's why Sam doesn't know how to talk to women; he just never learned."

Keeney noticed that Melanie was now making allowances for Sam's behavior. She said that he didn't know any better, that he couldn't help himself. He sensed that she was not just trying to find excuses for his behavior but also trying to give him the benefit of the doubt as well as holding out some hope that he could change.

Keeney could feel excitement building inside him. Up to this point he had been exploring things a bit, getting a feel for what might be going on. In part he was gathering information, but another part was plain stalling until he felt some intuitive stirring that might lead him in a particular direction. This is exactly the kind of process he experiences when he is working with indigenous healers in the Kalahari desert, the Brazilian Amazon, or the Aboriginal Outback. He felt a stirring, the barest glimpse of an idea, or a vision. Rather than trying to analyze or make sense of what was happening, he trusted his inner spirit and acted on what he sensed and felt.

Keeney recognized that they had now reached a point where they were no longer talking about Sam's alcoholism as the problem. They were now tacitly agreeing that there was much more to the situation than that, including larger systemic issues, and Melanie's own perfectionistic tendencies. Unlike most therapists, Keeney was not interested in making these interpretations or pointing these things out to his client (Remember, he has little faith in the mechanisms of traditional insight therapy). To Keeney, the action takes place at the level of acting out some therapeutic ritual. And now he felt ready to make a strategic move, to link Melanie's need to be a good mother with Sam's need to mourn his brother. Whether this was his finest hour or not, these moments of stirring intuition are certainly his finest moments as a therapist.

A Lengthy Wake

"I have a couple of wild ideas I'd like to throw out," Keeney said with a mischievous grin. He knew this would peak her curiosity and yet also give him room to maneuver if things didn't turn out as he hoped.

"Hell," Melanie answered with a laugh, "I'll try just about anything at this point."

"From what you've said," Keeney said, leaning forward in his chair and grabbing her full attention with his eyes, "it's likely that not only are you a good mother but an outstanding one."

Melanie visibly puffed with pride. She was trying, unsuccessfully, to restrain how good that comment felt.

"And," Keeney continued, "I think that's part of the reason why you came to see me today. Look how busy you are. Yet you came here because you'd do anything to help your daughter that you love so much."

"That's true. I already gave my daughter a bath and dinner and everything."

"I'm not at all surprised. I think I'm on the right track here." Keeney paused for a moment, giving her a chance to refocus on the next point. "I think that deep down inside Sam knows what a great mother you are as well. He may not have told you that very often, but he is well aware of your gifts that you bring to the home. It seems like he is struggling to learn how to be different in your home, to make it different than the one he grew up in. And this is really hard for him, especially at the same time as trying to recover from the death of his brother."

Melanie nodded all the time that Brad was talking, signaling her acceptance and agreement to what he was saying, this view of things in which Sam was seen to be struggling to overcome obstacles rather than merely being a drunk.

"This death," Keeney continued, "has been so hard for him to recover from. He is still in the process of his brother's wake, still trying to get out of the patterns that they grew up with."

"You know," Melanie said thoughtfully, "that's probably true. Sam talks a lot about wanting to change. He says he tries so hard to not be like his father."

"Exactly."

"The weird thing, though, is that he doesn't realize how he has become like his father. And I don't know how to show him." Melanie holds her palms open, as if to demonstrate she doesn't have any tools to do this.

Keeney recognized the paradox in her predicament and he wanted to underscore this. Her strong maternal skills draw Sam so she wants to take care of him. But if she tries to help him, she does so not as a wife but as a mother—and this pushes him farther away. Keeney did not see it as particularly important to bring this insight to Melanie's attention, but it did guide where he might go with her next.

Paradoxes

"There is a trap you seem caught in," Keeney explained. "People sometimes feel caught up in the same patterns they saw in their parents growing up. It doesn't often always help to point this out, but it does help you to understand what may be going on."

Melanie nodded her head.

"You have quite a challenge to face," Keeney added. "When he shows you disrespect, or speaks harshly to you, or gives you mixed messages about his commitment to the marriage, he may be expressing the exact opposite of what he really feels." Seeing a look of puzzlement on Melanie's face, he explains further: "I know this is a strange way to show love and affection, but that is what he may have learned in his family." As Keeney said these words, he was not sure if they even made sense to him, but he knew it wasn't the words that were getting through to her—she was getting the broad sense of his meaning—that their problem was not just the result of Sam's drinking but rather was part of the way they related to one another.

"So," Keeney continued, "maybe he's showing you how he doesn't want to be. He's hoping that you will respond in a way that can help him break out of his usual pattern, you know?"

"I thought my leaving would show him," Melanie responded. "But it hasn't."

Keeney nodded.

"If anything, he is drinking more than ever now. He says that he is willing to quit drinking if the marriage works, but if the marriage does not work, then why bother to quit drinking?"

So Melanie has caught on to the structure of their paradoxical interactions with one another. She has also moved to a point where she is now accepting that they have a marital problem rather than just Sam's drinking problem.

Keeney reasoned that it was now time to work on restructuring the ways they talk to one another. If things continued along their present course, the relationship wouldn't have a chance. He next wanted to find out more about the ways they communicated with one another.

"Well," Melanie said with some hesitance, "actually we only have one car so we still ride together. I give him a ride to the train in the morning so we talk. Then after he leaves it gives me time to think about things. It occurs to me now that he's always had someone to take care of him."

"So," Keeney reminded her, "that only confirms the idea that he considers you such a good mother that he wants you to take care of him as well as your daughter."

Melanie slipped back for a little while to complaints about Sam's drinking. Keeney wanted to get things back on track to a focus on their relationship and the resources they had available to them.

"What was Sam like before the funeral three years ago?" Brad asked.

"He was drinking," Melanie answered, "but he knew when to say when. We would talk. We communicated. But if I think back it was always his way."

Keeney was pleased that Melanie was continuing to elaborate and give support to the frames they had built together, the alternative view of the problem as expanded beyond Sam's drinking behavior. Even if this had been the sole problem, there was little that Keeney could do about that. Instead he saw Melanie showing increased hope for their situation; he sensed that she was ready for the next step.

Queen of Shock

Keeney asked Melanie what she planned to do next, to which she admitted that she had yet to make any definitive decision. This led her to talk about one area that she did feel particularly good about, and that was her work with handicapped people. "I'm totally into my job," she said with a huge smile of pride.

"So everything in your life seems to be connected to you being such a wonderful mother—to your daughter, to your patients, and even to your husband." Again he brought back the main theme of the session. "But this creates a dilemma for you. On the one hand, you say that Sam's behavior brings you a lot of pain that is making you crazy, but his childish actions are also a way to let you know what a great mother you are; otherwise he wouldn't act so much like a child. It's as if he's testing just how good a mother you can be."

Melanie nodded her head. "Yeah, I see it now that you point it out like that. It's like I'm trying to help him to grow up."

"I know this must sound bizarre to you," Keeney pressed the point. "This is certainly a crazy way to compliment your mothering skills. It seems to me that this business of increasing his drinking after his brother's funeral is his way of saying that he wants his childish behavior to die, to pass on."

Of course, Keeney had no idea whether this was the case or not, and it didn't matter that much to him. He was just looking for leverage that would allow him to pry loose Melanie's conviction that Sam's drinking was the only problem between them and that she should keep blaming him for it.

"I think Sam knows that he can't continue going on like this," Melanie agreed. "It's going to kill him. Literally."

Melanie seemed to recognize the trap she was in. Sam acts like a child. This invites Melanie to do what she does best: respond like a mother. This pushes Sam further away. And the vicious cycle continues.

Using what a narrative therapist would call a "unique outcome," or a solution-focused therapist would call "looking for exceptions," Keeney invited Melanie to consider a time when they didn't relate to one another as mother and child but rather as husband and wife. "I'm wondering if you can recall a time, even just 5 minutes in the course of a week, when you don't feel like a mother to Sam, when you . . . "

"No," Melanie immediately interrupted. "There really isn't."

"How about 1 minute then? Can you think of a single minute when you relate to one another as wife and husband?" There's no way Keeney was going to back off. He was determined to help her find an example of when things were going well.

"I don't honestly know," she said, shaking her head. "When we first met, we were soul mates. I still sometimes feel like I connect with him. We can almost think for each other at times. It sounds very weird, as much as I could strangle him at times. I also feel like I know what he is going to say before he says it." She pauses for a minute, then says: "And we used to go for long walks and talk all the time."

Keeney saw an opening when Melanie mentioned a specific time that she and Sam once felt intimate. "If the two of you would go for a walk now, where would you go?"

Shrug. "We can go on the forest walking path, around the block, almost anywhere."

"And if you were going to go for a walk together, how often could you do this?"

"For this? For my husband? I could probably make time." Her face lit up again. "We used to take our daughter for walks together. We'd go to the video store and rent a movie. We'd have a good time."

"When was the last time you did that?" Keeney asked her.

"Oh gee. A couple of months at least. We just don't seem to have the same interests anymore. The talking is all gone."

"But you said when you used to walk together you had plenty to talk about."

"Yeah," she answered wistfully. Melanie looks thoughtful, as if she's re-living those good times.

Now seemed like a perfect moment for Keeney to push her to change the situation in some way instead of just accepting the slow death, the wake of her marriage. "What do you think Sam would say if you asked him to go for a walk tomorrow?"

Melanie laughed. "Well, he'd probably say his feet hurt. He'd probably come up with some excuse."

Rather than letting this go, Keeney reminded Melanie of things she had said earlier—that she is resourceful, that she has good analytic skills in solving problems, that as a good mother she's good at figuring out how to get people to do things. "So," Keeney said, "I wonder if you have the skill to figure out how to get Sam to go on a walk?"

"No."

"No?" Keeney said surprised. "You don't? I find that hard to believe that you couldn't figure out something to do, someone as good at mothering as you are."

"Well," Melanie admitted, "probably if I tried really hard I could."

"How might you do this? That is, if you wanted to."

"I suppose I could approach him one night and ask him if instead of having a beer we might take a walk together."

Keeney could tell immediately that this was something she's probably already tried—and that probably hadn't worked. He knew that by the time people come into therapy they have already tried the usual things that they can think of, most of which haven't worked. He views his job as helping people to free themselves up to be creative enough to come up with new solutions—the wackier the better.

"Melanie, I'd like you to turn on your imagination for a minute." As he said this, Keeney wore a mischievous grin that drew her into the conspiracy. "I want you to picture a way that you could ask Sam to take a walk that would completely shock him, that would knock him out of his socks."

"Hey," she responded playfully. "I'm a mother, remember?"

Keeney laughed with her. "Let's just say that you wanted to do something that was weird, mysterious, even a little crazy, something that would capture his attention. This could be an idea, a gesture, a phrase, something, anything."

"A gesture maybe."

"A gesture. That's good!"

As infectious as all this was becoming, Melanie started to feel scared. She backed off, not just with words but visibly in her posture. "I don't know. I just don't know."

Recognizing her hesitation but refusing to let her off the hook, Keeney still encouraged her to access her creative resources. "You know, the really nice thing about pretending is that you can just make something up. I'm not asking you what would work. I'm just asking what you think might shock him."

Thinking she had found a way out, Melanie pleaded that nothing would shock her husband. "I've shocked him so many times before with other things."

"Oh?" Keeney grabbed this opening. "So you're really good at shocking people?"

"Yeah, I'm very good. My mother says I'm the queen of shock."

"Really? You're telling me you are the queen of shock and you can't come up with something that would work with Sam to take a walk with you? I think you're holding back."

Melanie laughed. She said that she must have been watching too many *Barney* movies with her daughter and she's out of practice.

The Shock Is Back

"Okay," Keeney said, deciding to approach this a different way. "How have you shocked Sam in the past? I mean, you are the queen of shock and all."

"Probably I'd have used his beeper to send him a message."

"Oh yeah?" Keeney answered, intrigued with her expression. "So you're pretty skilled at this. I'd like to hear more about how you do this."

Melanie explained that in the past she would occasionally send a message to Sam on his beeper using a special code. If she wanted to tell him that she loved him, she'd do it by sending the corresponding numbers. When Sam would call and ask if she beeped him, she'd say yes she had, but he'd have to look at the numbers and figure out what she'd said. "It probably took him a half-hour," Melanie explained, "but he really liked doing it."

"So you really do have a special talent for shocking Sam. And it's proven to be wonderful for your relationship." Again and again Keeney was emphasizing that Melanie did have the power to act in creative, resourceful ways.

Melanie shrugged modestly.

"If you were going to invite your husband on a walk, and do it by sending him a coded message on his beeper, how would you do that?"

"I'd just write it out with a pen first and then code it in." As she was saying these words, it was clear that she was already figuring it out in her head—how she would do this, when she would do this.

"We've hit some interesting territory. That is, we've found a skill that you held back from telling me." Keeney smiled playfully as he teased her. "I wonder if you've ever done anything that even shocked yourself?"

"Not that I can think of."

Again Keeney was not willing to let her first denial go. He asked her what it would mean for Melaine to do something that was so surprising that she would even shock herself. This invitation encouraged her to reach deeper inside for resources that she had yet to acknowledge, much less access.

"I just don't as much anymore," Melanie confessed. "Sam tells me this too. I just don't joke around the way I used to."

"You know what I think you need to do?" Keeney asked her.

"What's that?"

"You need to announce loudly and clearly that the shock is back in your life. You need to say it to yourself, 'I'm bringing back the shock. The shock is back!' "

"The shock is back," Melanie repeated with a giggle. In so doing, Keeney recognized that she had changed. She was no longer talking about problems but about resources. They spent the next few minutes reviewing some of the ways she had been shocking in the past, playing tricks, being childlike, laughing, feeling more alive. Melanie talked about times she had hidden things from Sam, making him go through a maze to find them. Or buying him a present that could only be found on a treasure hunt. After each example, Keeney responded enthusiastically and encouragingly.

"It sounds to me like you are willing to announce to the world that the shock is back."

"Yes, I guess that's true."

"You can be a good mother and yet still be a good, a great shocker," Keeney clarified. "One does not exclude the other."

"Yes," she agreed.

"What this relationship needs most is some shock. And you're just the person to do this. You've lost a lot of your laughter."

"That's for sure."

Next, Keeney wanted Melanie to recruit Sam into the shock conspiracy. It was one thing for her to become more proactive and playful in their interactions, but it would take things to a whole other level if they could work together as a team. He wondered what would happen if the two of them together found someone else they could shock. He was trying to strengthen the bonds of their fractured coalition.

"Have the two of you ever shocked anyone together?" He asked.

"Hmm," she answered thoughtfully. "I don't think so."

"Well, now that the shock is back and you intend to beep him to take a walk together. While you are walking you can plot together how you might surprise someone. How might that be?"

Melanie thought for a moment and nominated her sister-in-law. She was the person they both knew who was most likely to respond favorably to a playful interaction or practical joke. It was also quite noticeable how much Melanie's demeanor had changed since they had begun this conversation—she was smiling, laughing, showing animation and spunk. She really was acting the part of the queen of shock.

As the session drew to a close, Keeney returned to their created theme: "So you promise me that the shock is back in your life?"

"I will try, yes."

"Not good enough," Keeney said.

"I will definitely try."

"Still not good enough," he said again. "When you first walked in, you were really worried and upset. And now you have hope. And I don't want you to lose that. So I want you to tell me what you intend to do. No excuses. I want you to promise me that the shock is back in your life for at least one week."

"A whole week? I can promise you that."

Keeney reminded her that she had been facing a lot of adversity, and in the face of these challenges she must draw upon any resources she can. "You have a gift," he told her, "and you have to use that as best you can."

14 A Family Epiphany

A Case from Peggy Papp

Peggy Papp is one of the most prominent family systems theorists in the field, for which she was recipient of the American Association for Marriage and Family Therapy's Lifetime Achievement Award. She has developed an approach that examines how gender roles, beliefs, and expectations influence relationships and families, combined with her own compassionate and caring style.

A few of Papp's major books include The Process of Change, The Invisible Web, *and* Couples on the Fault Line. *She is Senior Training Supervisor and Director of the Depression Project at the Ackerman Institute of Family Therapy in New York.*

Family Background

"My finest hour was preceded by one of my worst hours," Peggy Papp recalled in speaking of her experience with a family in which privacy was valued above all else and secrecy was a way of life. Initially she was blocked by the family from obtaining the information she considered vital to helping them with their situation. The subjects that were taboo were the ones that she believed held the key to understanding the events that led to the problem. Papp's dilemma was how to unravel the family story without them feeling their privacy was being violated.

While it would be unnatural, and also unnecessary, for a family to reveal every unsavory episode of their history, there are certain events that are so emotionally charged that the reverberations continue to affect relationships for years afterwards. Often these events are difficult to talk about and so become forbidden subjects in the family. They then fester underground and reappear in everyday life in distorted perceptions, blocking communication, and creating symptomatic behavior.

This blocking began with this Latino family's reluctance to attend the family sessions recommended by the psychiatric hospital where the 17-year-old son, Mario, had been hospitalized. Several appointments were broken and numerous telephone calls went unanswered before the family finally came to a session.

The following history was learned from the hospital before the first session. Besides Mario, there were four other children in the family. When Mario was an infant, his father, Nando, took him to live with his paternal grandmother in Venezuela. When Mario was 15, his grandmother became ill and Nando brought Mario to live here in the United States with his present family. Because of the close relationship between Mario and his grandmother, Nando didn't tell the boy that the separation from his grandmother was to be permanent but pretended he was only coming for a summer vacation. The grandmother died before the summer was over and Mario was never able to say goodbye to her. He became psychotic on the anniversary of his grandmother's death.

During the previous year, Mario had told his father he was having "bad thoughts" and wanted to see a counselor. Nando dismissed his son's anxiety as a stage in his adolescent development. He considered Mario to be a strong, normal boy, and he had high expectations of him. Mario was an excellent student who had received a college scholarship. But his thoughts got worse and worse until finally he reported to the school counselor that he was having thoughts of killing his stepmother. She immediately notified the family and recommended hospitalization. Mario was told in the hospital that he became "sick" because of his "suppressed rage" toward his stepmother.

When Papp read the report, she wondered what the connection might be between Mario's "suppressed rage" toward his stepmother and his psychotic symptoms on the anniversary of his grandmother's death. She believed it was important to find out about the relationship between the grandmother and the stepmother.

When Papp was finally able to reach the father by phone, he told her there was no need for family sessions because Mario had decided to drop out of school, give up his college scholarship, and return to Venezuela. Peggy suggested they come to a session to discuss the details of Mario leaving the family. The father agreed and brought Mario and his stepmother, Miriam, to the first session.

The Wall

Mario turned out to be a very polite and articulate young man, but his speech was slowed a little by the antipsychotic medication he had been given at the hospital. Each time he spoke, he seemed to pause for a few seconds to gather his thoughts, which were clouded by the drugs.

Miriam, his stepmother, was a small, pretty woman with a shy and guarded manner. Papp took this as a clear signal that she should approach Miriam with particular caution and sensitivity. She wanted Miriam to feel respected and heard, yet not blamed.

Papp began by clarifying the reason for the session, saying that since Mario was leaving this family and entering a new one, it might be helpful to talk about how the separation and rejoining would take place and how different family members felt about it. Did that sound okay with them? They nodded in cautious agreement. Papp then asked Mario where he would be living in Venezuela.

"I will live with my father's sister, my aunt, and a lot of my cousins," he replied with an anticipatory smile.

Turning to Nando, she asked, "And how do you feel about his leaving?"

"It's okay with me. He will be with my family."

"And Miriam, how do you feel about Mario's leaving?"

Miriam seemed embarrassed and confused. She looked at her husband and said falteringly, "I didn't know he was planning to go back."

"You didn't know he was going back to Venezuela?" Papp asked in surprise.

Miriam was quick to cover up her initial reaction. "But that's okay. They never include me in their decisions."

"You wouldn't like to be included and know what is going on?" Papp asked.

"Mario doesn't feel comfortable having me participate. I'm not the boy's real mother. Neither of them wants me to participate."

"You don't feel comfortable having your wife participate in your decisions related to your son?" Peggy asked of Nando.

"She'd have to show more interest. She complains she doesn't know what's going on but she shows no interest. But it's not a problem." He said this emphatically, indicating the subject was closed. Miriam readily agreed.

Papp shifted back to Mario and asked what made him decide to return to Venezuela. He said, "Because something in this house made me sick. I have been having bad thoughts ever since I came here. I want to move away to a healthy place."

"What in the house do you think made you sick?" Papp asked.

"I don't know" he glanced again at his stepmother. "Just something." After a long pause added, "Sometimes I feel left out of the family."

"Is that why you are angry at your stepmother?" Papp asked.

Mario shrugged, hesitant to say more.

"You don't know why you might be angry at your stepmother?" Papp repeated.

Mario again glanced at his stepmother. "She treats me different than the other kids. I feel left out of the family."

"That's not true!" Miriam responded defensively. "I treat everybody the same. I always have."

Not wanting Miriam to have to defend herself in this situation, Papp drew out her version of the story in the most neutral way possible. Miriam insisted she showed no favoritism, that she always included Mario and everything was fine in the family. She kept reiterating that there were no problems at all, and she didn't even know why they were here.

"What do you think?" Papp asked the father, whom she could see was becoming increasingly upset by this interaction.

"I don't know. Maybe they don't understand each other. All families fight a little. But it's not a problem."

Miriam regained her composure and reiterated, "No, it's not a problem."

Picking up on the theme, Papp commented that both Miriam and Mario seemed to feel "left out" of different aspects of family life. She wondered if Miriam had been left out of the decision for Mario to live with them when Mario's grandmother became ill?

Miriam lowered her head and spoke in a barely audible voice, "I don't want to talk about it."

"Oh, I see. Okay—uh—uh—well—ah—," stuttered Papp, not knowing where to go from there. "So, this is something none of you want to talk about?"

All three heads looked down.

Papp searched for another way to engage the family and decided to ask about Mario's birth mother. "Maybe you could tell me something about Mario's birth mother. Where is she?"

"We were divorced a long time ago," Nando said simply.

"You were divorced?" Papp repeated.

"Yes, it happened many years ago. She is not around anymore."

"She's not around any more? Where did she go?"

Nando looked at his wife, then held out his hands, palms up. "Nobody knows."

"Nobody knows what happened to Mario's mother?" Papp repeated, stalling until she could think of some other way to approach this.

"That's right," Nando agreed. "*Quien sabe.*"

"I see," Papp responded. It was clear this was also a taboo subject in the family.

The family continued to put up a high wall, and no matter how Papp tried to collect the most rudimentary information, she felt consistently blocked.

Papp laughed at this point in our discussion. She still shows the video of this intake to her students as an example of how even experienced therapists can be stumped. As she continued her failed attempts to enter the family, she began to realize she was being "left out" like all the other family members. Mario was left out by the stepmother. The stepmother was left out by her husband. The grandmother had been left out of the decision to take her surrogate son away. The birth mother was left out of the whole story. And now Papp felt left out as well. Being "left out" was a theme that seemed to run through three generations of the family.

The Closed Door

At this point Papp decided to introduce the subject of the grandmother's death and asked what effect it had had on the family. Initially this was met with generalizations about "God's will" and "Everyone has to go sometime."

Turning to Mario, she said, "Tell me about your grandmother. What was she like and how did you get along with her?"

"Oh, we got along very well. We were very close. She was like a mother to me. I loved her very much."

"It must have been very difficult for you to leave her. How did your grandmother feel about your coming to live with this family?"

Again Mario glanced at his stepmother and said uneasily, "Well, she didn't like it."

"What was her objection?" Papp asked.

"Well . . . you see, she sort of didn't get along with my stepmother. I don't know why."

"You didn't get along with Mario's grandmother?" Papp asked Miriam.

Miriam again lowered her head and pressed her lips tightly together. Papp wondered how long she should wait out the long pause, when Miriam finally spoke. "I don't want to talk about the grandmother. She is dead. I don't want to badmouth the dead."

"I see . . . ummm . . . hum . . . so . . . uh . . . you want to respect the dead. Ah . . . well. . . . I understand your feelings and I will respect that." She was really quite confused about where to go with this.

Miriam nodded but did not speak again. All of them just sat silently, uncomfortable in the room. No one was making eye contact with any of the others. They just seemed to be waiting until the therapist dismissed them and this ordeal could be over.

Papp believed the door that guarded the family secret had been opened a crack by Mario, only to be slammed shut by Miriam's refusal to "badmouth the dead." She was convinced that the "something in the house" that had made Mario "sick" lay behind the door. If this was not dealt with, it would probably continue to have a profound effect on his mental health even after he left the home. How could she respect Miriam's right to privacy and still gain access to the forbidden family history?

Finding Another Entrance

It was time to retrenchment and try a different approach. Since everyone was reluctant to talk about family secrets directly, Papp decided that the details were less important than the effect on their present relationships. When people are reluctant to open up, rather than pushing them further, it is often best simply to ask them how this situation has affected their lives.

"We don't have to discuss the details of your relationship with his grandmother," Papp said to Miriam. "What is important is the effect it had on the family, because the way in which Mario entered the family will have a great deal to do with the way he leaves it."

Turning to Mario, she said, "You entered this family in a difficult way, so let's talk about how you can leave this family and enter the new one with your aunts and cousins in a good way so there are no ill feelings about your comings or goings. Okay?"

Mario nodded, a bit reluctantly.

"Since you were very close to your grandmother, she must have influenced you in a lot of ways."

"I guess."

"She must have influenced your feelings toward your stepmother."

"In a way. I saw the situation and I didn't like it."

"Whose side did you take?" Papp asked him.

"My grandmother's, of course." He said this as if it was obvious.

"So then, when you came here, would you say your stepmother already had two strikes against her?"

There was a long pause while Mario thought about this. "I guess so."

Turning to Miriam, Papp said, "Maybe that is why you didn't feel comfortable showing him more attention? Maybe you didn't know how to do this. Maybe you didn't know if he even wanted your attention."

Miriam just looked straight ahead and refused to speak. She seemed to have a lot to say about this subject, but she was not allowing herself to say it. Papp turned back to Mario. "How do your aunts and cousins get along with your stepmother?"

Mario hesitated. "They don't get along."

"You agree with that, Miriam?" Papp asked.

"Well, I don't know exactly. What do you mean when you say we don't get along?"

"How do you think they feel about you? Do you feel left out of the family?"

"It's not the first time," Miriam stated with a touch of bitterness.

"You've felt left out before?" Papp reflected.

The use of the thematic phrase, "left out," seemed to ignite sparks of anger in Miriam's eyes. "Well, in the beginning, when Nando and I got married, there was a conflict in the family. You see, I don't know why because they . . . they . . . they . . . you know—it's a long story."

"Could you share the story with me?" Papp asked.

Miriam took a very deep breath, sighed, and then said that when she was 17 she had married Nando, who was 33. He took her and Mario, who was an infant, to live with his family in his native country. Nando's family resented his marriage because they felt Miriam had taken away their prize son, their financial and emotional pillar. Also, Miriam was darker-skinned, different in class and religion. The family was extremely possessive of Mario and accused Miriam of trying to steal him from them. "He is our blood kin, not yours," they told her. Every day Nando's brothers would come and take Mario to the grandmother's house, where she kept him all day. Nando felt caught in the middle and admitted he was his mother's favorite and that his mother was jealous of his wife. "My mother wanted me to be for her and Mario only."

Miriam's voice became stronger and stronger, finally rising to a crescendo in recounting the "injustices" that had been done to her. As she regained her lost voice she actually seemed to gain in stature, like a character in a Greek tragedy. She recalled her agonizing years of being alone in a foreign country, unable to speak the language, and rejected by her husband and his family. When Miriam gave birth to a baby girl, the grandmother told Mario, "Your father will never love any child but you. They told him terrible things. Things they shouldn't have told him." Finally, the situation became intolerable for Miriam and she left Venezuela with her infant daughter for the United States. Nando followed soon after, leaving Mario to be raised by the grandmother.

Nando seemed taken aback by his wife's rage and made various lame attempts to justify his part in the family saga. "I took your side . . . sometimes."

"Not very often!" Miriam thundered.

Mario sat spellbound. He had listened to the telling of the story as though transfixed. It was the first time he had heard it. Papp began imagining how difficult it must have been for Mario to join this family after 14 years of being turned against his stepmother. It was inevitable that he become his grandmother's emissary, committed to carrying on her agenda. No wonder he had angry thoughts toward Miriam! Papp also imagined the degree of animosity Miriam must have felt toward Mario, since she had been told she was unworthy to raise him and then he was suddenly thrust upon her without her consent. She was now excluded by the alliance between father and son as she had been excluded by her husband's family. From the beginning, it was a setup for a disastrous conflict.

"So, Mario, I guess if you were to become friends with Miriam you might feel disloyal to your grandmother," Papp suggested. "Maybe this was your way of keeping the memory of your grandmother alive. You continued with her thoughts and feelings toward your stepmother."

Mario, still stunned and trying to absorb what he had heard, replied, "I don't know."

"It's something to think about. If you were to become friends with your stepmother maybe you would feel you were betraying your grandmother— that would mean she was wrong about some of her thoughts and feelings."

Mario looked long and hard at Papp and then said, "That's something to think about."

"Why don't you just think about it?"

Papp ended the session by thanking Miriam for having the courage to share her story. She described the bad feelings between Miriam and Mario as the fallout from an unfortunate family history that had prevented a caring woman and a fine young man from being able to have a good relationship. The family agreed to another family session and left in deep thought.

The Letter

Mario came alone to the next session, saying his father and stepmother had other business to attend to. He opened the session with the following statement: "Mrs. Papp, yesterday I met my mother for the first time in my life!" Papp was flabbergasted.

Mario went on to say that after the session he had gone to his father and told him, "I want to know where my mother is," and his father responded, "I guess it's time that you knew." Nando sent him to his aunt, who had his mother's address, and told her to give it to him. Mario discovered that his mother lived in the same city but in a different neighborhood. When he knocked on the door his mother answered and exclaimed, "That face. I know that face."

"And Mrs. Papp, I found a whole new family, with many aunts and uncles and cousins and nieces and nephews and even a new grandmother!" He had telephoned before coming, so the whole clan had turned out to welcome him.

Papp's voice choked up as she described how moved she was by Mario's experience. "As long as I live I shall never forget the glow on his face as he described his newly discovered world. He said, 'All my life I've wanted a mother and now I have one,' and it was all I could do to keep from crying.

"You know," Papp said slowly, taking a break from the story, "I thought I would never be able to talk or write about this case because it sounds too much like a soap opera or fairy tale. Especially when Mario told me his mother had written letters to him over the years telling him how much she loved him and wanted to see him. She had given them to Nando's sister to mail but the sister had never sent them, fearing the grandmother's response. Now doesn't that sound just like an old melodramatic movie? Or perhaps a testimony to the old adage that life is stranger than fiction."

Mario learned that his father had been given custody of him because his mother was "unable to take care of me when I was born." When she recovered from her "sickness" she tried to find him, but by then his father had taken him to Venezuela.

"They always told me my mother didn't love me and that she was a tough woman. So you see, Mrs. Papp, she really did love me!" Mario exclaimed. He reported he didn't hate his stepmother anymore. "Now I understand she wasn't treated right by my family and she felt angry."

After rejoicing with him, Papp asked him what he thought his grandmother would think about what he was doing now.

"She wouldn't approve," he admitted. "She saw my mother as a bad woman and my stepmother as an enemy. But I think she was wrong."

Papp asked, "So you've begun to separate your thoughts and feelings from your grandmother's?"

"Yes," Mario answered, "and it's also better for my mental health to see things fair." He went on to say he appreciated everything his grandmother did for him, but she had made mistakes.

Papp then suggested he write her a letter, expressing all his feelings and saying goodbye to her. He agreed and brought the following letter to the next session. This is what he read to Papp:

My Dear Grandmother,

First I want to assure you that I love you as deeply as you love me. I know that we long to see each other but that is impossible. I want you to know that even though death separates us I am not going to suffer in this world because I have grown and I am able to take care of my own happiness now. I have changed much since we saw each other. I am able to think with an independent view of fairness towards others and I have come to the conclusion that everybody makes mistakes. Some mistakes are made for love and others are made to protect our loved ones. I think you had disagreements with my stepmother because you wanted my father to be only for me. You did it because you loved me and only wanted the best for me. But you shouldn't search for my happiness by making other people unhappy. In this case my stepmother was unhappy. I am not judging you for this. It wouldn't be fair in the eyes of God to judge those who sin for love. My purpose isn't to judge anyone. If so I would also have to judge my stepmother because she wasn't always the victim but sometimes the oppressor. I want to make you see things from a higher point of view, beyond love and hate and towards fairness. I have decided not to bother with feelings of hate because I want my life to be higher and healthier than that. Grandmother, not only are my father and I your sons but my stepmother is also your daughter. I feel good now and my life will be beautiful and full of success because I have found happiness in my own moral and spiritual goodness.

Adios,

Mario

Papp was struck by the eloquence and wisdom of the letter. "Through this letter," Papp said, "he ended the family feud, bringing the two warring factions together in his mind with forgiveness and a sense of 'fairness.' Nobody else in his family was able to do this. He was able to differentiate himself from his grandmother's powerful influence. In so doing he freed himself from the onerous family legacy, and once he had done this all his disturbing symptoms vanished."

One important lesson that Mario had learned from his grandmother was the importance of working hard to succeed. He decided not to return to Venezuela but to stay in this country, return to school, and go on to college. He was planning to live in the college dorm and still maintain contact with both families.

One more family session was held before Mario left for college. Miriam and Nando both claimed they were happy with the turn of events and that Mario's relationship with his newly found family was "not a problem." Miriam described him as "a different person, no longer angry at me." Both parents claimed that the relationship between the two of them had not been upset by Miriam bringing up the past. Papp felt it was their prerogative not to pursue these issues any further.

■ ■ ■

Questions about Change

For weeks afterwards, Papp puzzled over what had taken place in that one session that led to the sudden and dramatic changes. What led Miriam to finally tell her story? What gave Mario the courage to ask for his mother's address after all these years? Why did Nando decide to give it to him at this particular time?

Papp speculated that her use of the family theme of being "left out" provided a catalyst for the expression of buried thoughts and feelings. Sometimes the use of key words and phrases that are laden with special meaning can serve to break through taboos and shatter myths that are having a profound effect on the family.

"I think my offering the family an empathic description of their situation in terms of their own personal metaphors permitted them to venture into previously forbidden territory. Once they had broken through the barriers of silence, many different options were opened for them.

Finally, this case illustrates how sometimes successful therapy can be chaotic, frustrating, unpredictable, and bumbling until its conclusion. Peggy Papp cannot recall feeling more inadequate with a family, nor more discouraged about the probable outcome. Yet by trusting the process of what she was doing, by trusting herself, and mostly by trusting the power of the family members, surprising things can happen.

CHAPTER 15

"We Have to Seduce People into Trusting Us before We Can Spank Them"

Cases from Frank Pittman

Frank Pittman is notorious (and he'd be proud of this label) for a number of eclectic contributions. He is, first and foremost, a psychiatrically trained family therapist who has logged more hours in session than perhaps anyone else alive. This vast clinical experience informs his other avocations as a columnist for Psychology Today, *a film critic for* Psychotherapy Networker, *and author of several notable books about fidelity, intimacy, maturity, family crises, and male psychology.*

Some of Pittman's best-known books include Turning Points: Treating Families in Transition and Crisis, Private Lies: Infidelity and the Betrayal of Intimacy, Man Enough: Fathers, Sons, and the Search for Masculinity, *and* Grow Up! How Taking Responsibility Can Make You a Happy Adult.

Further Introduction

Apart from this standard introductory stuff, we asked Frank what are some things about him that most people don't know or understand. "People think I'm some kind of moralist," Frank began, referring to a reputation sometimes associated with being rather conservative if not scolding. "But my life has been spent trying to empower people."

Pittman is also a film critic and screenwriter, as well as a psychiatrist, so he relates many ideas to particular movies he has seen. In this case, he cites the films of Martin Scorsese as an example of someone who looks at the lives of people who do evil things (like Robert DeNiro in *Taxi Driver*) and forces the audience to see them as human beings. "He doesn't distance people just because he knows they are wrong and doing bad things."

Pittman likens his own role as a therapist to a similar stance. People assume he is scolding and rejecting and distancing just because he forms judgments about patients' behavior. This, of course, was one of the earliest admonishments that many of us received in our own training—that being judgmental was antitherapeutic and antithetical to what we were supposed to be doing as loving, caring, compassionate healers. But Pittman takes issue with this and doesn't see how it is possible for us *not* to make judgments about those we are helping, especially when they are doing things that are spectacularly stupid or self-destructive.

Frank would much rather be known as someone who is extremely optimistic about people's capacity for change and their ability to do things differently. "I want people to learn," he said, "that they don't have to hurt others with their behavior, or hurt themselves, and they don't have to keep doing the same dumb things over and over again forever."

It puzzles Pittman that any therapist can avoid taking such a stance. "Much therapy is relatively harmless, but a lot of it is extremely destructive and creates far more problems than it solves, because it attempts to relieve people of guilt and assures them that whatever damn fool thing they do is not really their fault."

"Is that why some people call you incorrigible?"

"Some therapists kind of throw flowers at people as they drive the wrong way down a one-way street."

"Well then, now that we've got the introductions out of the way . . . ."

Convincing People to Give Away Their Money

If Pittman can be critical of his patient's behavior, he is just as "frank" about his own. When asked about a session that stood out to him as representative of his best work, he could think of many bad times but precious few that met his own high standards. We weren't sure if it was because his standards are too high, or if he was just doing his "Southern modesty" stuff, but we challenged this reluctance. "Surely," we pressed, "you can think of something you've done recently when you've nodded to yourself and thought that was a good piece of work."

"No question," Pittman replied. "I say that to myself after just about every hour. Then the next week I discover it wasn't as magical as I thought it was. It's one thing to make people aware of something they are doing, or something they could do differently, and it's another to help them take action in such a way that they bring about a permanent change."

"I might have a session with someone and he feels good about it, and I feel good about it. But a week later he's still screwing the bimbo and lying to his wife about it, or beating his kids, or getting drunk."

"So then," we interrupt, "tell us a good story, one in which against all odds you managed to help someone anyway."

"Well, now that you asked, I think the best therapy I've ever done is to convince wealthy, depressed people that they would feel better about themselves if they gave away more of their money."

We laughed appreciably, not sure if he was kidding or not.

First Generation

It was talk about money that prompted Pittman to settle on the case he wanted to discuss, one that spanned three generations. The couple first came to see him presenting a number of conflicts that resulted partly from their cultural differences: Xerxes was Iranian and Gretel was Dutch. As could be expected, Xerxes was patriarchal and tried to be controlling in the relationship, especially in relation to anything to do with money issues. This was consistent with the way things were done among the men in his family in the Old Country, where they not only controlled the money but also had lots of extramarital affairs. Gretel picked her battles wisely, and devoted herself to keeping him so sexually exhausted at home that he would never have the strength to screw around. Xerxes was subdued in the proudest of all possible ways, but he saw his fidelity as a sufficient contribution to the relationship: he saw no need to share what he thought of as "his" money as well. As he became richer and more successful, his money management became increasingly weird.

"I first saw Xerxes and Gretel over 30 years ago," Pittman recalled, "when they first moved here from Europe to start a branch of the family carpet business—cheap, machine-made ersatz Oriental rugs. They had three daughters and, finally, a son. Xerxes refused to give Gretel even an allowance, but required that she come to him before she could make even the most meager purchase. This was even more galling as the wealth began to roll in. On a trip to Paris, Xerxes had bought Gretel an extravagant designer dress she was wearing when it began to rain. She picked up a cheap umbrella for sale by a street vendor and Xerxes refused to pay for it, since she had plenty of umbrellas back at home. When they got home, the dress was ruined, and Gretel put in calls to both me and a divorce attorney. Fortunately, I called back first.

"The dynamics were clear: Xerxes, growing up around his father's wives, could not imagine anyone would love him for anything except his money. Gretel, whose father had run away from the family, lived in fear of losing Xerxes, so she was reluctant to take strong stands. She was (and remains) a woman of extraordinary, placid, blonde beauty, but she could stand toe to toe with her stormy husband."

"I don't know why you think you have a right to any of this money," Xerxes would scold his wife in the most condescending voice. "I made every goddamn cent of it!"

"You're such an ignorant peasant," she'd reply with even greater disdain. "Only people who live in tents in the desert could have that sort of attitude."

Xerxes told her, "You just want money because you're a women's libber. You can go stick your finger in a dyke, or maybe your tongue."

Gretel replied condescendingly, "Go bugger another camel."

And so it would go. They would fight and argue and attack and look for any leverage they could against one another. He would sometimes try to humiliate his wife by refusing to pay for their housekeeper. "What do you need a maid for anyway?" he would challenge her. "If you weren't such a pig and learned to pick up after yourself, you wouldn't need the bitch in the first place."

As Pittman watched these rather spectacular fights, he couldn't help noticing that Xerxes failed to catch on to most of the basic concepts about marriage: one, marriage is not a contest in which there is a winner and a loser; two, you have to treat one another as equal, total, permanent partners; and three, manners count. He had never seen such a marriage before. And Xerxes resisted the model Pittman was offering him, especially when the far classier Gretel could humiliate him so totally and did not hesitate to do so in any company if he got controlling.

Pittman tried to confront this misguided gentleman and teach him the error of his ways (by judging the way he was behaving as counterproductive and inconsistent with the standards of this century, maybe this millennium). Pittman's message was not "you're perverse," "you're evil," "you're stupid," but "you're misinformed." Pittman was saying in effect, "this is the way we do things on this planet," in the tone in which he would point out that the poor man was dialing the wrong telephone number or arriving at the wrong time. Pittman even pointed out that Gretel could always get her divorce attorney to explain that all they had was half hers, even if she had to divorce him to get it.

Even that was slow going until Pittman let Xerxes in on a secret. Pittman said, "There's been some research on this, Xerxes. Men who are afraid to let woman be equals to them in marriage have far smaller dicks than the average guy. When you try to lord it over Gretel, the rest of us guys think we know what you're hiding."

Xerxes promptly loosened the purse strings on the family fortune, no longer holding his wife accountable for her purchases.

But sure enough, Gretel decided to make up for lost time and began spending money as fast as Xerxes was raking it in with his various business pursuits. He was building things, manufacturing things, importing and exporting things, earning more money than he knew what to do with. Gretel similarly occupied herself with balancing the economic situation by ensuring that others profited from their privileged position. She began to invest in art. One day she brought home a Van Gogh. When Xerxes hit the ceiling, she warned him that if he said one more word, she'd buy a Vermeer. I not only had him tabulate the percentage of their holdings she was spending (it was minis-cule), I sent him to an art dealer who explained what a good investment Gre-tel's purchases were. I also had Gretel thank Xerxes for making this all possible. He muttered only that it took him almost as many hours to pay for the Van Gogh as it took Van Gogh to paint it. The couple had reached a sort of accommodation that worked for both of them. And through the years they just got richer and sexier and happier, and spread the money around to their families.

The Second Generation

The couple spoke very highly of Pittman's work to their family and friends. Xerxes had been especially impressed with the direct yet respectful way that Pittman had spoken to him: "Are you crazy? In this country we judge a man's worth not by how totally he can dominate women, but by the equality of his marriage!" Of course, with his soft voice and unthreatening appearance, Pittman claims that he can get away with saying things to people that most people would never hear from anyone else.

Xerxes and Gretel, who checked in from time to time over the next few decades, came in with concerns about Xerxes' young brother Darius, whom Xerxes had brought from Iran as the business expanded. Upon arriving, Dar-ius dumped his Iranian wife and five kids. He insisted he was not in an affair, but had fallen out of love with his wife and needed a divorce by Saturday night in order to protect himself from lifelong misery. This sounded too much like bad daytime TV. I explained to Xerxes that the likelihood of an established first marriage ending in divorce without infidelity is miniscule and nearly al-ways involves guns, knives, or wimpy therapists. Pittman sent Darius a copy of his book, *Private Lies: Infidelity and the Betrayal of Intimacy.*

Darius refused to see Pittman, got the divorce, refused to read the book, and left it behind when he went off to La La Land with Bambi, whose exis-tence he continued to deny as his problems mounted. He finally came to see Pittman when Bambi, after wrecking Darius's family, ran off with much of his money and his personal trainer. Darius was distraught. Pittman explained, "The fact that Bambi would screw you is not, I'm sorry to tell you, a testament to your beauty or charm, but an indication that she does not harbor the best interests of your family, your life, or you. She's a spider woman, who requires human sacrifice. She's probably a child of divorce [Darius nodded] who gets off on breaking up other people's marriages. You're an amateur at this—only amateurs marry women who screw around with married men." Darius read *Private Lies* and tried to get his first wife back from Iran. Sadly, her family back in Iran would not let her return. Darius had ruined everything in his life and knew it, and he dedicated himself to maintaining whatever relationship he could with his children until they could grow up and come here.

The Third Generation

Meanwhile, Xerxes and Gretel's dark, exotically beautiful daughters went off to careers in modeling and acting, and married poor but attentive young men. And in due time, their glorious son, Hans, came in for premarital counseling before he married Melanie, an Atlanta debutante and orthopedic surgeon. Hans and Melanie were both determined to break the molds shaped by their own parents and so were clearly motivated to work on their relationship. The young man, in particular, although a second-generation Iranian American, felt the legacy of the past (related to infidelity and control of money) was something from which he wanted to be free. Of course, he didn't try to escape the fortune that was being lavished on him.

Things went extremely well until Melanie became pregnant and experienced some problems during the pregnancy that required bed rest. Until this time they had an extremely active sex life and now the husband felt abandoned and cut off. Since having a physical affair was something he wished to avoid, he sought outlets first in pornography and then in cybersex on the Internet. This led him further to become involved with prostitutes, and then with Vasselina, a Bulgarian stripper. Hans hired Vasselina full-time and put her on salary in one of the family businesses. He set her up in an apartment so she would be available to him as a sexual outlet whenever he wished. His sadder but wiser Uncle Darius figured out what his nephew was doing and brought him his copy of *Private Lies*. Hans, already uncomfortable with the situation, read it and called Pittman.

Gentle Persuasion

If you know anything about Frank Pittman then you can readily imagine what he would say to such an "infidel" who is screwing around on his pregnant wife.

"Just what the hell do you think you're doing?" Pittman challenged the cowering man. "You've got a wife and pretty soon a child to be a grown-up for. Get this woman out of your life."

"But," he protested, "I do not love Vasselina. I would never leave Melanie. Ever. It's just that I have my needs."

"Let me get this straight," Pittman said in his deceptively soft, gentle voice. "You are having sex with a Bulgarian stripper you put on the family payroll. Your wife is lying in bed in agony waiting to give birth to your child. But this is perfectly acceptable because you don't love the hooker?"

"She's not really a hooker," the man protested. "She's a dancer. She works in clubs. I told you that . . . ."

"What you told me, long before this," Pittman interrupted, "was that you didn't want to behave the way your father and uncle and grandfather and all the other crazy men in your family did. You told me you had no respect for them because they didn't respect their wives and thus they didn't respect themselves. You told me lots of things back then, but something has messed with your mind. The reason you decided not to screw around is that it messes with people's minds and changes their brain chemistry and distorts their alliances and connections. It even gets you under the control of someone with a very different agenda, who does not have the best interests of your family at heart. She's got to go."

Pittman hugged the young man, told him to extract himself from Vasselina, tell Melanie all, apologize profusely, and call a family conference to tell the rest of his family it was all his fault, not Melanie's. Pittman was heading off for a week in Florence and agreed to meet the whole family shooting match as soon as he returned. Hans complied and invited everyone, including Uncle Darius. But Pittman had a heart attack and couldn't fly back in time, so he called Hans from cardiac care, explained his situation, lauded Hans for what he had done so far, and urged the young man to proceed with the meeting. On his return, Pittman got the gory details of the meeting from Melanie, who laughed lovingly through the whole recounting, as Hans appropriately blushed.

Public Confession and Apology

The young man took decisive action. According to Pittman, guilt is not such a bad thing if it motivates people to make amends for the hurtful things they do to themselves and to others.

"I wish to tell you all something that is very difficult for me to say," the young man began.

Everyone looked more than a little confused, wondering what was going on. Melanie, 8 months pregnant but tough as nails, was very uncomfortable physically but proud of Hans for doing this right.

"I wish to tell you all, what I have already confessed to my dear and forgiving wife, that I have been unfaithful. I cannot live dishonestly with her and I cannot live dishonestly with you."

The reactions were instantaneous and dramatic. There was crying. There was wailing. There were accusations and blame. Only Melanie remained still, proudly observing an adult emerge from what had begun to look like a spoiled prince.

"Why are you telling us such a thing?" Xerxes cried out.

"Why would you *do* such a thing?" Gretel asked.

"I am telling you all this because I wish to apologize to all of you, especially to my wife of course, but in this family we all affect one another and my behavior affects you just as much as your behavior affects me." He now looked at his family with absolute terror, wondering how he had gotten himself into such a mess.

"I know you have all seen me as somebody who is perfect, who has never done anything wrong before."

This may have been true for his parents, who saw him as the baby, the Golden Boy, but it was clear from the look his in-laws gave their daughter that they had never seen him as good enough for her, even with the obscene family wealth.

"I have been so self-righteous," he continued. "I have been condescending toward you for things you have done." He looked at his uncle and father. "I thought I was different from you. But I am not."

Hans looked down in shame, not knowing what to say or do next. "Melanie says she'll have me back, and I hope she will keep me," he said, looking at his wife, who still stared at him with eerie composure. "But I wanted you to know that she is a good woman, a good wife, a good surgeon, and she'll be a wonderful mother. She has done nothing wrong."

He then went on to talk about the old ideas from back home in Iran, and how they influenced the ways men behaved in the present. "I got this from Frank's book and this is what it said."

This was not the case. Pittman had not written about breaking from one's cultural traditions, at least not at this time. But readers are also authors of the books they read, including their own perceptions, interpretations, and beliefs. Nevertheless, he was impressed with the courage and level of responsibility that Hans had shown. He made no effort to make excuses or to blame anyone else beside himself. It was clear that his wife was also pleased with the outcome, even if she was ashamed of what had led to this meeting in the first place.

If anyone was angry with Hans, it was his mother, Gretel. She had idealized her son and now had to accept that he was not as perfect as she pretended. This confession also forced her, as it did everyone else in the family, to confront the destructive legacies of their past.

As Hans talked about the experience of reading *Private Lies*, and finally making sense of Uncle Darius's disastrous divorce and remarriage, Darius opened up about his errors and what it had cost him to treat his wife as less than an equal partner. He complimented his nephew on his honesty and insisted that his own affair became a disaster because he tried to keep it secret. He broke the Iranian tradition of men always seeing the man as right. The most loving thing a brother, or uncle, or therapist, can do is to tell one another when they are doing something wrong.

Pittman is in awe of men who have the balls to tell other men that what they are doing is wrong. "Guys usually tell each other that whatever makes them happy is just fine." Uncle Darius went out on a limb for his nephew. It was one of the finest hours in his misspent life.

Needless to say, Melanie not only accepted Hans back, but admired his honesty and courage, even as she kept him on a short leash for a while after she let him back in the house. She particularly admired his new-found humility. Before, he had been a bit intimidating even for someone as strong as she. If Melanie had been less self-assured, this therapeutic crisis might have been a marriage-wrecking disaster.

Hans and Melanie celebrated their reconciliation by buying a Rembrandt, together. And then they made plans to give it away, after they had spent a few years admiring the man who was brave enough to look squarely and deeply into his own face.

◼ ◼ ◼

The Most Loving Thing
That Someone Can Do

What was Pittman's role in this outcome, we asked him?

"I didn't have to be there to produce this splendid result, and after my heart attack I know I can't always be there, so I love the idea that my books can be there for me," he said with typical modesty. "Hans had seen me as someone who was dispensing wisdom without condemnation, without rejection. Even more than our conversations, it was when he heard my voice in the book that he could take in the messages without feeling threatened. Of course, he came to me after already hearing what a magician I was from his parents. This certainly helped."

What can others learn from this case, we wondered? It was not as if we couldn't see some clear lessons, but we were curious how Pittman would respond. He didn't disappoint us if what we were looking for was more provocation.

With nary a pause, he said: "We have to seduce people into trusting us before we can spank them."

"What do you mean?" we asked, already knowing what he meant but needing time to digest his statement.

Pittman recounted that he's seeing four different men in therapy who are in the process of leaving their wives and children for a stripper or a hooker. Amazingly, nobody will tell these guys that they are wrong. So Pittman has to do what a friend or uncle should do all the time, recognize that men have the best of intentions and a faulty instruction book, hug them, accept them as just guys, and tell them they're wrong.

Good Therapy as a Slap and a Hug

Pittman recalled another patient, who came from another state. He was a very wealthy, successful man in town (another millionaire whom Pittman would have loved to convince to give away more of his money to needy others). The man was desperate and on the verge of divorcing his wife, who was an unreasonable drunk. He didn't have the greatest respect for therapists, since his wife had been seeing one for some time.

"The guy just told her that if something makes you uncomfortable, then don't do it. Then he charged her—he charged *me*—a hundred bucks." He shook his head as if there was no end to such craziness.

Since the woman did not feel particularly uncomfortable continuing her drinking and carousing, she felt she had been given permission by an expert to continue her behavior. So this led the husband to see his own therapist, who told him that if he was not happy he should just leave her and move on.

So, the husband went home and announced to his children that he was going to divorce their mother. That got her attention, to the point that she stopped drinking and changed her ways. But the husband's therapist insisted that the results would never last and she was sure to relapse. That led to the impasse that brought them both into see Pittman.

"I've had enough," the husband insisted. "I'm only here because she dragged me in here. But I've had enough. I've had enough of her drinking and her abuse. I want a divorce."

"You want a divorce," Pittman repeated.

"Yes. I don't love her anymore."

"Love?" Pittman replied. "What's love got to do with it?"

"Excuse me?"

"I said: What does that have to do with it? We are talking about marriage here. This love business is a chemical state in the brain. It is a form of temporary insanity. It will pass. Forget about it."

The man was stunned by this response. He had by now become accustomed to the unconventional things that therapists might say, but this really took the prize.

"But I don't even like her," he protested.

"I don't blame you," Pittman countered. "I don't like her either. My mother was a drunk. I wouldn't live with one either. At least not until she sobers up." As he said this he winked at the wife, as if to say that he didn't mean it personally but she had to admit that she had made herself pretty unlikable.

"But what if she changed her behavior for good?" he asked. "Then what?"

The husband could only shrug. And they ended up staying together, Pittman added.

■　■　■

Pittman cites this case as another example of how important it is in therapy for the professional to be direct and honest, to tell people things that nobody else will, and to tell them in a way that they can hear it. According to Pittman's gospel, that is what good therapy is, and that is what he includes as part of his finest hours.

"So many therapists do therapy in such a way that they want to make themselves feel better," Pittman elaborated. "They refuse to take a stand, even if it doesn't help anyone except alleviate their own responsibility."

"It sounds like you cast yourself in the role of warm, loving, but scolding father."

"I'm a professional uncle," Pittman agreed. "The therapist has got to be unafraid of life. Unafraid of relationships. Unafraid of danger. Unafraid of taking risks. And unafraid of taking a stand."

"And being unpopular and criticized," we added.

"I feel much better when I am unpopular than I do when I am being ignored."

Core Fears

The case he had just mentioned reminded Pittman of an assortment of other men he has seen over the years, who have become involved with women outside their marriages as a way to pursue fantasies of unthreatening emotional acceptance. "It seduces people, like bad therapists who do the same thing," he added.

"So many of the guys I see in this position are successful men who have mobs of people that they have to pacify or satisfy. They look for some sort of safety and peace in a woman who is so self-loathing that there is no possibility that she is going to judge him as harshly as others do. He feels like some sort of hero with a woman he hasn't hurt yet. He sees the other woman as Marilyn Monroe or Eliza Doolittle—someone in the gutter who needs to be rescued. What he is seeking is the same things that a lot of other people are seeking: unconditional adoration."

By contrast, Pittman pointed out that when a man looks at his marriage and family, with all the accompanying emotional baggage and messiness, he might have fantasies of a woman dancing naked on a table whose only purpose in life is to serve him without demands of her own.

"This might sound crazy," Pittman said, "but it is an indication of how scared guys can be of emotional life when they have never been taught to process relationships very well. Yet if they find this perfect love in therapy, it has the same effect of making them unable to tolerate the messiness of a real relationship. What I'm saying is that the totally forgiving and nonjudgmental therapist screws up real relationships."

Concerned that this might come across as far more rigid than he might mean, we asked him to elaborate.

"Look, people are human to the degree that they respect the humanity of others, and they are respectful to the degree they have been respected. They get frightened when they don't feel that they will live up to their obligations and fulfill their responsibilities to the relationship. I spend my life trying to convince people that they can tolerate their imperfect marriages. They can work on their marriage and family even if their feelings aren't as romantically ideal as they would like them to be. I want people to understand and be aware of what they are capable of doing. The conservative aspect of this is that I do think that people have to fulfill their obligations, and a letter from the therapist saying that little Johnnie isn't feeling very well and doesn't have to finish out his life. . . ."

". . . is not very helpful," we finished the thought.

"Right," he agreed. "Eleanor Roosevelt said that most of the work in the world is done by people who aren't feeling very well that day. I am a strong believer that the survival of our civilization requires that we act contrary to our emotions."

"But it sounds like you are advocating that we should not trust our feelings, that we should live only according to our obligations, regardless of where they might lead."

"It comes down to this," Pittman summarized, "you can't trust your feelings when you have a stronger alliance with the woman who is dancing naked on the table than you do with the woman who is nursing your children."

16 Both Sides of the Story

A Case from Stephen Lankton

Stephen Lankton is a leading Ericksonian therapist and trainer. He combines hypnosis with several other theories that reflect his earlier training in Gestalt therapy, psychodrama, transactional analysis, cognitive therapy, and bioenergetics, thus presenting a model that is both highly flexible and infinitely more powerful.

Among the dozen or more books that Lankton has written or edited are Practical Magic, The Answer Within, Enchantment and Intervention in Family Therapy, *and* Tales of Enchantment. *In each of these practical handbooks, Lankton has integrated concepts from a variety of approaches with methods of clinical hypnosis into a model of brief therapy.*

Lankton works as a consultant, corporate trainer, and family therapist in Phoenix, Arizona.

A Collaborative Effort

This story is written in a style and format quite different from any other in the book. Rather than interviewing a single therapist about his or her finest hour, we have had the rare opportunity to talk to *both* participants in the process.

When we first approached Steve Lankton about participating in this project of talking about the best representative of his work, he immediately suggested that we include his client, Cassie, in the conversation. Although we should not have been as taken aback by the proposal (since it makes perfect sense that our clients should be included in all discussions about the meaning of our work), we did have some concerns about logistics. For that matter, we wondered why Lankton decided to proceed in this way.

There were a number of cases that he could have talked about that fit his criteria of a "finest hour." At first, he considered those clients who presented long-standing, chronic pain and who responded to treatment in a single (and only) session. He talked to several colleagues about other cases he could have brought up, but most of them were difficult to remember with any sort of detail. It was at that point that it occurred to him that it was too bad he didn't have a former client who might join him in the enterprise. This would lend a degree of authenticity and accuracy to the details of the relationship that could not be retrieved any other way.

Cassie was one former client who seemed perfect for the enterprise, since they had collaborated once before on a magazine article in which they wrote about their different experiences related to their therapeutic relationship. In addition, the case certainly qualified as a dramatic success.

So, that's how we found ourselves talking to both a therapist *and* a client about their collaboration and partnership in creating a successful outcome.

A Different Person Altogether

Our first question (as it might be yours as well) was directed to Cassie, wondering how and why she agreed to participate in this conversation.

Cassie nodded, as if this made perfect sense to her as a place to begin. "Well, I agreed mostly because my experience in therapy was so beneficial. I had originally gone to see Steve to deal with marital issues."

It was a series of panic attacks on top of generalized anxiety that first led Cassie to seek help. She felt so incapacitated by her increasingly severe symptoms that she found herself unable to take care of her usual business interests, which lay on the other side of a bridge from her home. As soon as she approached the roadway that led to the other side of the peninsula where she lived, her heart would begin pounding to the point that it felt like her chest would explode. It would take all of her self-control to pull over to the side of the road and catch her breath.

"My world was rather limited," Cassie admitted in an understated way. "There weren't too many places I felt safe. And the prospect of driving over the bridge seemed more and more remote. It got to the point where I didn't even want to leave the house."

This admission was particularly difficult for Cassie because she was a public person in her community, well known throughout town. It seemed to take her as much energy to pretend everything was normal as it was to get through her day without falling apart.

"I remember it was so difficult for you," Lankton recalled about their first meeting.

"What else do you remember?" we prompted him to continue the narrative.

"Well, there was some discontinuity that had taken place. I had seen both Cassie and her husband a few times when there was talk about making their marriage better and more emotionally intimate. It turned out that her husband was withholding the information that he was having an affair."

It was this extramarital relationship that led to the divorce and the adjustment period afterwards. Lankton didn't see Cassie for quite some time after their marital/divorce counseling ended.

"When Cassie returned a few years later, I was shocked by the way she appeared." He paused for a moment and then asked her for confirmation. In fact, throughout our whole conversation, Lankton repeatedly checked his perceptions with her own to make sure that he was neither speaking for her, nor distorting any of the essential details.

Previously, Lankton had seen Cassie as an incredibly accomplished, articulate, confident woman. Yet when she returned to resume therapy she was like a completely different person—helpless, out of control, and virtually a prisoner of her agoraphobia, which only seemed to be becoming worse.

"At first," he recalled, "I couldn't believe she was the same person. I thought she must be exaggerating how bad things were. But as we spent time together, I realized just how much pain she was in."

From the End to the Beginning

Lankton thought that the best way to tell the story of what ensued in their relationship was to start from the end and work their way backwards.

"The way I first got the idea of us collaborating on a magazine article, and then this chapter, occurred while I was watching television one evening. I saw this show about flying and I was thinking about taking lessons myself. I was only paying half attention when I heard this familiar voice, one I would never forget."

As if to make that point, Cassie laughed in her rich, distinctive voice.

"I looked up at the screen and saw my ex-client sitting there, telling viewers about her interest in getting a pilot's license. I couldn't believe that this was the same woman who had been so terrified of crossing a bridge, or even leaving her house. And now she was going to learn to fly!"

Lankton was particularly impressed by this dramatic change because they had only met for a total of eight sessions. During the relatively brief time they spent together he recalled what a difference it had made to talk about her early years of grief and loss related to giving up her baby for adoption. To add to her trauma, the young man who fathered the child was involved with someone else and abruptly ended their relationship.

"Steve helped me to reconnect with that young woman of 18 who had been in so much pain," Cassie said. "This allowed me to integrate that part of myself that I had been ashamed of and tried to hide from for so long."

Lankton continued the story by summarizing those early years they explored together and the possible significance to her later problems. "Here she was pregnant, with no place except her parents to turn to, and what she gets instead of support is a barrage of criticism. She was told repeatedly that she was unable to do anything right, or take care of herself, much less a child. She wanted love and tenderness and understanding rather than the barrage of anger that came her way. All this really stuck with her over the years."

Lankton and Cassie spent some time talking together about the connections between the past and her present predicament of acute, debilitating anxiety. Rather than not living up to her parents' expectations, she felt she was now disappointing her husband. Over and over she kept hearing scolding voices in her head that she was just no damn good and would never amount to anything.

"I think that was why the agoraphobia existed at that time," Lankton explained. And this provided him with some clues about structuring a series of interventions designed to bolster her confidence and come to terms with the past. But rather than taking years to do so as a psychodynamic or other insight therapist might do, Lankton sees this case as an excellent example of the power of brief therapy.

A Collaborative Effort

Cassie talked about how quick the turnaround was, such that she could drive across the bridge again and venture back out into the world. In addition, she felt sufficient support to divorce her husband, who was neither trustworthy nor supportive.

"I was able to put together a wonderful network of friends. I started to do things again that I hadn't done for a long time."

"So," we asked, impressed with the outcome but puzzled by what had transpired between them, "what exactly did Steve do?"

"Well, the session that I remember the most was actually the very first time we met. My husband and I had come together to work on our relationship, but he stayed in the waiting room while I talked with Steve alone. He had me relax and asked me to do some visualizations. I had never had an experience like this before. I don't remember what the conversation was that led up to all of this unfolding, but it was very emotional for me at the time."

As Cassie was describing her experience of what happened, immediately we were struck by the clear examples of therapeutic variables that are often mentioned in outcome research. In the single statement above, for example, we already noticed (1) the trusting alliance that was quickly created ("I talked with Steve alone"), (2) the prospect of hope and positive expectations ("He had me relax and asked me to do some visualizations"), (3) a novel interactive experience ("I had never had an experience like this before"), and (4) emotional arousal ("It was very emotional for me at the time").

"During the visualization," Cassie continued, "I could see myself at 18 and I was in the delivery room. It was extremely uncomfortable for me to look at this young woman I used to be. I just wanted to run. I wanted to get away from her. All I can remember saying about this woman I saw in my own image was: 'Oh, she is sticky.' "

Cassie remembers exactly the tone and quality of Lankton's voice when he responded to her. "Tell this young woman," he said to her, "this younger version of yourself at age 18, that you want to stick to her too."

"Oh my God!" Cassie said, startled by the power of these words.

"At that exact moment," she continued the story, "I could feel that it was finally okay to embrace this girl, this part of myself. I realized I wasn't so horrible. I didn't need to hide this part of myself anymore."

"So, how and why did this impact you so powerfully?" we asked her.

"I guess I needed someone in a position of authority, someone I respected, to tell me that this part of me was okay. I had nothing in my own history to validate this experience."

Of course, just as therapists make up theories to explain why their interventions may have worked, so do clients. Cassie is quick to point out that this is just her impression of what happened, leaving open other possibilities. One of these might be an even simpler explanation: "I think Steve is an extremely intuitive person. Later on, after my divorce, I did some dream work with him and it was like working with Sherlock Holmes. He took me on a journey to connect on a really deep level with different parts of myself. A lot of it was magical to me."

This mutual admiration between therapist and client is so evident in the respectful, caring way that each responds to the other. Both Lankton and Cassie took turns throughout our dialogue attributing the most important work to one another. Like any great helping relationship, they had developed a solid partnership that had so much collaborative effort that neither one could figure out who did the most work.

Creating New Memories

"What's your version of the story, Steve?" we asked him. We were curious how he might explain things in the language of his preferred theory.

"The only word I can think of to describe what happened is 'nonremarkable.'" Lankton shrugged apologetically, looking for a better word but unable to capture what he considers a rather pedestrian intervention. He realized that Cassie was not comfortable with herself and so he helped her to take a small step toward feeling more comfortable by accepting her choices of the past. At first glance, a simple visualization is not much of a big deal, but we think that what is missing in the explanation is the deep connection that they developed in a relatively short period of time.

Lankton conceptualized the case in terms of helping her to realize the resources at her disposal to cope with her faltering marriage, her shameful past, and her overwhelming anxiety. By putting her into a relaxed trance, he was then able to use her visualizations as cognitive mediations to retrieve earlier memories and enhance them.

"The first step," Lankton explained, "was simply to help her retrieve the experiences that had to do with strength and confidence and optimism. That was a general umbrella for all of the variety of things I could think of that would reduce her immediate anxiety and also facilitate her exploration visually. When I talk to someone like this, and see all the pain and suffering reflected in her face, I try to follow the indicators that lead to the source."

It didn't take long at all to find the pregnancy incident, and its aftermath, as a critical incident. "I think that asking someone to visualize herself at a younger age is a metaphor that can be played with much more readily than any that I could supply. It is a thinly veiled metaphor to be sure, but as you think about yourself at an earlier age you begin to stimulate the neurological activity that corresponded at that time.

"If I start thinking of jokes I used to tell when I was a kid, or the playing of something with my dog, I will begin to age regress a little bit and I will become more jovial. I think of childhood associations I wouldn't have otherwise considered. By doing so, I can activate some earlier experiences that are cognitive, kinesthetic, and visceral."

By encouraging Cassie to activate memories of a time when she felt helpless and hopeless and out of control, she began to experience those feelings again. Every time she thought about those times, she felt the same exact despair and shame. But as an adult, looking back, the person now has resources and skills that were not available at the time.

"If I can use the relaxation to partially inhibit the occurrence of those experiences, and then associate those positive experiences in the context of seeing those images, then I guess you could say that there are little neurological changes being made where the brain is firing off positive resources paired with the previously negative memories."

This is how Lankton believes that neural connections and associations can be changed. Bad memories take on a much less controlling and negative context once they are paired with a different set of interpretations and perceptions. New memories are thus created.

"Cassie," we kidded her, "maybe you can summarize what Steve just said because we aren't sure we understand all this."

"Hey, don't look at me!"

■   ■   ■

Power of Relationship

Again, we wanted to hear Cassie's version of the same events, so we asked her to elaborate. She mentioned several other factors going on at the time that also had accumulated influence. As in all cases of transformation, it is virtually impossible to find "truth" that explains fully and completely what took place. To add to the complexity of this case, she mentioned that before seeing Lankton she had been attending a support group for agoraphobics and also had been seeing a more "conventional" practitioner. "Still," she added, getting to the heart of the matter, "I felt a deeper, more soulful connection [with Lankton]."

"What do you mean?" we pressed her.

"Just that Steve is not so intellectualizing. He . . . ." She stopped for a moment and talked directly to Lankton: "You are really in touch with feelings and you let me stay there, to have these strong emotions. I felt safe with you. I felt supported by you. I call it now this 'snot flying' session of therapy where we got to this really deep place. I don't think there are many circumstances in our culture that allow for a person to reintegrate those things."

We've rarely heard such an articulate description of the power of relationship, especially one in which the client not only felt held and supported but also given permission to explore forbidden territory and experiment with new options.

We are moved not only by what happened in the past in their work together, but what is still going on as they talk about what has already occurred. We are pretending this is just a conversation about events that have already transpired, but the work continues as each partner in this process makes sense of what each experienced.

As a final question, we wondered what Steve and Cassie thought that others could learn from this case. For Cassie, the main theme is that people in pain don't have to accept that this is the way life has to be. There are choices. There are ways to come to terms with the past.

Lankton readily agreed, but had one final point to add. "For me the answer lies in the fact that therapy can be very brief and very profound and long-lasting. We are talking about events that took place over 7 years ago and yet the effects still last today. Therapists often think that this type of work has to take a long time, but if the work is structured and directed toward finding resources, instead of talking about problems, you can make remarkable progress in much less time than people can imagine."

17 The Gardener Who Dug Very Deep

A Case from Alvin Mahrer

Alvin Mahrer is Professor Emeritus at the University of Ottawa and one of the major voices in humanistic/existential therapy. He is the author of thirteen books and three hundred publications, most of which are about his unique brand of "experiential therapy" that seeks to promote radical transformation through the power of relationship. When asked about the significance of this theory, Mahrer observed wryly that it may be regarded as a very creative departure from traditional methods—or as a quixotic tilting at windmills.

Mahrer is most proud of his book, The Complete Guide to Experiential Psychotherapy, *first published in 1996 and since reissued. Another of his classic works,* Experiencing, *was originally published in 1978 and first set forth the origins, structure, and development of personal and social change within the context of his model.*

Mahrer has been named one of the "Four Living Legends" by the Psychotherapy Division of the American Psychological Association and has been named Researcher of the Year by his university.

An Overview of the Method

Although Al Mahrer is one of the most notable theorists and experienced practitioners around, he reported quite a lot of apprehension related to choosing a "finest hour" to speak about. At first, he considered choosing a session that displayed his consummate skill, fine wit, a time when he put on a dazzling, miraculous performance, cured cancer, or brought a dead person back to life (or at the very least brought someone back from the throes of dark depression). Instead, what he decided was to choose a session as most memorable because it was so personally moving to him.

Mahrer works differently than most therapists, not just because of the distinctive style of "experiential" therapy he developed, but also because of the unique way he applies the method. It all begins with the setup of his office—two comfortable, cushiony lounge chairs, recliners that can be tilted way back. But rather than facing one another in the traditional therapeutic configuration, they are placed side by side, like seats in the first-class section of an airplane.

A client is directed to recline in the chair, eyes closed, as Mahrer does the same: this is therapy in which both participants pilot this experience together. A client is invited to begin by taking deep, cleansing breaths, inhaling and exhaling explosively. Because he works to unlock a person's control, and wishes to activate strong emotional reactions, the office is completely sound-proofed—clients are encouraged to makes noises, yell, scream, wail, whatever comes out.

"The person begins," Mahrer explained, "by looking for some incident or situation in which there is a strong, full, deep, saturating feeling. The scene is typically a recent one rather than something from a long time ago. It can be dramatic or rather mundane, public or private, pleasant or painful, internal or externally displayed. The feeling may have been brief and intense, or lasted quite some time. It is up to the person to choose."

Once they begin with an emotional incident, Mahrer seeks to use the experience as a beginning point to promote some sort of personal transformation. The first scene is deepened in such a way that the client's experience is made more intense, more authentic, so that he or she may embrace the episode more fully. "The next step," Mahrer said, "is both dramatic and grandiose. The person is encouraged to dive, head first, out of the ordinary person that he or she has been, and to plunge into another, radical self that has far more potential to become something else."

In the final stage, clients are helped to integrate this new, deeper potential for experiencing into the person they wish to be become. "The new person is free of the old person's painful scene that had been so front-and-center in the beginning."

This outline of the method did little to help us imagine what this might really look and feel like in a session. We could picture the two chairs, side by side, but after that it became a little hazy. Always accommodating, Mahrer offered to show us what this was like with the case he wished to discuss.

The Peak Moment

Melanie was in her early fifties and from a small town. She had married at 19, had three children right away, and spent her life raising her family and helping her husband take care of the gas station they owned. Her life revolved around spending time with her family, taking care of the garden, and having an occasional beer. Her children were now grown and had children of their own.

A few months earlier, her husband, Frank, had died of a sudden heart attack while fishing with a friend. Melanie missed him terribly and had had trouble sleeping ever since his death. Although grieving and lonely, she took some consolation that one of her sons and his children lived just a few doors away.

In their first two sessions, Mahrer collected some basic background about Melanie and her family, although his focus tends to be more on present feelings and reactions rather than past events. The particular session that Mahrer wished to present, perhaps his "finest hour," occurred during their third session together. It began, as usual, with them reclining their chairs and closing their eyes.

"I have to let go of the usual controls," Mahrer said aloud in a booming voice. He wanted to model for her, as much as possible, the possibility of letting herself go. "I have to unbuckle all the controls that I usually have." He took several deep, punctuated breaths, then he announced: "I am going to scream and yell for about a minute. Join me if you can. Is this okay?" He opened his eyes for a moment and looked to the side to see how she was doing. He noted that she seemed relaxed and comfortable, then he saw her head nod.

Mahrer, quite experienced and uninhibited in this experiential process, began screaming and yelling as loud as he could. Unintelligible but passionate sounds. Blood-curdling shrieks. He really started to get into it, and as he did so, Melanie joined him with screams, yells, and shrieks of her own. In fact, it started to become quite silly and they both began giggling as they kept the screams going.

For the rest of the session, Mahrer continued talking in an unnaturally loud voice. At the time, he kept thinking that it didn't sound like him at all, but he wanted to continue to activate her. The more he yelled, the more worked up she became as well.

"Okay," Mahrer said in a more normal voice, signaling they were making some sort of transition. "I want you to find a time, perhaps a scene or incident when you experienced a really strong feeling. Can you do that?"

"Oh yes," she replied instantly. "I've got one already, a good one."

"Excellent! Let's hear it!"

"This happened yesterday—No, it was the day before. I was working in the garden. I've told you before that I love being in the garden. It's the one place where I don't feel so lonely, so . . . I don't know . . . so empty."

"Go on," Mahrer encouraged.

"So, I was working in the garden, pulling out some weeds, when I heard Frank call out to me from the porch."

"Frank, your husband?"

"Exactly. He called out to me asking if I wanted some coffee. It startled me so that I looked over that way. I knew it couldn't really be him, but the voice sounded so clear, so real."

"Then what happened?"

"Well, I was just so confused. I didn't know what to think. I knew it couldn't really have been Frank, but I know I heard his voice. It felt like. . . ."

"Go on."

"It felt like I was up in the air looking down on myself, like I was floating in the air. Isn't that strange?"

Mahrer felt right there with her. He could imagine it perfectly. It wasn't at all like he was just a listener to the story, but that he was sitting in the garden right with her, as if he had heard Frank's voice as well. So it didn't seem strange to him at all.

When Mahrer didn't respond immediately, Melanie added: "I guess it's because I miss him so!"

"Yes, my God!" he said in a loud voice. "I know he's dead but I hear his voice with you. Is it really his voice?"

"I . . . I think so," Melanie said, taking deep, gulping breaths.

"So, as you look back on what happened now, when during this scene did you have the absolute strongest feeling? That is what we are looking for."

"It was the moment when I heard Frank's voice."

"Yes," Mahrer agreed. "It felt like that for me as well. It felt wonderful, and yet terrifying and awful."

"It was like being in the air," she repeated again. "I felt sort of removed, serene, above it all. I don't know how to say it but. . . ."

"Just say it."

"Well, it was like I was God."

"What about right now?"

"Yes, I can feel it right now, this moment. I'm up in the air but I'm scared because I am so high."

"Yes, I am with you," Mahrer said. "I can't even see a thing down below because I am so far up."

"No, no, not like that. It's just, maybe 10 or 15 feet, just hovering above."

"Okay, then, what am I seeing?"

"I'm looking at me," Melanie said in a voice that Mahrer could barely hear. It was like the frightened voice of a child.

What struck Mahrer as so remarkable about this whole experience was that it felt like he was absolutely there with her. Whatever Melanie was seeing and describing, he could see and experience as well, *as if he was there.* He could feel them both getting closer and closer to the strongest feeling, for which they were searching. Once they were at that place, then the real work would begin.

"I am living in that scene with her," Mahrer recalled with awe. "I am up in the air with her. I am looking down and seeing myself—herself—and then I am looking for the instant when the feeling is strongest. Of course, nobody can ever find that moment. You have to live again in the scene and slow it down. Like a detective, you have to look around carefully."

"Slow it down," Mahrer said to Melanie. "Go slowly here. Take each frame one at a time, each second, and explore it fully. You are still kneeling in the garden. Now you are turning."

"Yeah," she said in a whisper. "I'm turning now. I see the back porch."

"You've got that shovel in your hand."

"Yes, I'm weeding."

"And now you're up in the air, right?"

"Yes."

"Now slow things down even more. Exactly which moment is the feeling strongest?"

"I have this funny, funny feeling," Melaine said. She was speaking in a slow, lethargic voice, as if when the tape was slowed down, so was the soundtrack. "I see myself in the garden. . . ."

"Wait a minute," Mahrer interrupted. "Is the feeling strongest when you are seeing yourself down there? Is that it, or is it when you are up here 20 feet and you are having thoughts and ideas?"

Melanie shook her head. "I don't know. Wait, there it is. It is definitely as I'm hovering in the air, looking down. That's it!"

It Was Mystical

Once they discovered this peak moment, Mahrer asked her to hold very still. He wanted them not only to freeze the moment, but to dilate it. The deepest potential for experience lies in that moment, whether it is painful or ecstatic. But for Melanie, the moment was not so much uncomfortable as it was rapturous. It seemed to her as if, all of a sudden, things made sense to her even if she couldn't put them into words.

"I don't know what I'm feeling," Melanie said, but didn't seem to be bothered by the confusion and ambiguity.

"I'm with you there," Mahrer said. "There is no way to describe the moment because. . . ."

". . . it doesn't matter," she finished. "I don't know if I am feeling good or bad, but there is something like knowing everything."

This whole dialogue does not make much sense to us right now, but it certainly seemed clear to Mahrer at the time. It was simply magic, the moment of transformation, and he believes that it is beyond understanding or analysis.

"This whole thing went on for about a minute, which is a long time. Melanie kept saying that this was all so strange and I am saying professional things like, 'Wow!'"

"It's like a miracle," Melanie said after a long pause.

"Like seeing something nobody would ever believe."

"Yes!"

It was as if they were both transported to another world. Mahrer has had many other experiences similar to this in which he joins his clients on their journeys, but this was the first time he had felt totally *there.*

"Since then," Mahrer recalled, "I have come across similar kinds of deeper things in other people, but I never had this kind of reaction. This kind of reaction was so powerful, and it lasted so long, that it was absolutely amazing. I am still moved by how mystical, wonderful, noble, grand, and majestic, and marvelous this feeling was that we both shared. It was like we were witnessing something deeper in her that made us feel like little people in the presence of something miraculous."

Later, Mahrer went over the tape of the session with students, trying to figure out what had happened. Yet all they heard on the tape were exclamations of "Oh God!" and "Wow!" interspaced by long silences.

It was as if Mahrer and Melanie had discovered some deeper wisdom. Melanie had also found something deep inside herself that created a possibility for knowing and understanding that had previously been beyond her. "This just isn't me," she kept insisting.

"But it *is* you now," Mahrer responded. Then they both giggled uncontrollably.

"I don't know what this means, or what to do with it all," she said.

"This means you have an opportunity to change your life, if you want to."

"But I'm no brain," Melaine said. "Hell, I never even finished high school. I'm just a country girl who now has grown kids. All I've got now is my garden."

"That's the way you *used* to be. But now things are different."

One Hundred Minutes

The rest of the session seemed ordinary by comparison. Mahrer and Melanie explored a few other scenes that struck Melanie as significant. In each of the enactments she appeared wise and knowing in ways she had never felt before. This all felt totally out of character for her. She had never before thought of herself as special or smart or talented in any way, but now she felt blessed.

Just before the session ended, Mahrer asked her what it would be like if she became this way in her real life.

"That would scare the hell out of me!" Melanie laughed. "It would ruin everything."

"Ruin it how?" Mahrer asked.

"Well, my sister for one. She'd wonder what the hell happened to me. She'd think I had some kind of screw loose or something. My whole family would slap me on the ass if I acted like this."

"Let's pretend that your family and friends wouldn't be upset if you became more like you were here today. What would that be like?"

"What do you mean?"

"Let's say when this session is over you walk out of here and get in your truck and drive back into town. What's the first think you're going to do when you get home?"

"I'm going . . . I'm going . . . " Melanie stuttered for a minute, then finished: "I'm going to start writing."

"That's good," Mahrer said. "What are you going to write?"

"Well," Melanie considered. "I think I'm going to start by writing in a journal."

"A journal?"

"Yup. I'm going to write down my ideas and my thoughts."

"You mean like the potatoes are rotting and I have to plant some more?"

They both laughed. "Hell no! I'm going to write about life! I know you're wondering what I know about life but. . . ."

"No," Mahrer protested. "I'm not thinking about that at all. Just the opposite."

"Really?"

"Absolutely. Okay Melanie. Time to open your eyes."

They both looked up at the clock and saw that they'd been in their reclined positions for almost 2 hours! But never had 100 minutes made such a difference in a person's life.

Melanie pried herself out of the chair, groaning a little from the stiffness of sitting still for so long. Only her vocal cords had gotten a workout, and her voice was hoarse. She looked at Mahrer and smiled at him still sitting in his chair. "I know. I know," she said. "You don't have to say a word."

And he didn't.

20 Years Later

On that day many years earlier, Melanie had indeed gone home after the session to begin writing. She started writing in a journal about her thoughts and feelings, just a few minutes each day. Then she extended this to several hours each day, writing about her life, her town, and her family. Eventually she moved on to writing fiction and enjoyed a spectacularly successful career, moving out of the garden and into the public eye. She wrote many novels, short stories, and essays that were published all over the world. She won many literary prizes. Although she had never graduated from high school, she was awarded several honorary doctorates.

Melanie still lives in the same town. Some things have not changed for her even though she is a person who transformed herself.

As for her therapist, Al Mahrer is still blown away by what happened in their 2 hours together. "This is what I thought of immediately when I considered my finest hour," Mahrer said. "It was like seeing God or the center of the universe."

After this transcendent session, he came to believe in a much higher potential for what therapy can do for people if we think beyond the relatively modest goals of making symptoms go away. There are deep, deep possibilities in every person that remain unexplored. "Ever since that day," Mahrer said, "I have wondered if we have even the slightest idea of what is inside people and where it comes from? It felt to me as if I had been an explorer with Melanie and that we had discovered something that nobody had ever found before. This encouraged me to ask people to go deeper inside themselves. Who knows what we will find?"

18 Solving Unsolvable Problems

Cases from Richard B. Stuart

Richard Stuart is one of the leading theorists in the specialty of couples therapy, combining his original training as a psychoanalyst with behavioral and social learning methods to create a structured approach for helping couples deal with a variety of concerns by addressing the interactive patterns with which they relate to one another. His earlier work examined failures in therapy (Trick or Treatment), *behavioral marital therapy* (Helping Couples Change), *behavioral strategies for dealing with weight loss (*Slim Chance in a Fat World, Act Thin, Stay Thin, *and* Weight, Sex, and Marriage), *and other clinical applications of social learning theory (*Adherence, Compliance, and Generalization in Behavioral Medicine, Second Marriage, *and* Violent Behavior: Social Learning Approaches to Prediction, Management, and Treatment). *More recently, he has become far more pragmatic and integrative in his approach, combining features from a number of other systems into an integrative approach.*

Stuart is Emeritus Professor of Psychiatry at the University of Washington and also teaches and directs the program offering Respecialization in Clinical Psychology at the Fielding Graduate Institute.

Success and Failure

We began from a philosophical perspective before delving into a particular case. Stuart wanted to distinguish between what he considers good and bad therapy. In order to do so, he first considered that both good and bad things happen in everyone's lives, therapists included. In other words, we all have our finest hours, and others that are somewhat less than fine.

According to Stuart, a definition of being well-adjusted would include four components:

1. The ability to avoid some of life's predictable misfortunes
2. The ability to minimize the effects of unavoidable situations

173

3. The ability to capitalize on opportunities that are presented
4. The ability to create additional opportunities as needed.

Although therapists are inclined to claim credit for our clients' successes, we blame the clients for being resistant when there are negative outcomes. Stuart was reminded how during his training years he was taught to assign any difficult client a label of being character-disordered, as a way to be freed of any responsibility for promoting change.

Just as he thinks that clients should take most of the credit (or responsibility) for any outcome in the treatment, he also recognizes that a number of influences beyond the therapy itself may affect the results. With this said, Stuart defines great therapy as "helping patients identify their underutilized talents, helping them make the best use of their resources (the ones they know they have), and helping them build necessary but absent skills."

This may sound simple, but it takes a really great therapist to function outside of what is expected in order to promote all of these goals. This means not being restricted by any single conceptual ideology, but also being willing to work with the sort of creative inventiveness that one associates with the process of scientific discovery. According to Stuart, great therapy is akin to the process of bringing out the best that people have to offer, making the best possible use of their resources.

It is not nearly enough to behave well in session. "Patients can have a wonderful relationship with me," Stuart said, "but if they don't have a wonderful relationship with people in their real world, the therapy is not much of a success."

Short-Term Wonders

In sorting through his caseload to select his best piece of work, Stuart thinks in terms of categories. The first kind is the "short-term wonder," those times when people are helped within a matter of a few sessions. The client comes in absolutely paralyzed by some traumatic incident or life event and then responds very quickly to a dramatic intervention.

Ann had become pregnant by a man she had dated for only a few weeks. She couldn't decide whether to carry through with the pregnancy and have the baby, or to arrange an abortion. Stuart had his own opinion that it would be a mistake for this woman to have a baby at this time in her life, but he kept this to himself and took the usual route of helping her to make her own choice. They explored the alternatives, and the consequences of each, but before the final decision was announced, Ann left therapy and never returned.

Like so many of the stories we hear, the endings are unfinished. People move. They call to cancel without explanation. They don't return calls. We are left to write the endings ourselves, based on our own predictions, projections, or fantasies. And so it was with Ann that she vanished from Stuart's life without a hint of where she was going or why.

Several years later, Stuart and his wife were out hiking in the woods when two people approached them.

"You may not remember me," the first person, a woman in her twenties, said, "but 6 years ago I came to you for a few sessions and you helped me to decide about whether to have a baby or not."

"Of course I remember you!" Stuart responded. And indeed he did. As so often happens, we recall the unfinished stories best of all.

"You were the only person I talked to at that time in my life who didn't tell me what to do. You let me think things through myself."

"Yes, I remember that quite well," he agreed, recalling that he had taken great care not to express his own opinions.

"Well, it's funny running into you here like this. And I don't mean to bother you but I wanted you to know that I decided to have the baby. I'd like to introduce you to her. This is Grace, Dr. Stuart, and she is amazing."

Looking up at him was indeed the most adorable little girl. She was holding her mommy's hand and was curled around her legs in that shy way that kids peek out at strangers.

As Stuart studied the little girl and her mother, he thought to himself that this was not at all the outcome he expected, nor the one he would have thought to accomplish. As they walked up the hill together, he was reminded again about how important it was not to meddle in other people's lives but to allow them to make their own choices, and accept responsibility for them.

Solving Unsolvable Problems

The second category of extraordinary therapy involves helping people to solve problems that they believe have no solutions. Stuart thought of a case that represented this type of "cure," in which a boy with a strange eating disorder came to see him. Roy was insistent that he would not eat anything that was once alive. In addition, he had problems in school and had also been diagnosed with a psychotic disorder.

Since the eating problem was the one that was most immediately life-threatening, Stuart did a thorough evaluation of Roy's eating preferences. Once he discovered that the boy liked to build models as a hobby, Stuart decided that they would collaborate to work on a color-coded menu of foods. They identified foods in several color-identified food groups that were acceptable to him and then built menus that incorporated nutritionally balanced diets. In very little time, Roy began eating normally.

While preparing these menus, it became evident that the boy also had a reading problem. Further investigation revealed that it was a visual tracking error—he would see the first two letters of a word and then guess what it meant before reading further. This led to a lot of mistakes and misinterpretations.

Again, Stuart resorted to a creative problem-solving role. Working together with Roy's sister, they obtained rolls of adding-machine paper, the kind that scrolls out in long curls. They typed up fifth- and sixth-grade-level word lists on the paper rolls.

Roy was asked to find an empty cigar box and a dry-cell battery. Together they wired the box so there was a small light bulb on one side and a buzzer on the other, with two wires running down each side to a toilet-paper roll that had been wrapped with the word list. It was now possible to train Roy's sister to move through the list of words while testing Roy, teaching him to track each word to the end and sound out the meaning. The light and buzzer were used as a reinforcement. In a matter of a few sessions, Roy's visual tracking error was corrected. His other problems, including his so-called psychotic condition, cleared up once his eating and reading difficulties were solved.

Reparenting

A third kind of excellent therapy that Stuart mentioned occurs within a longer-term context. This is the kind of relationship-oriented work with which we are all familiar, in which a person's sense of self-efficacy and personal relationships are improved. It is through the therapeutic alliance that we teach people to develop more trusting connections to others while appraising the impact of their own behavior. Yet where Stuart's more behavioral approach may differ from others is the emphasis he places on giving clients both positive and negative feedback within the relationship.

"You feel victimized," Stuart might acknowledge with a client, "but let's see what *your* role was in creating this situation."

Stuart pointed out that this is a delicate process, one in which it is important for the clinician to be sensitive and supportive, yet can have a great impact in that it helps people to develop a new set of interpersonal behaviors that they can then generalize to other relationships in their lives.

An example of this "reparenting" kind of therapy took place with a young woman who was the girlfriend of one of Stuart's graduate students. It was reported to him that Mandy was both addicted to a number of substances and also sexually promiscuous and unable to remain faithful to her boyfriend. Indeed, it turned out that she was using quite a number of hallucinogenic drugs and other substances, but Stuart discovered this was mainly as a form of self-medication for a progressive bone disease that was likely to kill her within the next few years. She seemed to be living a high-risk lifestyle as a way to distract herself from the rapid deterioration that was taking place and her approaching death.

Stuart was uncertain about to what extent he should tamper with Mandy's situation, and if so, how he should do so. "It isn't my place," he said "to tell people which defenses they should use. She was already uneasy about coming to therapy in the first place."

Rather than taking a more direct approach, Stuart instead concentrated on helping her to find more meaning in her life in the time she had left. Since music was a main love, he encouraged her to pursue this more seriously (as a parent might). She eventually formed a rock band and made a few records and then started collaborating on musicals in the drama department. She ended the relationship with Stuart's graduate student and started seeing someone else, in a much more healthy relationship. Mandy and Alan, her new lover, got married, went to graduate school together, and Mandy pursued a successful career as a composer in the music industry.

Mandy and Dick Stuart kept in touch over the years, sometimes doing phone sessions. One day she called him to say that her bone condition had dramatically worsened—her hip had just plunged through her pelvis, puncturing her liver—she was going into the hospital to die.

By this time, they had been doing phone therapy for 6 years, on top of the 5 years he had seen her in regular sessions, so they had a very deep and honest relationship.

"Dr. Stuart," she asked him in a weak voice, "how can I do this? How can I cope?"

"Mandy, you have written the book on coping. You have done so much over all these years to take care of yourself. You have minimized the effects of this illness and led a pretty normal life. You have lived far longer than anyone expected you to. You have been successful in your career beyond your wildest dreams. You have a rock-solid marriage. Why don't you teach me about coping?"

They stayed on the phone for several hours, both of them crying and reviewing their relationship. Mandy felt better and ready to face her death with as much dignity as she possibly could. Finally they said goodbye for the last time.

* * * * *

Twenty years have elapsed since this last phone conversation, in which Stuart said goodbye to his dying patient. A few months ago, he received an e-mail that read as follows:

Dear Dr. Stuart,

I don't know if you remember me. You talked to me when I lived in _____. I just came across your name on the Internet and thought I'd say hello. I wondered how you were and how things were going for you. We speak of you often. My husband and I are celebrating 32 years of marriage and I give you most of the credit for this. Had I not been seeing you at the time I met him, I would not have been able to SEE him. And you helped us through some pretty tough years.

It was signed, "Mandy."

Stuart didn't know what was going on. Could this be some horrible joke? Was this a ghost? He didn't know whether to feel angry or amazed or just confused.

But it was indeed Mandy! She had looked Stuart up using a search engine on the Internet and decided to contact him after all these years, her surrogate father whom she had lost track of.

Stuart immediately e-mailed her back:

Dear Mandy,

UNBELIEVABLE! I am so glad to hear from you. Not only do I remember you and almost everything about the transitions in your life that I was able to watch, but I have something you once gave me sitting on my desk. It has been there all these years. I would love to know what is happening with both of you for the past 32 years.

Stuart also told Mandy in this first message how much of an impact she had had on his therapy ever since. He invited her to call him, which she did soon thereafter.

"So what the hell happened to you?" Stuart asked her. "The last time we talked you had gone into the hospital to die. Your bones were literally falling apart. There was no hope."

Mandy laughed. "Well, it's a long story, but basically somebody at the National Institutes of Health found out I had this rare bone disease. They had just discovered that the cause of the disease was due to an enzyme deficiency. And it so happened that they were experimenting with this new drug that was supposed to cure the disease."

"Wow, that's amazing."

"Wait, you haven't heard the best part. They developed this orphan drug for me. They gave me a prescription that cost $400,000 per year. That's what these experimental drugs cost. Anyway, I've been taking it for 25 years."

Stuart realized that this contact was not just to report good news after all these years. Something must have happened recently that led Mandy to reach out at this time.

It turned out that Mandy's bones were starting to deteriorate again. She'd had three hip replacements already and was now planning for a fourth operation. This time, she was not sure she would survive.

Stuart and Mandy resumed therapy, but this time neither in face-to-face sessions, nor on the phone—they began doing sessions via the Internet.

Mandy reported that her career had really blossomed and she had been extremely successful. She was especially proud that she had done so well in such a cut-throat business considering her debilitating illness. Rather than discouraging her, she felt the disability only helped her develop more resilience and strength.

Making Sense of What Happened

There are at least two parts of the work therapists do. The first component consists of the interventions that, hopefully, produce desired changes in clients' lives; the second involves making up a theory or reason to account for what happened. In this case, we were especially curious how Stuart would make sense of what took place with Mandy.

Sounding very much like a narrative therapist rather than the behaviorist of yesteryear, Stuart talked about the ways that Mandy had been dominated by her feelings. "She operated on the basis of what she felt. Emotions are problematic gods because emotion is stored history and in somewhat disabling ways she would decide that the most relevant aspects of situations were the ways she felt about them."

What's an example of this?

"Relationships can be useless," Stuart explained. "Relationships can be exploitive. I felt that she was seriously exploited by her father as a young child. She thought and believed that because she felt exploited in her relationships with men and boys; she thought that relationships just had to be that way."

"Wait a minute," Stuart would challenge Mandy. "Let's think about what we know about relationships. Have you ever seen a movie that had a relationship that seemed to be a good one?"

"Yeah, sure," Mandy agreed. "They might look that way in the movies but it doesn't happen that way in real life."

"All I'm trying to say is that life is not objective. Life is what you believe."

"Okay then," she responded, digging further into her position. "There is a gangster coming into my apartment and pulling out a gun. Am I supposed to believe that he is my best friend coming for dinner?"

"No, of course not. But if you believe that you have no choices then you have no choices. If you believe that you can do something to influence what happens next, then there is a possibility that you can do that."

In the style of reparenting therapy that Stuart has been describing he has seen a lot of people who are totally ruled by their emotions, which they allow to define their reality. He realizes that if the therapist challenges these emotions, the client is likely to feel misunderstood. But if you accept them, reinforcing their helplessness, then it is difficult to make much of a difference.

Mandy is the person who taught Dick Stuart most about doing therapy. He learned from her how to walk the delicate line of helping clients to feel understood at the same time that he was challenging their distorted perceptions of reality. Until this point he had been operating psychodynamically, giving a lot of weight to disabling life experiences. And Mandy had quite a few to review.

Focusing on her pathology only made Stuart feel more helpless. If clients could redefine their reality, then so could he reconceptualize the nature of their conditions in such a way that both he and others felt more empowered. "What I had to do was be aware of the impact of the past," Stuart explained, "but also co-create with her a very different present and future. The focus was always on what comes next. And this is a cognitive rather than a feeling phenomenon. Mandy would come to therapy in order to move from emotion, which had been her dominant process, to cognition, which was her towering strength. But at the time she didn't know it."

■ ■ ■

Making a List

One reason why Stuart selected this case seems rather obvious—the intensity, length, and depth of this relationship, which lasted throughout most of his adult life. We find it interesting (although Stuart might disagree with this) that although he was helping his client to move away from her feelings into the realm of cognitions, it was his own strong emotional connection and attachment to this woman that made her so memorable and influential in his own life and theory development. Their attachment to one another was both mutual and enduring, even after three decades of not having seen one another. Stuart taught Mandy about relying on all her resources, not only to overcome the influences of the past, but also the disabilities of the present. Mandy taught Stuart about the power of relationship and the courage that is possible when someone resolves to survive.

Dick Stuart likes a sense of order. And he likes to make lists. So when we asked him what else he did in this case that best represents the ways he is generally helpful to others, he presented us with several main points.

1. He resisted the usual habit of using diagnosis to chart Mandy's psychopathology and instead looked at her as a person with both resources and limitations.
2. He focused on her strengths rather than her weaknesses.
3. He helped her to develop additional resources to compensate for what she might have been missing.
4. He normalized her experience. He helped her to feel that the ways she was responding to such a horrendous situation were appropriate and understandable.

5. He demystified the complexity of her experience. He helped her to understand and find meaning in what she was living.
6. He helped Mandy to clarify what she really wanted most (to feel more control; to cope better with her disease; a more loving relationship; a career in music).
7. He negotiated with her to formulate achievable goals. He stresses that these should be the client's goals, not the therapist's objectives.
8. He put his client ahead of his theory. In other words, he abandoned and altered his theory to fit the needs of someone who didn't fit his current conceptual paradigm. This is what allowed him to evolve his ideas to help others.
9. He taught pragmatic problem solving. As with the case of Roy mentioned earlier, Stuart taught Mandy ways to cope with a situation that had seemed intolerable.
10. He used a collaborative relationship as the context for modeling solutions.
11. His most important principle of all was the importance of remaining optimistic and planting hope for the future.

Stuart summarized these ideas by pointing out his belief that people don't come to therapy to be understood.

"They don't?"

"No," he said. "They generally come to therapy because they want to have rationalizations for continuing to do what they have always done but have different outcomes."

That is what he means when Stuart talks about teaching people alternative ways of solving their problems. Mandy had felt overwhelmed when she first came to see him. "If I had been Mandy," Stuart said, "I would have just given up 30 years ago. I am so in awe of her ability to adjust to everything she had to face. It really surprises and delights me when people allow me to help them master challenges. That is the exciting part of doing therapy. It almost makes working with managed care worth it."

19 Treating the Trauma of Alien Abduction

A Case from John Krumboltz

John Krumboltz has been instrumental in the promotion of Learning Theory and Behavioral Counseling, as well as developing one of the major theories of career decision making. Throughout his distinguished career as Professor of Education at Stanford University he has stressed the potential of changing one's thinking and behavior.

Krumboltz believes that his theoretical orientation originated from growing up in a small town in Iowa, where practical, useful results were valued. His father used to say, "If it don't make the corn grow taller, or the pigs grow fatter, it ain't worth a damn."

Krumboltz has written a number of influential books, including Planned Happenstance, Behavioral Counseling: Cases and Techniques, Counseling Methods, Changing Children's Behavior, *and* Assessment in Career Development.

Disturbing Memories

Bill was a pretty ordinary guy, early thirties, married, with several young children. He seemed more nervous than usual when presenting the problem he wanted help with. John Krumboltz was curious about why that might be so, but decided to be patient and let Bill tell his story in his own way.

With a number of starts and stops, plus awkward silences, Bill eventually confessed that he was having some disturbing memories.

"Disturbing memories?" Krumboltz asked. "What sort of memories are you talking about?"

"Well, the kind that are really bothering me. I can't seem to concentrate on anything else. They just seem to be getting worse and worse."

"I can see that you are indeed quite upset, but I'm still wondering what kind of memories you are having."

"Well," Bill said hesitantly, "I know you are going to think this is pretty crazy, but I was once abducted by aliens." As he said this, he looked down, although Krumboltz could see that his eyes were studying him carefully for his reaction.

"Actually," Krumboltz said, "I don't think that is crazy at all. Why don't you tell me more about it?"

What Bill did not know at the time was that John Krumboltz, although known as a distinguished scientist and theoretician, was also very open-minded and "agnostic" when it came to looking at any unexplained phenomenon. He was not inclined to reject, out of hand, anyone's experience as "crazy" without examining the evidence for himself. So when he told Bill that he didn't think his report of being abducted was completely out of the realm of possibility, he was not being disingenuous.

Bill reported that he had been abducted by aliens two different times in his life, once when he was about 6 years old and a second time when he was 14. Some of the details were sketchy about what happened and how it all took place.

Krumboltz decided to treat the case as if it were posttraumatic stress. In many ways, Bill seemed like a war veteran who had been through brutal combat. He showed many of the same symptoms as a shell-shocked soldier. Most of all, he was paralyzed by fear.

"There's only one way for us to work with that fear," Krumboltz explained, "in that you have to face it directly while you are safe. In that way you learn from your own experience that there is no longer anything to fear."

"I guess I'd be willing to do that—I'd be willing to do *anything*," Bill said. "I just don't know how to go about it. I can't remember much of what happened. I just have the foggiest images."

"We could try hypnosis," Krumboltz offered.

As one of the originators of behavior therapy, Krumboltz had long worked with desensitizing people to fearful stimuli. Yet in order to help Bill face his haunting images, he would have to be put in a relaxed enough state that he would not shut down.

"I *might* be willing to try something like that," Bill said with real reluctance. It was clear that he was really saying he would rather not.

"I don't want to pressure you do anything you don't want to do," Krumboltz explained. "Hypnosis is often misunderstood. It is not a state where you relinquish control. Instead it is a cooperative arrangement in which we both work together to help you feel more relaxed and comfortable."

"I see," Bill responded.

"And it may very well help you to remember things."

The Trance

Bill was actually quite a responsive subject to hypnosis, and he went deep into a trance. Krumboltz was both amazed, and a little concerned, by just how intensely Bill seemed to be reliving his reported experience. Manifesting all the behavioral cues that are associated with a trance state, Bill spoke aloud about what he was experiencing.

"I'm afraid . . . Can't look back . . . My heart is beating so hard . . . I can't move . . . Can't hide . . . I know someone is there . . . But I can't move."

Krumboltz noted that Bill's feet were shuffling and his eyes were moving back and forth, almost as if he was trying to escape the chair he was sitting in.

"Want to run . . . Need to move . . . Can't run . . . Getting darker . . . I'm holding onto a tree . . . But something is pulling me . . . From behind . . . Can't hold on . . . Losing my grip."

Bill opened his mouth further as if he were going to scream, but then abruptly closed it and tightened his fists.

"Can't scream . . . Can't talk. . . ." As he said this, his head fell forward.

"I hear someone walking, coming closer . . . Not a dog . . . They are all around me . . . I see feet . . . Dark feet . . . No shoes . . . Nothing on the feet . . . I see knees . . . I'm afraid . . . Afraid to look higher."

"Just relax," Krumboltz reassured him. "Just stay calm. You are not alone. I am with you. Take a deep breath and continue. Just let yourself remember. I will make sure nothing bad happens to you."

Slight nod of acknowledgement, then the stream of consciousness continued. "Feet are gray . . . Black, thick hair . . . Not human . . . A hand touching my shoulder . . . Another touching my chin . . . I don't want to see . . . Close my eyes." As he said this, his eyes squeezed tighter.

"Cold hands on my face . . . They are opening my eyes . . . See a dark face . . . Not as tall as me . . . Wearing a hood . . . His hands are like the paw of a dog . . . They are making noises . . . Holding me down . . . Squeezing my arms and touching my back . . . Touching my chest . . . All of them touching me."

Bill's voice was becoming more and more alarmed and high-pitched. His body was starting to shake and Krumboltz wondered if he should let Bill continue. He looked nervously toward the door because Bill's screams had become so loud they could be heard in the outer office.

"They are unbuttoning my shirt . . . Taking off my shirt . . . Put their fingers in my ears and mouth . . . Pulling my tongue out . . . Can't bite . . . Touching my chest and pinching my nipples . . . Now they are unbuttoning my pants . . . Pulling off my pants . . . Then my underpants . . . Can't fight . . . They are touching me all over . . . Making strange sounds . . . One of them touches me between the legs . . . Stop . . . Please stop . . . But they don't . . . They put powder in my face."

Bill started to cough and had trouble catching his breath, which was becoming more labored.

"Can't move . . . Touching me . . . They put a tube on my part down there . . . Feel suction . . . I don't want this . . . What are you doing? . . . Why are you doing this to me? . . . Say they won't kill me . . . They want my life essence . . . Just my essence."

Eventually, in this halting narrative, Bill described himself on the ground again. He walked home and was surprised that nobody noticed that he had even left. Nobody asked him where he'd been or what happened to him. And ever since he was 14, he'd never told anyone about this story for fear they would think he was crazy.

"You aren't crazy," Krumboltz reassured Bill after he awakened from the trance. "You must know that you aren't the only one who has had an experience like this. It could very well have been a real experience and not something from your imagination. I am familiar with the literature on this subject and there are many, many documented cases similar to yours. You are not losing your mind. You have experienced a very rare event. You can think of yourself as being privileged for having had an experience that very few people in the world have ever had."

Facing Fears

We interrupted the narrative at this point to ask John to what extent he believed what he had told Bill. It had seemed to us that some alternative hypothesis might be more viable—for instance, that Bill had been sexually abused as a child and had created this fantasy as a way to live with the experience. We were also concerned that John Krumboltz, one of the living legends of our field, might be seen as a little strange for confessing that he believes in alien abductions.

"I suppose you guys are entitled to think I'm cuckoo for believing my client, but I have to tell you, I've been studying this phenomenon for many years. You may think this sounds crazy, and I used to be rather skeptical as well, but I had some experiences when I was in the Air Force that convinced me otherwise. A few times I actually sighted some UFOs that were confirmed by a witness. Now, I am not sure what to make of these things, but it did teach me to be open to what people report, whether it happened the way they said it did or not."

Ever since then, Krumboltz has made a systematic study of UFO-related phenomena. As a scientist and behaviorist, he has been interested in applying the same level of objectivity and skepticism that he has used to examine any other subject. That is why he came to this relationship with an open mind rather than making immediate judgments that his client was delusional.

Throughout their 8 hours of sessions together, Krumboltz and Bill had decided to record their sessions together. Krumboltz invited his client to take the tapes home and listen to them, maybe bringing back other memories, but also providing a record of their conversations.

About a month later, Krumboltz received the following letter:

Dear John,

Enclosed here please find the cassette tapes of our interviews. Thank you so much for spending so much of your valuable time with me. I really appreciate the help you gave me in dealing with the serious and frustrating issues of my encounters. Since most people consider encounters, or even sightings of UFOs or their beings, to be nonsense and fabrication, it was great to find someone like you who is open-minded enough to consider the possibility of such an event.

Our world is very small compared to what is out there in our universe. I have always believed that it is extremely simple-minded and arrogant to assume that we are alone in this great universe. I am one of the few who knows, without a doubt, that we are not alone but we share our skies with many different and intelligent beings. Some of these beings are nearby, and others travel from far away galaxies.

Although I know, as a member of our planet Earth, our understanding and technology is extremely limited and only a particle of that which our visitors possess. But with all of their superior intelligence and advancement, some of these beings are malicious in intent. Even so, they can have no power over us except that which we yield to them from our own fear. Thank you for helping me to understand that power is knowledge and fear is the absence of knowledge. It is only our fear that gives any adversary power over us. Thanks again.

Bill

■　■　■

Why This Case?

We wondered why John Krumboltz selected this case as the one to share as his finest hour. As a preeminent career development theorist, behavior therapist, and Stanford scholar, this was probably the last sort of thing we imagined he would disclose. We figured he might tell us that the case was seminal in developing his influential ideas, or one that solidified his thinking as a behaviorist.

Krumboltz was particularly proud of this case for several reasons. First of all, the client was a man with life-long fears that had developed in childhood. After spending a mere 8 hours together, the symptoms had vanished. Second, Krumboltz likes the way it shows how important it is to validate a client's experience. "He was just an ordinary guy who had a very, very unusual experience."

"John," we asked him, "for therapists whose last connection with you was 10 or 20 years ago when they were students who studied your theory of career development, or behavior therapy, how does this case represent your way of working with people?"

"Here was a client who wanted to overcome his fear of disturbing memories. I was using a very standard behavioral technique of desensitization. The way I explained it to him was that the way to overcome a fear is to experience that fear, but in safe circumstances. So I created an environment that was safe and comfortable so that Bill would be willing to relive what he had experienced long ago. This is classical conditioning. We paired old fear responses with an experience of relaxation and safety. It's just that the content was very unusual."

Krumboltz went on to elaborate how, in using desensitization methods, the intent is to help people overcome their fears. "If a people are afraid of heights, for example, you can get them gradually to experience increasing levels of height, and gradually expose them to the stimulus that they fear. But with something like an alien abduction, there is no way to reproduce it in reality. It can only be reproduced through imagination or through memory."

Krumboltz has found that most fears, even those that appear to be irrational, are grounded in something that has happened in reality. It may not even be necessary to know what the original source of the fear was, but it is important to recognize that the fears are real. So in one sense, it doesn't matter if Bill was really abducted by aliens or not. Krumboltz believed in him, and accepted his reported experience as real. Bill felt understood and accepted and validated. That helped him to feel safe enough to deal with the fears he had been avoiding his whole life.

20 Killing Herself Slowly

A Case from William Doherty

William Doherty developed an approach to family therapy that encompasses the larger community to which clients belong. He has sought to expand the bounds of traditional therapy to include the areas of medical illness, morality, and citizenship.

Doherty serves as Professor and Director of the Marriage and Family Therapy Program at the University of Minnesota. He is also Past President of the National Council on Family Relations and Co-Chair of the Collaborative Family and Healthcare Coalition. Doherty has written a number of best-selling books, in-cluding Take Back Your Marriage, Take Back Your Kids, The Intentional Family, *and* Soul Searching: Why Psychother-apy Must Promote Moral Responsibility.

A Terrible Prognosis

Lynn had a host of medical problems, mostly related to her diabetes. She had been hospitalized several times because of complications related to her refusal to take her insulin doses. Her physicians were frustrated and at a loss as to what to do with their patient: Lynn knew what she needed to do to take care of herself, but she simply refused to comply with the medical plan. Given her obesity and lack of self-care, her prognosis was terrible; at age 29, it was highly likely that some of her major body systems would soon begin to fail.

Bill Doherty was known in the community as a specialist in working with chronic illnesses, especially noncompliant patients and their families. Since individual therapy had already proven unsuccessful, a referral was made as a last-ditch effort to save this woman's failing health, if not her life.

Guilty as Charged

When Lynn first called for an appointment, she readily admitted to all the charges leveled by her medical consultants. "It's true," she said. "Totally true. I don't take my insulin like I should. I don't do what the doctors tell me to do."

"What's that about?" Doherty asked. He didn't want to get into much on the phone, but he was intrigued that Lynn made no effort to make excuses or deflect blame.

"Well," she said directly, "I know I need to lose weight. And I'm supposed to be taking some medications. But . . . I don't know . . . I just. . . ." Her words trailed off, as if she didn't have the energy to explain. Or maybe she just didn't know why she wasn't cooperating with what her doctors and family wanted.

Although Lynn was not living at home, she saw her family frequently, which gave Doherty the opening to ask to meet with her and her mother and stepfather. He had already gotten some basic family history from the referring individual therapist and learned that Lynn's father had died in a farm accident when she was an infant. That left her mother with a 2-year-old, plus two other children, and no viable means of support. Within the year, the mother was remarried—to her husband's brother. He took over the responsibilities of running the farm, plus helping to raise his brother's three children and later one of their own.

In their first phone conversation, Lynn confessed to Doherty that she didn't like her stepfather much. She resented his intrusion into their lives and never felt that he was part of the family. "Don's always criticizing me," she told him. "It's always that I'm too fat, or I'm lazy, or some damn thing or another."

It was not long into their first meeting that Don himself confirmed this exact assessment: "Lynn could be a good-looking woman," Don said, "but she don't take care of herself." He went on to cite all the ways she was irresponsible, most of all her refusal to take her medication. "She's making herself sick and she's not doing a thing to help herself!"

Don seemed to be the antithesis of his stepdaughter. If Lynn was irresponsible, he was the model of dependability. He let it be known right away that he was taking care of everyone in the family and that he was disappointed that Lynn refused to do her share. He just couldn't understand how she could let herself go like that. "I'm a farmer," he said. "I work hard. And I don't have time for this psychological talk."

Lynn alternated between scowling expressions as her stepfather spoke and also a certain amount of shame. "Some of what he says might be true," she admitted, "but still, he's so critical all the time. He's always telling me what a disappointment I am. Whatever I do, I can't ever please him."

"And what about your mother?" Doherty asked, looking over toward Karen, who, until then, had been sitting quietly.

"We're close," Lynn admitted. "But she nags me all the time too. She's always . . . ."

"Honey," Karen interrupted, "you know we only want to help you. We're just worried about you, is all. You're going to die if this keeps up, and you know it. It's like you're trying to kill yourself or something."

Worried indeed. Lynn weighed well over 300 pounds. She was still gaining weight rather than losing it, and this is what had made her type II diabetes even worse. Still, she denied that she was trying to hurt herself. Instead, she mentioned how tired she was having everyone nag her all the time about her weight, about taking her insulin, and complying with her other medical requirements.

While Lynn and Karen went back and forth with one another, Don sat rather passively, staring straight ahead, occasionally glancing at his wife. When pressed, all he could offer was that he was just disappointed in his daughter and just didn't know what else to do.

A Family Problem

Although Lynn was living on her own, her mother was very involved in her life. They called her frequently, Karen asking Lynn whether she had taken her insulin (usually the answer was no). Sometimes Lynn did say that she had taken her scheduled dose, but more often than not, this was a lie. Karen was frustrated, and Lynn was dependent and resentful.

"So," Doherty wondered, "what is it that you'd like from your mother instead of her calling to question you about your insulin?"

Lynn nodded. "I just want her to trust me again."

Doherty replied, "As your mother, I don't think she is going be able to trust you if you are not taking care of yourself. What do you want from your stepfather?"

"I want to get along with him better and for him to stop being so critical."

"Again, that's a worthy goal, but a hard one to achieve while you are hurting yourself physically. But we can work on it."

It wasn't clear yet what Don wanted, except to feel less disappointed and frustrated, and for Lynn to become more responsible. It was very clear that while he was willing to come in and talk about things, he didn't place much stock in the value of therapy. He was a hard-working farmer, a man of the earth, who had always tried to do the right thing. He had stepped in to save his brother's family because it felt like the thing for him to do, but he didn't feel like he'd earned much appreciation for his efforts.

"I can't guarantee that I'll be able to come to these things every time," Don said as the session came to a close. "Spring planting is coming up and I'll need to be out in the fields if the weather is right."

Doherty indicated that he understood that reality. Since his wife's family were farmers, he well understood not only the culture of this area, but also the demands placed on people by the weather conditions. He couldn't tell if Lynn and Karen were relieved or disappointed that he might not be joining them regularly.

"I do have one question for you, Don," Doherty mentioned in closing.

"What's that?"

"I'm wondering if you are willing to hang in there in order to help your daughter?"

"Well, 'course I would."

"I hear that you're disappointed in her," Doherty pressed, "but I want to make sure that you will give the time to work this out."

Don gave his word.

Doherty surveyed them one more time. He realized this was a life-threatening situation. Lynn might very well die if she didn't change her ways, and do it rather quickly. Doherty was also concerned about the prognosis because Lynn had already seen quite a few other therapists but had never really stuck with any of them for very long. She'd become frustrated, or impatient, or feel picked on, and then quit.

Doherty emphasized that he didn't see Lynn's weight and diabetes problems as being hers alone. He saw these issues as embedded in their relationships with one another. Mom would continually pester her daughter about her medication, and this only made Lynn more stubborn. Dad would criticize Lynn some more, and this created a circular reaction that was even more obstructive. Somehow, Doherty had to break this cycle.

Some Parting Instructions

"I have something for you to do, Karen," Doherty said.

"Anything. I'll do anything to help Lynn. You know that. She knows that too." As she said this she looked over at her daughter.

"That's good," Doherty said, "but what I'm going to ask you to do is going to be really difficult for you. I know you want to help so I'm sure that even though this is going to be hard for you, you'll do your best."

Karen nodded, not sure what she was agreeing to.

"This is very, very important," Doherty said. "I want you to promise that this week, before you come back here, that you agree not to ask Lynn about her insulin or her diet." As he said this, he looked over at Lynn and saw her grinning.

"I'm serious about this. I don't want you to ask her one time if she's taking her medicine. Can you do that?"

Karen nodded, but not with a lot of confidence.

"You don't look sure that you can do this," Doherty pressed further.

"No," she said, "I can do this. If you think this is important." She was making it clear that she thought this was pretty stupid but she'd give it a try. By now she'd tried everything else.

"And you, Don, I'd like you to agree not to ask her about her diet, or her weight. Are you willing to do that?"

Don shrugged indifferently.

"May I take that as a yes?"

"Ayah," he agreed.

"Good, you see, you know your daughter is overweight. She knows she's overweight. She doesn't need you to point that out anymore. When you bring this up, it only makes things worse. She knows you are both worried about her but there are other ways to express this, and other ways to be helpful to her. She's got to sort this out in her own way. Am I right, Lynn?"

She nodded, clearly delighted that someone was getting her parents off her back. She was a grown woman, nearly 30 years old for God's sake, and felt she didn't need to be treated like a child.

"Lynn," Doherty said, "you are still struggling to make a place for diabetes in your life. This is something that you came down with a couple years ago and it is a real pain. It requires you to be monitoring your blood sugar, which you haven't been doing regularly, and giving yourself shots, which is a pain. I think you are still struggling with how to make a place for this in your life. When you are fighting your parents, you don't get a chance to figure out how you want to deal with this disease in your life."

Lynn looked at Doherty suspiciously, waiting for the other shoe to fall. She was expecting the usual scolding, but this time from him instead of her parents. But that is exactly what Doherty decided *not* to do.

"There was this power struggle going on," he explained. "She had been involved in this struggle with everyone—her parents, her doctors, her previous therapists. There was no way I was going to get sucked into it. So, I didn't ask her why she was not taking her insulin; I just accepted the fact that this was the way that things were. I framed it that she had not yet made a decision about making a place for diabetes in her life."

Family Secrets

Lynn and her mother returned for the next session without Don. They explained that he was working in the bean fields, since the harvest had begun. Although he was by no means highly motivated to return, they all understood that in this case he had little choice.

During their check-in, both Lynn and Karen reported they had liked the first session. Somehow, Karen had managed to avoid nagging her daughter and had chosen not to remind her to take her medication a single time.

"And what did you think of that?" Doherty asked Lynn.

"I liked it," she said casually.

One thing Doherty did not do was ask her if she had taken her insulin; she volunteered that she had, although only one time when she happened to be at home with her parents. "But I've been taking all my other medicines, my blood pressure pills, my cholesterol pills, and my antidepressants."

"That's curious, don't you think?" Doherty observed.

"How do you mean?" Lynn said.

"Well, you're taking all these other medications but not the insulin that you need the most."

"I guess it's how I'm hurting myself."

"But why are you doing this?" her mother interrupted. She was furious and upset. "Do you know how much I love you? Don't you know how much I worry about you? Why are you doing this to yourself? Why are you doing this to *me*?"

"Before I answer that question," Lynn said defiantly to Karen, "I have a question for you."

"What's that?"

"I want you to tell me about my daddy and why you married my uncle. I want you to tell me about your marriage to my father."

Wow, Doherty thought to himself, *this* was a Shakespearean moment. The timing of this was incredible. The daughter says, "I am not taking my insulin because I want to hurt myself." Her mother blows up. The daughter comes back with, "I want to know about my father. I want to know why you married his brother, this guy who has never accepted me."

"Where did this come from?" Karen said to Lynn with a bewildered expression.

"Everything that I have heard about my father is that he was so different from my uncle. You married Don after one year. One year after daddy died. We have never talked about it. I don't know anything. I can't start taking care of myself until I know about this."

Doherty was holding his breath. He couldn't believe the power of what had just taken place. He looked over and saw that Karen was weeping. "I've had a lot of hardships in my life," she said through her tears. "There've been a lot of losses. I've tried to just put them behind me and move on. You should do the same."

Before Lynn could respond, Doherty intervened. "How do you feel about what your daughter just asked you to do?"

She shook her head. "I . . . I've tried to put all that behind me. I can't open that all up again. I just can't."

This was the moment of truth. "I hadn't read about this in any of the books," Doherty recalled. "This had never come up in my supervision as a student or in case consultations. Now Lynn, who was slowly killing herself, was pursuing her mother who was running away. Somehow, I had to bring them together. One of the things that has characterized my therapy is a sense of what the moral issues are, what is fair and just. It was time to make a proposal."

Doherty said to Lynn that he didn't think it was fair for her to ask her mother to take this big risk, to open herself up to such pain and vulnerability, if she was not willing to take care of herself. "If you are so unstable medically that you can't be present emotionally, then I don't know how you could ever handle what your mother would tell you, how you would take it in and make sense of it." There it was, the challenge, the critical moment. Yet it was a fair and reasonable request.

Until this point, Doherty had been using remarkable restraint in not applying any pressure on Lynn to comply with her treatment. "I don't go after something where I have no leverage. I didn't have that much of a relationship yet, even the kind of relationship that her individual therapist had with her. Why would she start taking her insulin for me? But now here was something that she was asking for from her mother."

"So," Doherty said to them both, "here's the deal. Karen, you would have to answer all of Lynn's questions if she would agree to start taking care of herself in such a way that she could be mentally and physically ready to handle the answers. You both have to decide if you are prepared to do this."

"I'll do it," Karen said without hesitation.

"Me too," Lynn answered after some reflection.

Doherty had no idea if they would follow through on this, but it seemed worth a chance.

Restraint

Again, Lynn and Karen returned without Don, since he was still working in the fields. Doherty was concerned about this because Don would have now missed two sessions in a row.

Karen reported that she had found it easier to not ask Lynn about her diabetes. Doherty found this to be a good example of what can happen in families when they become less enmeshed.

"I appreciate you not nagging me so much," Lynn said.

"You mean, not at all," Karen teased.

"Yeah, not at all. But I don't know. . . ."

"What?" Doherty prompted Lynn.

"Well, it's just that I don't feel like we're as close."

"That's part of having better boundaries between you. Some of your closeness was related to these arguments that you were having about your diabetes. When you are not talking about that for a little while, you wonder what is holding things together."

Lynn said this made sense to her. She also added, quite casually, that she had begun taking her insulin every day. She admitted she was feeling much better.

Of course Doherty was dying to jump on that, but he restrained himself. "One of the ways I stay out of control struggles is not just by not hounding people to take control of their health. I also don't jump out of my chair the first time they say they are taking care of themselves, because it suggests to them that I was holding back all this time."

So Doherty nodded mildly in response to Lynn's report, as if he expected this all along. "So then, where are you now with questions you want to ask your mom about your father?"

"I've been thinking about that," Lynn answered. "I don't need for her to talk about this anymore because I know how hard it is for her. I think I understand why she hasn't wanted to bring this up."

Doherty nodded. He was amazed at how she was willing to let her mother off the hook in such a beautiful way. She knew this was painful for Karen, and she didn't want her mother to have to dredge up the difficult past.

But now Karen wanted to talk. She told Lynn about her father, what a wonderful man he was. He had been a caring husband and father. Then one day she got a call from a neighbor saying that there had been an accident. She dropped everything and ran out to the field, where the tractor had stopped at an odd angle, her husband's body crushed and mangled.

Karen had been a young woman at the time. But now she was a widow, with three small children, and a farm that she knew nothing about. She had no idea how she would support her family. And then Don came along, her husband's bachelor brother, and a farmer himself. He offered to pitch in and help out.

Don was a good man, and a hard-working man, and a responsible man, but in some ways a cold man. He was willing to take Karen and three small children under his wing, and this would keep the family together. They could keep the farm. They could stay connected with the larger family. So she married him.

All throughout the narrative, both Lynn and Doherty sat perfectly still. "I sat there with red eyes," Doherty recalled, "like I was part of this religious moment. My job was just to not get in the way. I asked no questions. I made no reflective comments. I did no paraphrasing. It was all just so out there beautifully that I just bore witness to it."

Finally, reluctantly, Doherty brought the session to an end. Just as he proposed a time for the next session, Lynn interrupted.

"You know," she said, "I just wanted to say that I've been feeling less depressed lately. And I told you I've been taking my insulin, maybe not every day, but most days. I'm starting to think I might handle this diabetes okay, maybe not perfectly, but a lot better than I have been." She looked meaningfully at her mother, who reached over and hugged her. They both had tears in their eyes.

It Took Some Work

Don returned for the next session. Doherty was glad to have him back on board and still excited about the glow from their previous meeting. But he was surprised to find Don extremely angry. "I don't want to be here," he said, red-faced, working himself up. "I got better things to do than drive all the way here. We still got things to do at the farm."

This was not the follow-up session that Doherty had in mind. He did something that he does not normally do and asked Karen and Lynn to leave the room so he could talk to Don alone. He was afraid that Don was about to explode and start ripping into Lynn again.

Once the two women left, Don, with considerable relief, just poured out his anger and resentments. "I've never been part of this damn family," he said. "I've lived in the shadow of my brother for 25 years. I took on his farm. I took on the financial support of his family. But I don't get any support myself."

"Your brother must have been very important for you to have done this."

Don nodded and averted his head. All his anger seemed to turn to grief. Now he talked about his brother with such love and affection, how he had always looked up to him, admired him, respected him, even worshipped him. And then his beloved brother was struck down, leaving Don to pick up the pieces but never to feel adequate to the task. He had saved his brother's family but never gotten inside it. Again Doherty was struck by the Shakespearean-like drama of this man's life.

"Look," Doherty said to him carefully, "I think I have an idea to help you get into this family. I really believe that Lynn wants you to be her father and I know that Karen wants you to be her husband. You have a solid partnership that can become stronger."

"I'm all for that," Don agreed.

"It's not going to be easy," Doherty warned.

Don gave him a look that seemed to say: "Do you think I'm the kind of guy who's afraid of a little work?"

"Okay then," Doherty began, "you are going to have to learn to be less negative and more positive towards your daughter, because that is the biggest thing that is keeping your wife distant. You are a hard-working man. This is what you have centered your life around, and from everything I hear, you do a great job. This is the way you look at the world and so when you don't see Lynn working hard enough on things in her life, you come across as very disapproving. She backs away from you and your wife feels protective of her daughter."

Don nodded as if this made sense to him. Although he claimed not to trust this "psychological" stuff, he did seem to grasp the main ideas and take them in.

"So," Doherty continued, "if you want to join this family more fully, you are going to have to change. I can help you with that if you're willing."

"Yessir," Don answered solemnly. "But you gotta understand that I can't come all the way over here like this. I've got fields to tend and work to do."

In other words, Don would work on this, but he was not willing to come to more sessions. This would be it.

Doherty nodded his own understanding of their deal and then went out to retrieve Lynn and Karen. In the ensuing conversation, he facilitated a deeper conversation between all three of them, inviting Lynn to engage her father. In turn, Don admitted that he very much wanted better relationships with each of them.

"Well," Lynn responded, "I don't think we have the kind of relationship right now where I'd go over to the house just to see you, but I'd be willing to call you. I know that you care about me and you want to help."

This was a huge concession on Lynn's part, to give her stepfather the benefit of the doubt and acknowledge all the sacrifices he'd made on her behalf. He also agreed to back off and give Lynn the space she needed. He admitted that he'd been far too critical.

Each of the three of them further contracted to make some adjustments in their behavior. It wasn't the specifics that mattered as much as their commitment to make improvements. They decided that this would be their last family therapy session.

Doherty received a phone call from Lynn a couple of months later. She reported that Don had given her a wonderful birthday present with an attached note that said: I hope the next 30 years are better than the first 30 for us." That seemed to be another turning point for Lynn, who finally felt ready to make Don her real father. It seemed almost an afterthought for Lynn to confirm that, yes, she was taking her insulin and other medications according to the doctors' orders. She was working in a new job and feeling much healthier. She'd even managed to lose some weight. (Her individual therapist confirmed these changes in a phone conversation with Doherty.) Lynn said she had hoped that there could have been more family therapy sessions but was surprised and delighted at what had transpired.

Doherty finds this case illustrative of the power of working with a family together. Nobody had tried to put them all in the same room and help them deal with their feelings toward one another. Nobody had looked at Lynn's problems in the context of her relationships. "I try to extend my orbit of care," Doherty summarized, "to each member, not just using them as adjuncts for treating the identified patient. I also believe there is a moral domain in families where each member is indebted to one another. I thought that Lynn was owed the story of her father. Lynn, in turn, owed her parents the intention to remain healthy."

21 Thinking Out Loud

A Case from Gordon Wheeler

Gordon Wheeler is a senior faculty member of the Gestalt Institute of Cleveland, as well as Director of Gestalt Press. He also works as a consultant, clinician, and trainer in private practice.

Wheeler has written over a dozen books and numerous articles in the field, most of them drawing on the Gestalt model to integrate a range of new approaches for understanding human experience. He seeks to articulate a postmodern vision of self and relationship. His most recent works include Beyond Individualism: Toward a New Understanding of Self, Relationship and Experience, The Voice of Shame: Silence and Connection in Psychotherapy, *and* The Heart of Development: Gestalt Approaches to Working with Children, Adolescents, and their Worlds.

The Resources Within

Joe had been in therapy with Wheeler for almost 14 years, most of that time in weekly sessions, but the latter years structured as occasional phone consultations.

"Fourteen years?" we asked him.

"Long-term therapy all depends on the client's ultimate goals," he explained. "Some people need an ongoing developmental resting place that may not exist elsewhere in their lives. Indeed, we have all seen clients in this type of lengthy relationship that spans decades, if not a lifetime. This may be because of the severity of the presenting problems, but most often it is because some clients either want (or need) regular contact with a professional who supports and challenges them in ways that would not otherwise be possible."

While Wheeler organized his thoughts, each of us thought about our own long-term cases, individuals we have seen over a period of many years.

It seems amazing to consider that we have spent more time in intimate engagement with them than we have with some of our own friends.

As is so often the case, Joe's core issues remained relatively consistent over the years even as he made progress on a number of fronts. If you think about it, Wheeler pointed out, there is no real reason why these developmental imprints should fundamentally change, since they are part of our very being. The goal instead is to help people to carry the issues within them in such a way that they become resources rather than liabilities and chronic injuries.

Flawed Merchandise

Joe was a gay man in his mid-forties who struggled constantly with a need to be liked and accepted by others. This severely limited the risks he was willing to take in relationships, because he was so terrified of rejection.

Over the course of the first few years they worked together, Wheeler witnessed Joe attempting to deal with his issues, but in a steadily widening scope of living. He particularly made progress in his professional life, learning to take small but incremental steps toward risk taking that were paying off for him in other areas of his life as well.

It was during their sixth year working together that Joe came in one day feeling particularly discouraged. He had just taken on new responsibilities at work and things were not going well at all; his worst nightmare was unfolding in that he was being told that his performance was not up to par. Just as he did in other situations throughout life when he received criticism, Joe overreacted in a rather controlling and defensive way. Not surprisingly, this only exacerbated the situation.

"I'm just not getting any better," Joe complained. His voice was tired, strained, and discouraged. "I think we're just wasting our time. I think this whole thing has been a waste of time."

"A waste of time?" Wheeler prompted.

"Yeah. I mean, what's the use? It's the same old song over and over and over again. I'm sick of it. I'm sick of myself."

"It has got to be frustrating for you when. . . ."

"Frustrating? You gotta be kidding? It's goddamn exasperating! We've been over this same crap three years. Maybe it was four years ago. Hell, it could have been five years ago. It's the same stuff we've been talking about for years. And I'm just tired of it. Nothing seems to make any difference." As he finished the tirade, it was almost as if his store of energy suddenly ran out. His shoulders dropped and his whole body seemed to fold inward. His head dropped forward.

Wheeler did his best to reassure Joe, to recast the latest disappointment in a larger context in which it might be viewed as a temporary setback rather than a major crisis. All the while Gordon was attempting to soothe and comfort Joe, he couldn't help thinking that, in part, he agreed with him. Joe *was* dealing with the same things that he had been when he first came in. Still, there had been a lot of progress thus far, and Wheeler did his best to remind Joe of what they had accomplished already. "What I didn't do," Wheeler reflected, "was to pay attention then to what I myself was really feeling—the frustration and irritation I was pushing down—and then find a way to use *that*. Not say it necessarily, in so many words: *use* it. And as long as I didn't do that, as long as I wasn't fully aware of my own process, we kept turning in the same circles."

"I know everything you are saying is true," Joe picked up again right where he'd left off, "and I already thought of all these things you are telling me. The thing is—I just think there's something wrong with me. It's kind of just like I'm flawed merchandise. You know, like those shirts you see for sale at half off because they are discolored or have a hole in them."

"I know that's the way you feel right now," Wheeler said, still trying to get things on a more constructive track. "And it's certainly understandable that you would feel that way after what happened at work this week."

"But it's not just this week. Look Doc, I know you are trying to help me and all, but. . . ."

"But what?"

"But all your reassurances don't work with me. I just can't take them in. That's what I mean—there's just something wrong with me. Everything turns to crap."

Wheeler recognized that Joe was spiraling downward and felt unable to stop the self-destructive spin. He felt such despair and hopelessness he just couldn't imagine that there was anything that would make any kind of difference, at least over the long haul. He would always be discolored and have a hole in him.

Shared Responsibility

"At this point," Wheeler explained, "I tried to step back and remind myself that we were co-constructing a relational system here. I tried to reach for a useful hypothesis because if there is any use to theory it is something that you can reach for when things are not going well."

"What do you mean?" we asked him, intrigued by this statement.

"When your instincts are taking you down a productive path, you don't need to stop and plan every step. You would fall over your own feet. It's when you're feeling lost that you most need a compass. In this case, my theory reminded me that if Joe was locked in a masochistic spiral, there had to be some way I was joining him, from a sadistic position. In a different model, this might be called 'projective identification'—which still suggests that the dynamic is entirely driven by the client. I prefer to think of it in a sense more simply, and I believe more productively: whatever is happening, we're both constructing it, together."

"So you're saying, then, that it is when you are having a problem that you need a good theory to make sense of what is going on and reorient yourself?"

"Exactly," Wheeler agreed. It is during those times when he is feeling most stymied that he falls back on his favored theory of relational meaning, in which interactions are deconstructed to find their essential core. In this case, he could feel himself resonating with Joe's own hopelessness; they were both feeling helpless together—and yet somehow Joe was the one carrying the brunt of this feeling. Any feeling Wheeler himself might have, of frustration or diminished competence, wasn't "on the table." It seemed time to bring things into the here and now, just as any self-respecting Gestalt therapist would.

"What might you be feeling right now?" he asked Joe.

"You mean right now?"

"Yes. Right now." Wheeler knew Joe was stalling. After working together for so long, his client could hardly be surprised by the nudge to get in touch with his immediate experience in the present.

"Nothing," Joe finally replied after a long pause. "I'm not feeling anything at all."

"Nothing?"

"Look," Joe said. "Don't get me wrong. This doesn't have anything to do with you. It's just my problem. You've been so helpful to me all these years. But. . . ."

"But what?"

"It's just that things are getting even harder to deal with."

Ignoring the plea for a moment, Wheeler chose to push a little further. "Joe, I'm wondering what I might be doing to contribute to making this even more difficult for you."

"What do you mean?"

Wheeler just waited.

"I can't think of anything," Joe said finally. "I'm sorry, but there's nothing you've done." He paused, then added, "There's just nothing you can do for me."

Wheeler realized that he had asked Joe the wrong question. Instead of shifting attention to their relationship, his client was now taking even more responsibility for his plight, blaming himself in such a way that he felt even more despair. It was at this point that Wheeler decided to take things to the next level by attempting to share the burden more directly. After all, in any relationship that reaches an impasse, it is almost always an interactive effect in which both participants bear some responsibility for the difficulty.

"Let me tell you what I'm thinking right now," Wheeler began a new tack. He finds it very helpful to approach delicate situations in this way, sharing aloud his innermost thoughts and feelings as delicately yet honestly as he can. "Maybe you can help me to sort this out."

Joe laughed nervously. In his own disoriented state, he couldn't imagine that he could help anyone else achieve clarity, especially his therapist. But he chose to go along with where Wheeler was leading him.

"Let's push the replay button," Wheeler continued, "and let's look at the last few minutes of our conversation, when your feelings of hopelessness began to get worse."

Joe nodded.

"Okay then," Wheeler said. "You came in feeling discouraged. Would you say that is accurate?"

"Yes," he responded without hesitation.

"So far what I've been trying to do is figure out what that is like for you and, hopefully, talk you out of it. But then, just now, I've been thinking about what this is like for *me*."

Joe looked quizzical.

"What I mean," Wheeler explained, "is that for a moment I stopped thinking about you and started thinking about me. I started wondering what this means for me as a therapist, how this reflects on me as a professional. After all, you've been coming in here for years and now you say you aren't making any progress. It's like, what am I, chopped liver? It sure doesn't make me feel very competent."

Joe laughed awkwardly. "That's not what I meant," he started to protest, defending himself.

Wheeler held up his hand. "No, that's fine. I can accept that. Maybe you're right and you really haven't made any progress. That might be the case; it might not be so. You might even be feeling a little disappointed and angry at me right now. . . ."

"No, it's. . . ."

"But let's leave that aside for a moment," Wheeler said, keeping things on track. "Earlier, I was reassuring you that you really are making more progress than you say you are. But I think I was really talking to myself, not to you. I was reassuring myself. Do you know what I mean?"

Joe nodded uncertainly.

"What I'm saying is that I was telling myself that I'm not really such a bad therapist even if I have this client who says he is not making progress. Maybe I needed you to admit you were doing better than you said you were so I could feel better about myself. My own feelings of inadequacy were touched and stirred by what you were telling me. So, what I'm thinking to myself is that really both of us are struggling with the same thing. I've also been sitting over here in my chair, as if I'm okay, telling you to feel better. But really, I've been feeling much the same way that you are—doubting myself."

Through this use of immediacy, Wheeler was attempting to co-construct a different sort of experience than the feelings of failure that both of them were feeling. By acknowledging his own feelings, by sharing the burden of responsibility, he was hoping Joe would feel less alone, and less hopeless.

"So what I'm saying to you, Joe, is that it was my own shame, my own feelings of inadequacy, that led me to export and transfer these feelings onto you. You're taking all the blame on yourself, and I'm being reassuring, speaking from a safe, superior position. We're connected, we're triggering each other and mirroring each other, but you've been bearing the whole weight."

This time when Joe nodded, it was with complete comprehension. The whole session now seemed transformed.

■ ■ ■

The Relational Process

In his Gestalt/constructivist model, Wheeler sees the therapeutic relationship as continually evolving as both participants co-construct their relational world. "When things are not going well," he said, "we make some attempt to deconstruct what just happened. We may do that informally, or with a friend. We may get formal supervision or get into therapy to deal with the underlying issues."

Wheeler is quick to point out that we are not to use our clients' therapy hour to deal with our own issues, in the sense of explore and resolve them. Rather, what is often productive (as in the session with Joe) is to disclose those feelings, and at times the issues underlying them, when that disclosure can function as an intentional, strategic intervention designed to clarify a stuck place and break through an impasse.

In Joe's case, he was disoriented to the point where he could not sort out what was going on. Once Wheeler supplied the missing piece, which was his own covert process, his client was able to get back to the work of understanding himself. Joe was then able to deal with feelings that he had been keeping at a distance because they were so hard for him to tolerate. He also realized that he was not alone in these feelings of inadequacy, that even his therapist could resonate with similar issues.

"I was modeling for him how to do it. Finally, Joe was able to see a model of the relational process that he could use in his relationships with other people which don't always go that well. He developed the capacity to stop and say to himself, 'Wait a minute. What is going on here? Am I doing something at this moment that is getting sticky? Maybe we can put our heads together and figure out what it is.'"

This process of putting their heads together not only changes the client, but in this case, also had an impact on the therapist. Wheeler had been writing about shame for years, but it was at this moment with Joe that things seemed to come together in a new way. Since this session, Wheeler has been developing this approach further. He frequently takes reflective time with clients, asking out loud: "Let's stop a moment and see where we are. Let's back up and explore what each of us is doing in this interaction and how each of us contributed to what is going on." This is almost always useful to the client, Wheeler stresses, and also useful to the relational process.

Undressing the Authentic

Joe remained in therapy for another 5 years, during which time he experienced one triumph after another—as well as recurrent moments of frustration, depression, occasional panic. There were many other factors that contributed to his continued progress, some of them in therapy and others in his life, but Wheeler still believes that the session described above was a principal turning point. Soon after that conversation, Joe began to develop intimate relationships that had not previously been possible. He received a significant job promotion as a testimony to his newly found interpersonal sensitivity; this occurred largely as result of his own persistence after receiving several rejections. He also repaired a number of relationships with estranged family members. None of this came easily to him; in fact, every step was a struggle for him; Wheeler believes that Joe is probably still struggling, as very little has ever came easily to him.

As for Joe's therapist, Wheeler continued to apply lessons learned from their relationship that were not only instrumental in helping him develop his theoretical ideas but also his personal friendships. He found that the same kinds of intimacy risks he took with his clients were equally constructive with loved ones. He resolved to be more open and honest with others. And he became determined to "think out loud" as much as he could whenever he found some block in a relationship.

More and more, Wheeler began using the "self" in his work, relying on his own experiences of the moment. Rather than "dressing up" his experiences in more palatable form, he became accustomed to presenting his thoughts and feelings in their most authentic way. These "real" experiences are more conflicted, more complex, more hesitant, sometimes more unpleasant, but they are also more powerful.

"How do you know the difference between the authentic and dressed-up versions?" we asked.

"I could have said to Joe: 'I experience you very differently than the ways you portray yourself.' That would have been true, since I did not experience him as a failure the way he saw himself. But that was the dressed-up version of what I was really feeling, which was far more complicated—and personal."

"So then," we pressed, moving into the realm of the experiential in this very conversation, "how is what we are talking about right now a dressed, careful version? What would be the more raw and pure honest version of what you are experiencing right now?"

"Well," Wheeler said, amused and intrigued by the challenge, "I'm aware of a slightly mobilized tension to try to cover all this and do a good job and make it a good story. Make it interesting. But now that I say that to you it changes, and I'm not feeling that way."

"What, then?"

"It's like what I said earlier, that the times you most need theory is when you are stuck. You don't think about your experience until there is some problem or question. That is what happened with Joe—we negotiated during those times when we were struggling. He would be telling me about how he handles his boss or something and I would try not to give him advice but still share concerns without shaming him. Over the years we got to read one another pretty well. He'd see some look on my face and ask me what it meant. That became an invitation for me to be more confrontive with him, but in such a way that he wouldn't feel paralyzed."

"So, what could others learn from this case of your finest hour?"

"You can always open up your experience to the client. There is always a way to do it that is not about you, but is about serving the client's growth. When you have a dilemma about how to share something without shaming the client, try sharing those concerns. If you start with this hypothesis, that your experience in the here-and-now is a crucial component of what is going on and needs to be more transparent, it will lead the two of you somewhere new and interesting and empowering, for the client—and for the therapist."

22 Finding Love in the Right Direction

A Case from John Gray

John Gray is one of the best-known writers about human relationships. He is a columnist, lecturer, and author of many books, including the best-selling, Men Are from Mars, Women Are from Venus, *which has sold over 30 million copies in the last decade. John has written other books in the Mars and Venus series, including* Mars and Venus in the Workplace, Practical Miracles for Mars and Venus, Children Are from Heaven, Mars and Venus on a Date, Mars and Venus in the Bedroom, *and his most recent,* The Mars and Venus Exercise and Diet Book.

Gray has extensive training in the area of meditation as well as communication and relationships. The focus of his work is to help people understand the impact of gender differences on their relationships and to learn methods for providing greater intimacy with others.

The Person Inside

When Trina first appeared, Gray was struck by the slouch in her walk: this was a seriously depressed woman. She had once been attractive but was now grossly overweight. Once she introduced herself, the reason for her appearance quickly became apparent. She was indeed seriously depressed, so much so that Gray considered her a suicide risk.

It was just a few minutes into her story that Trina displayed significant despair and hopelessness. It was as if she was just going through the motions of seeking counseling but didn't really believe, in her heart, that anything could help much. She seemed filled with self-pity and consumed with a sense of herself as a victim.

"Tell me a bit about your family," Gray prompted. He wondered what could have possibly happened in this woman's life to make her so profoundly debilitated.

"I was the black sheep of the family, you could say," Trina said in a voice that could barely be heard.

"Black sheep?"

"Yeah. My older sister, Nadia, got all the attention. My mother didn't seem to like me much." Trina laughed as she said this, but it was a hollow sound filled with pain—even after all these years.

"You must feel pretty angry about that," Gray observed.

"What do you mean?"

"Well, just that your mother didn't seem to love you, nor give you much in the way of support."

"That's for sure," Trina mumbled, mostly to herself. "I felt bad about it when I was a kid. I still feel bad about it. I'll always feel bad about it."

"That sounds rather final," Gray said, then added, "and unfair."

"Yes," she agreed, "it was always unfair that Nadia got everything she ever wanted, all the attention, all the kudos, all the love, that she could ever want. But I wasn't good enough. Maybe if I was good enough I might have been loved." As she said this, it was apparent that she didn't imagine that this could ever be possible.

"Let's just assume that you really were good enough," Gray responded, "and your mother was incapable of giving you the love that you deserved."

When Trina looked quizzical, Gray explained: "Perhaps you were so much like your mother that it bothered her—she couldn't deal with you because she didn't like herself. And you've indicated that your sister was quite different. Perhaps it was because she was different that it was possible for your mother to love her."

Trina thought about this for a moment, then shook her head as if about to reject the premise. She paused in half-shake, reversing the direction into a tentative nod. "Maybe," she said so softly that Gray could barely hear her.

"Was that a maybe I heard?" he said with a warm smile.

For the first time, Trina showed the barest glimmer of a smile. It seemed that beneath all of that suffering and anguish there really was a hopeful person inside.

The Yellow Dress

"Where's the anger in all this?"

"Excuse me," Trina said.

"I was just wondering where you are keeping your anger. I mean you've been telling me that your mother all but ignored you. She withheld her love without any compunction. No matter what you did to earn her approval, she rejected you—in the most hurtful ways possible. And ever since then you've felt abandoned and unable to sustain any kind of trusting relationship."

As he said this, Trina was nodding her head.

"So, where's the anger then?"

Trina shrugged apologetically.

"I was just thinking," Gray continued. "If I was to behave toward my daughter they way you were treated by your mother, I'd be certain that my daughter would hate my guts. She would despise me and be outraged at the way I had neglected and hurt her. She might start to feel unworthy after that sort of experience, but she would also be tremendously angry at me."

With such tacit permission, Trina acknowledged that she did feel a bit upset with her mother.

"I'm just curious," Gray pressed her carefully, "what is it that you are most annoyed about with respect to your mother?"

"I guess most of all I'm angry that she rejected me."

"Go on."

"I'm angry that she made my sister more important than me."

"More."

"I'm angry that I always wanted a yellow dress and my mother would never buy me one. She insisted I get a red one instead, an old-fashioned one that looked horribly out of date. I hated that damn red dress but she made me wear it." She stopped and looked directly at Gray. "Why shouldn't I have been allowed to have a yellow dress?" she asked him. "My sister was always allowed to get whatever damn dress she wanted. No questions asked. And no grief."

Gray noted that anger seemed to be a huge issue for Trina, or rather, her inability to acknowledge and express those feelings. She seemed to feel helpless to get what she wanted most. Even now, as an adult, she was still unable to either ask for a yellow dress, or give herself one.

"Look Trina," Gray said to her, "before you can ever get to the point where you can forgive your mother for the ways she treated you—or rather, *mis*treated you—first you're going to have to let yourself feel the anger."

Hope and Grief

"So," Gray asked her, "what is it that you really want most?"

Trina struggled for awhile with the question, unable even to comprehend its meaning. Finally, after several minutes of asking what he meant by the question, talking around and around, she finally blurted out what she wanted most: "I want to be loved. I want to be truly loved."

"Okay," Gray said. "What would that be like for you—to be loved?" He wanted to help her to create a picture in her mind of what it would look and feel like to be loved.

"I don't know," Trina said simply and honestly. She really didn't know what it was like because she'd never experienced love.

Gray helped her to flush out the image of what this might be like, what this could be like. He tried to help her to imagine this very possibility—that love was something that she could someday experience. Perhaps it would never be with her mother, but it might be with a friend or a lover.

"So," he prompted, "tell me again what you really want?"

Again Trina hesitated, unsure how to respond.

"What if it was your mother saying this to you, asking you what you want. What would you say to her?"

"What do you mean?" she said, knowing exactly what he meant.

Gray just waited until she nodded her understanding. "What would you say to your mother if you could ask her for what you wanted?"

"I'd want her to. . . ."

"Don't tell me," Gray interrupted with a grin. "Tell *her*."

Catching on to the role play, she sat up straighter in her chair and seemed to look over Gray's shoulder rather than directly at his eyes. "Okay. . . ."

"Okay Mom," he reminder her.

"Okay Mom. I want you to pay attention to me. I want you to notice when I do something good. And I want you to tell me that. I want you to praise me in front of Nadia. I want you to be less critical of me. I want you to love me. I want you to hold me. I want you to read me stories before I go to bed. I want you to be a part of my life. I want to be a part of your life. I don't want to be alone. I don't want to be left out."

Once she got rolling, Trina had no difficulty articulating a whole lifetime of wants that had been ignored and passed over. As she recited the list her voice took on a whole new passion and strength that had not been expressed in a very long time—if ever. Trina no longer looked or felt powerless. She no longer seemed to feel sorry for herself. Yet she was still very much afraid of these feelings that had brought her down for so long. She had always associated any feeling with her depression and despair.

Gray made this very point. "You aren't in touch with the deeper levels of what you feel most authentically because of your fear these emotions will destroy you. Yet as you get closer to the depth of your innermost feelings, you can actually feel more energized. You can feel a sense of passion. You can feel a sense of authenticity, a sense of sweetness. And this is the place from which love emerges. Sometimes it emerges first for yourself, and then it eventually emerges for someone else."

Trina hung on every word. These were the first signs of real hope that she had felt in such a long time. During the ensuing sessions, the more she concentrated on feelings other than depression, the more her anger bubbled to the surface. She became like an erupting volcano, easily triggered by the slightest provocation. But with the anger came an aliveness, a continued passion, that had been unknown to her.

Of course there was a learning curve for Trina: she had to manage the anger appropriately and not just lash out at those who did not meet her growing expectations. But as she gained experience, Trina found that she could indeed handle even strong emotions without hurting either herself or others.

"You'll need to expect other feelings as well," Gray warned her. "Like sadness and grief."

"You mean like with my mother?"

"Exactly. You may notice yourself feeling more sadness about what you missed growing up, what you still miss in not having your mother a supportive part of your life."

"I still want my mother in my life," Trina said defiantly. "I haven't given up completely yet."

"I never said you had," Gray answered. He was taken aback, yet proud of the way that her new-found courage was leading her to stand up to him as well. "You may notice more and more what you don't have in your life, things you used to take for granted would just never be part of your life. But now you are beginning to hope. And you are starting to grieve."

Intimacy and Rejection

During the next few weeks, as Trina began to feel the full brunt of her sadness and regret, she experienced a relapse of bad feelings. Her posture and demeanor slipped back into old patterns.

"No," Gray insisted. "You are no longer the same person. You are completely different than you used to be." He said this with the force of a hypnotist, willing it to be true. "Right now you are feeling sadness for what you didn't have because you deserved it. Unlike before, you are not in the dumps any longer because you think there is something wrong with you. Maybe there was something wrong with the way you were brought up, but certainly not with the person you have become."

Trina looked at Gray with tears in her grateful eyes. She nodded that she understood.

"When all this happened to you so long ago," Gray explained further, "you didn't have the words to express your pain. That's what we are doing now, going back to complete that work."

Again she nodded.

"I want you to imagine that you are that little girl and I want you to feel the pain that she once felt. I want you to talk to your mother."

Gray could see Trina change visibly as she adopted her child-like self. She seemed to collapse in on herself, becoming physically smaller.

"When you're ready," he instructed, "I want you to talk to your mother. This time tell her how you feel. Tell her that you don't feel important to her, that you never felt important to her. Once again, tell here that you want to feel special, that you want her love. Tell her that you want her to be part of your life, but only if she is willing to treat you with the love and respect you deserve."

Trina nodded her understanding. "I just need to feel. . . ." Her voice broke as she began, dissolving in tears. Once she pulled herself together, she started again. "Mother, I need you to love me. I need you to play with me. I need to be part of your life."

"That's great," Gray reassured her. "Now, I am going to be your mother. Imagine that I am her. Can you do that?"

Trina nodded and continued saying the things that she'd always wanted to say to her mother. During one critical moment when she looked at Gray (as her mother) and told him/her how much she loved him/her, he reached over in the mother's role and gave her a hug. Tears of reconciliation followed.

Trina reported that she felt terrific afterwards, as if a huge weight had been lifted off her shoulders.

"That's outstanding," Gray said. "But this is just the beginning. Now that you are in this place where you are feeling worthy of love, it's time to get some for yourself."

By this time, Trina was no longer feeling depressed. She had also learned to manage her anger and was reaching the point of forgiveness toward her mother, and her sister. Now that she felt she was deserving of love, she became involved in a relationship with a man that seemed to be going well. Remarkably, this was the first real such relationship in her life.

"You are starting to fall in love because now it feels safe to do so. You never felt worthy of love before. But just because you are experiencing love in this new relationship doesn't mean that you are with the right person." Gray was warning her of the distinct possibility that her first love attachment might not necessarily be a good match for her. In fact, he was fairly certain that she'd made a lousy choice her first time out, just as one might expect from someone so inexperienced.

Soon afterward, the relationship did begin to fall apart. This was particularly devastating for Trina because she had come to depend on this man, just as she had opened up to him. But he was not ready for a committed relationship. "I deserve something better than this," she confessed to Gray. "I'm ready for a real relationship with someone who can truly love me, and someone I can love in return."

"As you are starting to feel better and better about yourself," Gray reflected, "you deserve a different kind of relationship that is both reciprocal and giving. You are tired of feeling unimportant with those you are with."

"Yes," she agreed enthusiastically. "I really do want that."

"Good for you. It seems clear to you that this guy you've been seeing does not fit what you are looking for. It's not his fault; he's just not ready for someone like you."

"I know this is true," Trina said. "But it's so, so hard."

She was indeed reluctant to extricate herself from this relationship that was not meeting her needs. Eventually she did so, feeling even better about herself in the process. More than ever, she felt ready to tackle other challenges that might require her to look at deeper fears of intimacy and rejection.

Beloved Daughter

Again they went back into childhood to role-play some unfinished business. "Tell your mother what is most painful for you," Gray directed.

This was really, really difficult for her, not just to say these things out loud, but especially to her mother, who had been so distant and withholding.

With prompting, Trina talked about her fears of not being good enough, of rejection, of not being able to express herself, of not measuring up. Most of all, she admitted her fear that her mother didn't love her.

With each of these disclosures, Trina felt herself wake up just a little bit more. She could feel the fears just as she was saying them out loud. But to her surprise, they didn't flood her as she might have expected. On the contrary, she felt lighter and more confident.

Soon after this, Trina began to lose more and more weight. She became involved in another relationship with a man, and this time she confessed her secret hope that this was "the one." Gray advised some degree of caution, but Trina was feeling particularly courageous in taking risks related to love. "Don't worry," she said to him. "I can handle myself now. You've taught me well."

Gray smiled in return, but he was still worried. Trina had not been stabilized for very long and he was genuinely worried about the choices she was making. Nevertheless, she insisted that she was ready to take some time out from the sessions and test her wings.

A few months later, Trina returned, disturbingly depressed once again. Her new relationship had not worked out and she was losing hope.

"But surely you can't find that so surprising," Gray said. "You hadn't known the guy for very long. There must be something else going on for you as well in order for you to lose so much ground."

Trina nodded. "Well, over Christmas I went to my parents' house." Trina laughed, but it was a sound that left no doubt that there was nothing funny about this.

"I see."

"I'm not sure you do. I wasn't even invited to my mother's Christmas party. My sister was there, of course, as was everyone else. But I wasn't even invited, nor allowed to be there. It's the same crap all over again."

At a loss about what to say, Gray asked a question. "So, what did you do instead?"

"I went to my aunt's house, my mother's sister."

"She invited you?"

"Yeah," Trina said bitterly. "She actually invited me. Even if my own mother won't have me, at least her sister will."

"And what was it like there?"

"Oh, I had a wonderful time. My aunt is wonderful to me. In many ways, she is like a mother to me. My aunt's daughters, my cousins, were there. And their families were there. They are kind of like a second family to me since I can't be with my own family."

Gray felt excitement as he heard these words, realizing that Trina did not appreciate the significance of her own words. "Don't you see what has happened?" he said to her. "You have healed yourself so much that you have been invited into this wonderful family that supports you. This is a family that is even better than your own because you are valued and loved and appreciated when you are with them. Even better, they actually *chose* you to join them, which is far better than just being born into a family."

Trina broke out into a huge grin, nodding enthusiastically. This did make sense to her, since it felt like her aunt had always been her real mother. It was also true that her aunt's home was the only place she had ever felt truly loved and safe. For the first time she realized that she was a beloved daughter.

Happy Ending

Gray looks back on this relationship as one of his finest hours as a counselor because of the depth of the transformation that took place. Trina had been severely depressed and suicidal, completely without hope, and yet she had managed to achieve all of the things that she wanted most. She was able to deal with her feelings, yet also forgive her mother for her own limitations.

Eventually, she was able to find the life she wanted, even if it was not in a direction that she ever imagined. She had been looking for love with those who could not give it to her in the way she wanted, and the way she deserved it. But once she broadened her vision, risked facing the rejection and intimacy she most feared, she was indeed able to reconstruct her life with all the love she ever wanted.

"We always have what we need most," Gray summarized. "We are often just looking in the wrong direction."

23 When the Therapist and Client Influence One Another

A Case from Judith V. Jordan

Judith V. Jordan is one of the leading voices in feminist theory as applied to therapy. She has written, lectured, and conducted workshops nationally and internationally on the subjects of women's psychological development, gender differences, mothers and daughters, mothers and sons, empathy, psychotherapy, marginality, diversity, mutuality, women's sexuality, gender issues in the workplace, and a relational model of the self.

Jordan currently serves as Co-Director of the Jean Baker Miller Training Institute and Founding Scholar at the Stone Center at Wellesley College. She was formally trained as a clinical psychologist at Harvard University and previously worked as Director of the Women's Studies program at McLean Hospital. She is currently working on developing new models of human development, which might transform the current distorting impact of competition, hyperindividualism, racism, sexism, heterosexism, and classism.

Judy has co-authored the books, Women's Growth in Connection *and* Women's Growth in Diversity, *and has published more than thirty original reports at the Stone Center.*

An Experienced Client

The case Jordan selected as her finest hour occurred early in her career, when she was still a novice. The case was not her finest hour because her therapeutic skills were so masterful, but rather because she learned so much from this client, who was such an important teacher for her. Indeed, one of the distinguishing characteristics of Jordan's "relational-cultural approach" to helping people is the great emphasis placed on collaboration between the participants in the process. Therapy is seen as a journey in which the clinician is viewed not so much as an expert guide, but as an experienced companion who is learning and growing as well. Both therapist and client learn through the process of fluid expertise, a gentle, respectful awareness of the knowledge and wisdom that both possess.

Jordan was a bit apprehensive about first meeting Cindy, her teenaged client, and not just because she was still relatively new in the profession. Cindy may have been only 18, but she probably had more experience in therapy than Jordan did! Cindy had been hospitalized repeatedly for depression, anorexia, and suicidal ideation since she had been 12 years old. She had already worked with seven previous therapists, who had not been able to help her; in fact, several had been so frustrated by this young woman that they had "fired" her as a client. Those who had not given up on Cindy had been dismissed by her as shallow, stupid, or just "too shrinky."

"What do you mean, 'too shrinky'?" Jordan asked her.

"You know," Cindy said. "Too cold. Stiff. They don't listen."

Jordan took that to mean that Cindy didn't feel safe with them. "So, then, given that you have already tried this with so many others, what do you think would be different about working with me?"

Cindy shrugged. "I don't know. I heard, maybe, that you might be different."

"Different how?"

Another shrug, but Jordan couldn't tell if this meant she didn't care, or didn't know. "I guess someone told me you might listen," Cindy said after another thoughtful moment.

"What do you think that means?" Jordan pressed. She wanted to get a sense of what Cindy felt and anticipated as they began their relationship.

"I already told you," Cindy responded impatiently. "I don't know. But I can tell you this . . . " She stopped and smiled for the first time.

"What?"

"You're not as good as they said you were."

Jordan almost smiled herself. This young woman would indeed be a challenge to work with, and she could already see why Cindy's previous therapists had described her as so difficult.

A Secret Revealed

The first sessions did not go well at all. As Jordan tried to explore Cindy's depression and sadness, Cindy would frequently not speak much at all, except to tell Jordan how clueless and inept she was. She would tell her therapist continuously every time she felt misunderstood or every time Jordan made some perceived mistake or misjudgment. And after 6 years of intensive therapy with a half-dozen practitioners, this young woman knew as much about how the process worked as most seasoned professionals. Her initial assessment of her latest therapist: unimaginative, unclear, and far too passive.

There were other times, early on, when Cindy felt such despair and hopelessness she didn't seem to have the energy to be critical of Jordan. "Look," she said, "I know you are doing the best you can—just like the others—but this just isn't helping. Nothing is helping. I don't see any reason to keep going." Then she would go on at length about her suicidal thoughts, which were quite well developed.

They spent some time talking about family history. Jordan learned that Cindy was an only child. Her parents had divorced soon after her birth, and then her mother had remarried.

"What was your stepfather like?" Jordan asked. It struck her as unusual that in the family narrative Cindy had spent more time talking about her grandparents, with whom she spent considerable time, than she did her parents.

"He's an asshole," Cindy said simply.

"An asshole?"

"Yeah, my mother always takes his side."

"Maybe you could give me an example of this, of a time when your stepfather acted like a jerk?"

"Well, how about like the times when he comes to my room at night?"

"He comes into your room?" Jordan responded.

"You heard me. I told you he is an asshole. He's been coming into my room at night for years. Since probably I was about 8 or something."

"What do you mean he comes into your room at night?" Jordan wanted to be sure to clarify what she thought she heard.

"It's just what you think. He touched me and stuff. I usually tried to pretend I was asleep, hoping he would leave me alone. I just didn't know what to do. I told my mother about it but she didn't believe me. She told me to stop making things up." Cindy paused for a moment, fighting back tears. "Nobody believed me."

"How lonely for you! What about your previous therapists?"

"I didn't tell them about it. Only you."

"My gosh," Jordan said in genuine shock. "How awful for you! That must have been so terrible for you to carry this around with nobody to talk to and nobody to help you. And your mother not believing you!"

Jordan knew enough to realize that they had not yet established sufficient trust for her to probe into the details very deeply, yet she did want to communicate to Cindy as clearly as she could that she believed what she had been saying about the sexual abuse having taken place.

At this point, 25 years ago, Jordan had never worked with anyone who had reported sexual abuse, nor had she received any training in this area. The whole subject had been taboo, and not much was known about how to proceed with such matters. The only thing that Jordan was certain about was that she believed what Cindy had told her was true. It was not just the abuse itself that must have been so difficult for her to live with, but also the feeling that she could not feel safe and that she could not trust anyone.

Cindy blamed herself for the predicament she found herself in. She believed there was something she could have done, something she should have done, instead of just lying there passively. She should have run away, or stayed with her grandparents more often, or even fought back against her stepfather. Now she was filled with self-loathing and self-blame, as if it was all her fault.

Jordan not only witnessed Cindy's pain but actually *felt* it. This was more than simple empathy; she was evolving a style of therapy in which, rather than detaching herself from clients, distancing herself and objectifying the story, Jordan was resonating deeply with their experiences. Jordan actually felt some part of Cindy's shame, and her anger.

A Guiding Model

In order to understand the unique way that Judy Jordan and her colleagues from The Stone Center work within the relational-cultural model, it is useful to understand some of the core beliefs. Jordan explained that "growth-fostering relationships" lead to what Jean Baker Miller called the "five good things": zest, clarity, productivity, self-worth, and the desire for more connection.

"Disconnections in relationships," Jordan explained, "are ubiquitous— they happen all the time. It is not that you are trying to create a world with no disconnections; acute disconnections can actually produce real growth, especially of trust in both parent–child as well therapist–client relationships if the person who created the hurt is open to hearing about the other person's pain. When there is a disconnection and a person is misunderstood or hurt, if he or she can represent the experience of pain to the other person and can be responded to empathically, a strengthened connection results."

Jordan believes this is when people can feel most effective and competent, when they feel heard and understood. The growth revolves around the person feeling that he or she has had an impact on the other person. This is in marked contrast to alternative situations when the other person denies his or her role and responsibility, resulting in further humiliation and wounding. This is what happened to Cindy when her mother insisted that she was just making up the stories of her stepfather sexually abusing her. It was bad enough to be violated and molested, but then she was further wounded by her mother, who called her a liar. The messages she heard (even if they were not actually intended) were: "I don't care about you. You don't matter. I am not impacted by you. And you are not relationally effective." This is what Jordan refers to as "chronic disconnection"—when the person begins to relate less authentically to others and feels consistent isolation.

This is how Cindy learned to stop telling her mother (and others) about the abuse. She also became adept at hiding her pain, keeping it to herself, and trying to make everything okay by turning further inward. This was easy for her to do since she believed she didn't matter. It was also an understandable way of being—and a strategy for survival—for someone who had good reason to believe it was unsafe to trust others.

"Shame takes us into a spiral of disconnection and inauthenticity," Jordan elaborated. "The relational images that are formed during these periods of chronic disconnection are something like this: 'When I try to protect myself, when I try to protest, I am abandoned.' This is what we call a relational image." And this particular relational image perpetuates a sense of isolation.

We note in Jordan's way of speaking that there is almost always a plural pronoun, a "we" that is part of her speech. This is her way of acknowledging that the relational-cultural model is a collaboration not only with clients, but also with many other colleagues with whom she works. Whether in her writing, in presentations, or in an interview like this, Jordan speaks as a representative of a feminist perspective that values collective contributions rather than individual credits.

Also core to the relational-cultural model are the processes of mutual empathy and empowerment. "Mutual empathy is our understanding that in order for empathy to create healing in a relationship, a client like Cindy must see and feel and know the therapist's empathic response. In other words, we are saying that the client must have some empathic responsiveness to the therapist's empathy in order for the therapist's empathy to produce healing."

It is not enough for the therapist to impact clients; clients must also know that they have impacted their therapists. This mutual influence leads relational-cultural therapists to be open to, and search for, mutual change—not just in their clients, but in themselves. Jordan is thus not afraid of showing her clients how they have moved her, how they have changed and taught her. She does not intend this as either self-indulgent or merely reactive, but rather informed by clinical judgment and mediated by what is called "anticipatory empathy" toward the client's likely response. Thus, in this model, empathy constantly flows in both directions.

This is in contrast to the traditional psychodynamic model, as well as others, that emphasize individuality, individuation, separation, independence, autonomy, and so on. The messages people are taught, especially in Western, Eurocentric, male culture (and in therapy) are: "Stand on your own two feet." "Take care of yourself." "Show some courage." These are seen as internal traits, but not at all connected to the interdependent nature of our world. Jordan and her colleagues instead emphasize doing therapy in a relational context in which quite different messages are communicated, those that stress reaching out for help, depending on others as well as oneself, and moving out of isolation.

Thrown Off Balance

Jordan believes that the myths of therapy emerge from the larger myths of our dominant culture—that it is important to remain neutral and detached, that therapists should not be real and authentic, that only the client changes in the process. Any personal reactions on the part of the therapist are seen as distorting effects, countertransferences, projections, and indicative of poor boundaries. At the core is the therapist being fearful of his or her own vulnerability.

This idea has huge implications for our present subject of what constitutes great therapy. In traditional psychodynamic circles, excellence is determined, in part, by the clinician's ability to remain separate and detached from clients, guarding against influences that might compromise one's objectivity. Yet in the relational model, the therapist not only respects and honors the client's vulnerability, but his or her own as well.

"With Cindy I was constantly off balance with her in the beginning," Jordan recalled. "I really liked her, but I had a hard time knowing how to work with her. She didn't talk much. I felt inadequate a lot of the time. I felt like I didn't know what I was doing wrong."

Jordan struggled most when Cindy would become angry at her. One time they were talking and Jordan said something that demonstrated to Cindy that Jordan just didn't understand. Without warning, Cindy leapt out of her chair and ran full speed, ramming her head against the wall. Jordan had no idea what was happening, nor what to do. They were in a hospital setting but there was no time to call security.

"Stop that right now!" Jordan yelled out. "You cannot do that! Stop that this moment! We are here to talk."

Cindy looked back over her shoulder, but then lowered her head and rammed the wall again with even greater force. Then she backed up for another try, when Jordan ran in front of the girl. She held up her arms and yelled, "Stop!" just like the sixth-grade safety patrol kid she had once been. Rather than stopping the charge, Cindy just headed right through the annoying obstacle, knocking Jordan down in the process, tangling them both up in a heap on the floor.

Jordan was thoroughly shaken, not only physically but emotionally. She knew that Cindy had suffered a lot of abuse and neglect, that she was out of control at that moment, but she could still feel her own anger and frustration boil to the surface.

Cindy arose from the floor and looked at Jordan, still sitting on the floor, and said: "You feel like killing me right now, don't you?"

Jordan knew what her traditional training would prescribe for her to say: "What makes you think I am angry?" Or perhaps: "You must be feeling quite angry with *me* right now." But instead, she met Cindy's challenging gaze and said: "Yes, I am *very* angry right now. I am *very* shaken. But I actually don't feel like killing you. I just need a few minutes to collect myself."

All the energy seemed to drain out of Cindy at that moment. She just collapsed on the floor, uttering a tiny, childlike sound. Then it was time for the session to end: they both collected themselves.

"Look," Jordan said, "We can't solve things this way, by you hurting yourself or me. Therapy is for talking. I know you are frustrated by me. I am sorry that I misunderstood you. And I need to know when I don't 'get it.' I didn't mean for this to happen. And I know it leads you to mistrust me. But just like you, I'm trying as hard as I can and doing the best I can. But I can't manage such physical confrontations. . . . they scare me and when I get scared I actually listen even more poorly. So we have to work together to try to find a different way through these hard places."

Cindy nodded and then they parted.

Afterwards, Jordan was filled with doubts and misgivings. This was before she had any sort of theory in her head about relational therapy. In fact, she had just violated everything she had ever learned. When she confessed later to her supervisor, rather than getting the expected scolding, her supervisor reassured her that perhaps it was helpful for her to have been so real in the relationship. It was by literally being thrown off balance that Jordan had become vulnerable and real. She had let Cindy know that she had had a real impact on her, that she felt angry and frustrated and scared. And Jordan also let Cindy know that she, Jordan, had personal limits that Cindy needed to find a way to respect in order to help protect the relationship. "Stating one's limits" in a relationship provides important relational information and is quite different from "setting limits" on another's behavior, which implies a "power over," unidirectional approach.

In a subsequent session Cindy let Jordan know what this meant to her, that it was a turning point in the trust that developed between them. "That is when I knew that you really cared for me. I mean, I saw you cry sometimes before, like when I told you about the abuse and stuff, but when I saw you *that* angry—that's when I knew that I was important to you too. I knew I really affected you . . . and that you are vulnerable too . . . that's incredibly important to me."

The Abduction

About a year into their work together, things seemed to be progressing—slowly, very slowly, but still evidently. Cindy continued to be quite vulnerable and volatile, still depressed, but at least the thoughts of suicide had all but ended and her eating behaviors had become more stable. She was now working as a nurse's aide, which was surprising in itself—that she could tolerate being in a hospital after having spent a significant portion of her adolescence in one. One evening, while walking home from work, she was attacked at knifepoint and taken to an abandoned building, where she was held for several hours. After pleading for her life, screaming for help, fighting off her attacker, and finally breaking free, she managed to escape without physical harm.

It was 4 o'clock that same morning that Cindy called Jordan from the police station—Jordan was the first person she thought to contact. She was still numb but distraught.

"Oh my God! Are you okay?" This was the only thing Jordan could think to say, awakened in the middle of the night from a deep sleep.

"Yeah, I'm okay. They got the guy."

"That's good. But what about you?"

"I'm okay, I think."

"Do you want me to come down to meet you? I'll come now if you need me."

"No, that's okay."

"Okay," Jordan said. "Then I'll see you first thing in the morning."

When they did meet, Jordan seemed more visibly upset than Cindy. "This is so awful," Jordan kept saying over and over. "I'm so upset this happened to you. Are you sure you're okay?"

While Jordan was tearful and angry, Cindy seemed more composed, if not dissociated. Jordan was feeling so upset that this poor young woman who had already been through so much was now innocently victimized once again. All she could think about was how there was nothing she could do to protect her; she felt so helpless. She couldn't stop thinking of Cindy being terrorized by a crazy man with a knife. She had been alone in that warehouse and it seemed to trigger things from her past all over again.

Mutual Vulnerability

Cindy returned to the hospital as a patient again. She hated the very thought of that surrender, that defeat, but the trauma seemed to be too much for her to handle without ongoing support. The self-blame began all over again, the feeling that she had somehow done something that had invited this attack.

Once again, Jordan could tell that Cindy desperately wanted to reconnect, yet she feared further vulnerability. To complicate matters further, Jordan was feeling her own vulnerability. Throughout their relationship, whenever Cindy had become frustrated, or impatient, or angry with Jordan, she would call one of her previous therapists and complain about Jordan's ineptitude. Some of these previous therapists were former supervisors of Jordan's; a few were current colleagues. It felt that every single mistake or misattunement that she made would be exposed to these valued colleagues. There would be times Jordan would be in the hospital cafeteria and someone would come up to her and say, "Oh your favorite patient called me this week. She said you did something incredibly stupid. You wouldn't have said *that*, would you?!" (and of course she had, because Cindy was an absolutely accurate recorder of all of Jordan's empathic failures). Jordan felt exposed, and to a certain extent betrayed. She began avoiding the cafeteria altogether, which in effect produced the same kind of isolation that she was trying to help her client break out of.

"I was a new therapist," Jordan recalled. "I was already insecure. But now I felt anxious and incompetent. And I felt angry. I'm not proud of the way I handled this initially, but I would interpret her hostility towards me.

Basically what I wanted to do was get her to stop doing this. I was feeling very exposed."

Jordan eventually realized that through this increased vulnerability she was getting more caught up in her own narcissism and less able to really listen to the messages Cindy was sending. She was interpreting the "resistance" in the standard way, but didn't see that it was useful; if anything, the cycle seemed to make Cindy and Jordan feel less safe with one another.

Then the major insight kicked in, the awareness that led Jordan to nominate this case as one of the best (and earliest) examples of her work. She began to realize that Cindy was a kid who had been repeatedly abused behind closed doors by people she should have been able to trust but who had abused their power. Therapy to her represented a retriggering situation—it was also behind closed doors with a very powerful person who was asking initially for unearned trust. By making the goings-on more public, Cindy was, in effect, protecting herself against further harm. Each little empathic failure was held up to scrutiny; each mistake was brought out into the light of day for others to monitor. It was her way of telling this powerful therapist that if you try to hurt me, the way others have in the past, I've got some protection this time. She was not doing this consciously, of course, but a wise part of her was teaching Jordan about what to do to create a safer relationship.

Once Jordan had picked up this message, and the meaning of the behavior as self-protective and protective of the relationship rather than as being about betrayal, she was able to stop taking it so personally and settle down. This was actually brought into their conversations in such a way that Cindy no longer needed to "make the therapy public" in order to feel safe. By cutting her therapist some slack, by allowing Jordan to make mistakes and forgive them, she was also learning how to do the same with herself. But this could only be learned slowly and by experiencing the disconnections and reconnections together in the therapy. During the reworking of these small and sometimes large empathic failures, Cindy's reactive amygdala (the underlying brain sequela of chronic childhood abuse, which interpreted each empathic failure as life-threatening violation) began to quiet down. Connection was beginning to feel safe for her.

In turn, Jordan was learning to apologize for her lapses, something she had never learned in graduate school. She revealed to Cindy not only her remorse but her pain when Jordan did or said something that caused further hurt. This let Cindy know that she was affecting her therapist, who valued her, for whom she was important.

"I felt exposed and ashamed," Jordan confessed to her, "when you talked about me to other therapists in a negative way. But then I realized how clever and wise you were, that you figured out a way to protect yourself and our relationship. I am so grateful to you for that lesson."

The lesson for Jordan was that both the therapist *and* the client contribute to disconnections as well as connections and that both need to work to create safety in the relationship. "Cindy taught me the real meaning of 'fluid expertise.' She had some pretty important things to teach me. I really did come to truly and deeply appreciate and respect her ways of staying in the relationship even though they were hard for me. Respect is a big piece of this. I really respected this young woman in ways that others had not before."

Whenever Cindy's name had come up in conversations or case conferences around the hospital, she had frequently been referred to as "that flaming borderline." One previous therapist had described her as "an empty black pit." Yet Jordan refused to buy into these labels. In one sense she had to unlearn how to do therapy the way it had been taught; part of that meant moving away from the objectifying labels that provide the pretense of understanding and certainty but rarely illuminate the therapy.

■ ■ ■

Epilogue

Jordan worked with Cindy for about 4 years, 8 months of which took place during an inpatient hospitalization. From there, she moved to a transition facility, and then back into the world, where she remained. There were other setbacks for her—a difficult relationship with a man, the death of her beloved grandmother—but she grieved appropriately and moved forward. Cindy enrolled in college and did quite well, a remarkable accomplishment for someone who had never spent more than a few consecutive months at a time in a regular high school.

Cindy eventually moved out of town and Jordan heard nothing from her for some time. A postcard arrived, then another. Eventually Cindy called on the phone, wanting to know the answers to two questions: Was Jordan still in the same office? And was her hair still long?

"Yes on both accounts," she told her. "My hair is still long and I'm still in the same place."

"How about your desk?" Cindy asked. "Still have all those papers on the desk?"

Jordan laughed. "Yup. Still the same." She realized that partly what Cindy was asking was whether she was still the same person.

"Well, that's good," Cindy said. "There's one more thing."

"What's that?"

"I just wanted you to know that I'm getting married. It's a really good relationship."

Jordan not only felt like crying, she *did* cry. It was the same a year later when she got a birth announcement that Cindy had her first child. Jordan was just so moved by the courage and the resilience of this woman. Here was someone whom nobody believed could ever sustain a relationship with any-one, yet she had turned into a loving, warm person.

Although this is a happy ending indeed, that was not the reason why Jordan chose this case to discuss as her finest hour. "What I hope people will really take from this story is how important it is to respect the wisdom of the client. It is also important for therapists to work with their own growing edge and vulnerability. Therapy is about being with the client in real, growth-fostering interactions where there is humility, an awareness of the yearning for connection and honoring the inevitable strategies of discon-nection. The therapist holds responsibility for the safety of the connection but also respects and encourages the client's growing ability to create mu-tuality and connection. In this relational context, positive, therapeutic change happens."

24 Continuing a Relationship with a Dead Father

A Case from Robert A. Neimeyer

Robert A. Neimeyer has written extensively on constructivist and narrative approaches to psychotherapy, as well as on the experience of death and loss. His additional areas of research include depression, suicide, and psychotherapy outcome. He presently serves as Director of the Psychotherapy & Psychopathology Area at the University of Memphis. Neimeyer has published eighteen books, including Constructivism in Psychotherapy, Constructions of Disorder, Meaning Reconstruction and the Experience of Loss, *and* Lessons of Loss: A Guide to Coping. *The author of more than two hundred articles and book chapters, he is currently working to extend an understanding of grieving as a meaning-making process, and to advance a constructivist approach to psychotherapy through his scholarly work and training workshops for psychologists and other health care professionals.*

Neimeyer has served as Chair of the International Work Group on Death, Dying & Bereavement (2002–present) and as President of the Association for Death Education and Counseling (1996–1997), which conferred on him its Research Recognition Award in 1999. He presently is working to shape a national agenda for research on grief through his consultation with the Center for the Advancement of Health.

Spirals of Nervousness

Joanne had been experiencing fairly severe panic attacks that included symptoms of dizziness, rapid heartbeat, and a racing pulse. She was both articulate and thorough in the way she presented her complaints in her first therapy session, including the frequency of onset and corresponding precursors. "I have been told by my physician that they are of psychogenic origin."

Neimeyer was struck by the familiar way she used clinical terms and wondered about the private meanings beneath the objective language. "Can you tell me more about what that diagnosis means to you?"

"Well, as I mentioned, shortness of breath, racing pulse, and spirals of nervousness."

"Spirals of nervousness?"

"Exactly," she said with a smile. Joanne was not only a highly educated middle-aged African American woman, but also quite comfortable talking with professionals.

"And how is it that you ended up calling me?"

"It was my doctor's recommendation that I consult with you," Joanne said, again with a warm smile. "So here I am."

"I see. Maybe you could tell me about when these symptoms first presented themselves in your life." Neimeyer easily fell into the pattern of using "externalizing" language to separate Joanne from her symptoms. He was interested in the much larger picture of her life beyond the presenting problem.

"We were living in Baltimore at the time, that is, my husband Michael and me. He is a minister," she added.

"I see."

"Baltimore had always been our home, and my parent's home, until Michael was called to take a position as pastor of a large church here in this city. That meant we had to move very far away from our families, and especially from my mother and sisters."

Joanne spoke for a while about the many transitions she experienced after the move. She had become isolated and reclusive. Her bouts of panic were segregating her from the new congregation because she feared that her weakness would be discovered and people might think she was crazy. "I have certain responsibilities with the church and all," she said, "that don't allow me to lose control of myself like this."

Pot Holes and Landmines

"I am curious," Neimeyer changed the focus a bit, "what your theory is about how you came to have this difficulty?"

Joanne thought for a moment or two, then she smiled apologetically. "I don't really know," she admitted. "I'm just at a loss."

Neimeyer was struck by that choice of language and found it significant, the part about being at a loss. "One of the things that I routinely do in therapy," Neimeyer explained later, "is get very interested in people's previous experiences in therapy. It has been my experience that if we give people the opportunity to talk about their previous treatments they will tell us exactly how we can fail with them. They will lay out a very elaborate road map for precisely every pothole or landmine that lies ahead of us in the road. They will also tell us what paths work well for them in terms of pursuing the goals."

In Joanne's case, she had had only one previous experience in counseling and that occurred while in a training program for pastoral counselors through her church some years before. The trainees had been invited to work on some personal issue as part of the program and Joanne chose to focus on residual feelings related to the death of her father, who had recently passed away.

"How did he die?" Neimeyer asked.

"Cancer. He was stolen away from us." As she said this she started to cry.

"Stolen away . . . and the grief associated with that is still very accessible to you," Neimeyer reflected.

Joanne shook her head. "It's not only that. Well, of course that's part of it. But he just became so *mean* during that time, not like himself at all."

"Mean?"

"Yes. The worse the cancer got, the crueler he became. In some ways I was almost glad when he passed away. It was so hard on all of us. We were trying to take care of him, to do the best we could, but it was never enough. It's like we lost the father we knew even before he died." The tears were flowing in earnest now.

Neimeyer tuned in carefully to what Joanne was experiencing, as well as expressing. He likes to follow the "affect trail"—that is, when emotionally significant material comes forth. He finds that in such circumstances people are often making a request for us to join them exploring the meaning of their tears.

"In spite of how difficult he was for you to be around towards the end," Neimeyer observed, "it sounds like you still really miss him."

Joanne nodded her head and reached for a tissue to wipe her cheeks. "I do miss him. If Daddy had been around he could have given me advice about moving, and all the emotional changes it's put me through."

There was an emotional intensity to Joanne's last statement. Even though the death had occurred years before, the grief wounds still seemed fresh. Neimeyer was also struck by the way that Joanne implicitly had linked her panic attacks to the relocation.

The Empty Chair

"Joanne," Neimeyer said softly, carefully, "I wonder how you would feel if we were to invite your father to join us here today to reopen your conversation with him?"

"What do you mean?"

"Just that we could talk with him about things that matter to you, as if your relationship had never been interrupted by illness and death."

"How . . . How could we do that?" As she asked this, Joanne swallowed hard and took a deep breath, as if she were uncertain what would come next.

Many therapists are familiar with the "empty chair" technique popularized by Gestalt therapists. For a constructivist like Neimeyer, the same device might be useful not to deal with "unfinished business" but rather to reconnect with a "lost relationship," to help revitalize a continuing bond. Neimeyer moved a chair in front of Joanne and gestured toward it. "Let's place your father in this chair, this *comfortable* chair," Neimeyer suggested, choosing his words carefully to offer a position of comfort to Joanne's ailing father. Neimeyer's attention to the nuances of language in therapy convinced him that every word was potentially an intervention, and that nothing said in therapy should be superfluous. "And just give you a chance to say what still needs to be said," he continued. "Maybe we could start with where it hurts most. You might begin the conversation by expressing something to him of what you needed from him, or what you need still."

"Daddy, I just . . . ," she began, and then dissolved into tears.

Neimeyer waited patiently, slowly nodding his head. "Just. . . ." Neimeyer prompted. "What words come next?"

With gentle encouragement, Joanne began talking to her father, and between her sobs, told him about her disconnection from her church community and the growing separation she felt from her husband. "Daddy, I just feel so lost. I just don't know where . . . I don't know what to do anymore. LaToya, my little girl, is growing up so fast. You wouldn't believe it Daddy—she's almost a grown young woman now—almost 12 and shooting up like a weed."

Joanne stopped and bowed her head. For a few minutes she just wept silently, then she started to speak again. "Daddy, I'm sorry. I'm so, so sorry that I abandoned you by moving away from Baltimore. I'm so far away from you now. It's where we were from, where we spent our lives, and now I'm not there anymore for you."

That this did not seem rational was beside the point. Joanne obviously felt tremendous guilt in having abandoned her father, not only after his death, but perhaps also during his long, agonizing demise.

As Joanne fell silent, Neimeyer quietly invited her, "Joanne, I wonder if you would now change positions now and take your father's chair, and loan him your voice so that he might respond to you. What would he say to this daughter who is sharing these concerns and feelings with him now?"

Tentatively at first, Joanne switched seats. Sitting upright in the chair, she immediately ceased crying, with a swipe of her hand across her eyes. She paused for a moment, placed her hands on her knees, then stared straight ahead at the chair she had just vacated. In a deeper, if somewhat uncertain voice that was still her own, Joanne said, "Don't worry, baby. Don't worry about 'nothin. It don't matter where you go, I'll still come visit you." Joanne as her father then fell silent, as if he didn't know how to proceed. While this fatherly reassurance was tenderly offered, the words seemed to ring hollow. They didn't seem to square with the keen sense of loss that Joanne had expressed just moments earlier. It seemed to Neimeyer more like a token offering than an authentic continuation of the dialogue.

"Why don't you return to your own chair?" he asked her.

After Joanne was repositioned as herself, Neimeyer said, "I'd like you to repeat something, if you don't mind."

Joanne nodded. At this point she seemed almost pliable, as if the tears had so thoroughly soaked her body she was just raw emotion.

Neimeyer waited until she looked up at him again. "Repeat after me," he instructed. "You can't visit me Dad. You're dead."

As she voiced those words Joanne choked with sobs. All her grief poured forth in a way that she couldn't hope to control. After a few minutes, she again became still and quiet.

"Why don't you switch chairs again," he said to her, and that's all the direction he needed to give.

"Despite my death," Joanne's "father" said in a steadier, more resonant voice, "I will always be with you. I will always believe in you. I trust your decisions no matter where you live and whatever you choose to do." Nodding her head slightly, Joanne then grew silent and thoughtful, as if she were grasping something in a different way.

"Come back over here," Neimeyer directed, inviting Joanne to resume the conversation with him by repositioning her father's chair so it no longer faced her. From experience Neimeyer knew that "unstaging" the chair work in this way allowed people to reenter direct discussion with the therapist, without a sense of their loved one "eavesdropping" on the conversation. "I am wondering," he continued after she was reseated, "if anything occurred to you that was important during that talk you had with your father. Is there anything that percolated up for you that we should give some attention to?"

"There *was* something," Joanne replied. She was smiling now through her tears.

"What's that?"

"Well, I realize now that I *can* keep my father. He *can* be with me."

Finding Her Voice

As she spoke with Neimeyer about this insight, Joanne found a way to build a bridge to her father's continuing presence, by once again including him in family conversations, sharing cherished memories, displaying boxed-up mementos of his long life as a community organizer, and carrying forward some of his projects in her own life. This living bond with her deceased father could again become a major resource for her. But as Joanne focused on restoring the connection with her father, she began to realize that her bond with her mother had been disrupted as well. Once she moved away from Baltimore, she had experienced deeply the sense of loss associated with the distance from her family.

Seeing this as an elaboration of the same basic theme, Neimeyer again invited Joanne to do some "empty chair" work, this time with her speaking to, and speaking for, her mother. Joanne readily took up the challenge. "I already lost Daddy," she said to her mother, her lower lip trembling with feeling. "I can't stand to lose you too."

After only a few conversational turns, Joanne realized with absolute certainty that she had to do something more proactively to stay in closer touch with her mother, sisters, and friends back home. There had to be a way to cross the geographic distance that separated them—a distance that she sensed had served as a buffer against their mutual sense of devastation following her father's death. Yet this was only one way she felt lost and powerless. Another aspect of this sense of dislocation revolved around her position as "first lady" of her husband's church. She had her own ambitions and dreams, and many of them were put on hold while she served to support her husband's career. "You don't understand what it means to be the pastor of a black church," she told Neimeyer. "It requires total devotion. If I were to pursue my own career, people would think I'm selfish."

"It sounds like a real dilemma," Neimeyer reflected. "It feels like you have to choose to either take care of your own interests or those of your husband."

Joanne nodded agreement. "I think I'm just needing to speak my mind."

"To find your voice," Neimeyer said.

"Yes. That's it. My voice. I've been noticing lately that I need to speak out more, make decisions instead of waiting for my husband to take care of everything. Like with my daughter for instance, I need to slow her down from growing up too fast, making the wrong choices. There are some things only a mother can do."

"And you really want to be that kind of mother," Neimeyer added.

"Yes, that's so," Joanne agreed, nodding her head with new-found conviction. "But it's even more than that. I need to stand up for myself in the church as well as the family. I've got my own ideas about what we ought to be doing in the church community, rather than just the things they've always been doing."

"It sounds like you are beginning to feel a kind of strength and clarity about what needs to be done," Neimeyer observed.

Joanne grinned. "Yeah, I guess that would be right, wouldn't it?"

"It would," he smiled back. He could begin to see how the symbolic reconnection she had earlier in the session made with her father and family was helping her reconnect to her own internal resources as well. In narrative therapy terms, she was able to resist the dominant story of her powerlessness and panic in favor of an alternative, preferred story of her own creation.

It's Hello, Not Goodbye

Whereas in Gestalt therapy the "empty chair" technique is often used to help people to take care of "unfinished business" with deceased loved ones, Neimeyer has found that what is often most needed is *not* saying goodbye or finding closure. "I regard all of these concepts as rather pernicious twentieth-century metaphors on how to adapt to a loss. Instead I see the goal of thera-peutic work more commonly as finding a way of *continuing* a relationship rather than ending one.

"It is interesting to me that we are so captivated by what is essentially a capitalistic discourse of grieving. Listen to the terms we use. We should fin-ish unfinished *business*. We need to seek *closure*. We ought to *withdraw* emo-tional energy from the one who has died in order to *invest* it into other relationships. What I would say in response to all of this is that business may be finished but relationships rarely are. And we usually don't seek closure. Closure is for bank accounts, not for love accounts. Those remain open.

"Love is not like money. It is not available in limited supply. It is poten-tially boundless, so the more open we remain to continuing loving relation-ships with those who are not physically present, the more love we have available to give to contemporary relationships with those who are living. The notion of withdrawing energy as if it were just so much emotional capital that can be reallocated to another higher-interest-bearing account strikes me as bizarre."

Neimeyer advocates helping people resist letting death intervene artifi-cially to end their sense of relationship to those who have died. He is rarely interested in using an empty chair, or any other technique, in order to help people to say goodbye or let go of those who have played a critically impor-tant role in their lives, unless that role has been thoroughly destructive, as in instances of severe abuse or oppression. Instead he is interested in helping people to rebuild their connections in a different sphere and context. For Joanne, this meant recapturing a sense of her father as a significant part of her life story, of her history as well as her present and future. With remarkable ease, she was able to relocate his voice inside her, providing strength and sup-port in a way that had not been present before. The effects of this shift became more and more evident across their remaining three sessions of contact.

Joanne was not the only one to notice this difference. During their fourth session Neimeyer noticed the change in her appearance. In the past she had always come in dressed elegantly in the most fashionable business attire, everything perfectly coordinated and in place. Now he noticed that she was dressed neatly, but far more casually, and this was reflected in her more re-laxed demeanor as well.

"Something has lifted for me," Joanne reported. "I no longer feel like a puppet at the end of a string."

"You do look different indeed," Neimeyer agreed.

Joanne went on to talk about other benefits that were taking place. She had begun an exercise program. She felt more involved in her daughter's life, "setting down her foot" when her daughter started drifting toward "the wrong crowd."

"Have others noticed these developments as well?" Neimeyer asked. "What are their comments on the person you seem to be becoming?" He wanted to anchor the development of the new narrative about who she was as a person in the responses of a relevant audience.

"Michael respects me more," she said. "He's been asking my opinion about things that he never did before. It's like I'm really finding my voice as a woman, and he respects that." Joanne then went on to describe parallel changes in her relationships with various church ladies, who at first seemed surprised by her new-found assertiveness on congregational committees, but were starting to appreciate the novel ideas she was contributing to the church's mission.

"And to what do you attribute these changes?"

It was perhaps no surprise that she talked about the dramatic dialogue with her father in the empty chair. It was the first time since his death that she really felt her father's love and devotion, and his strong confidence in her ability to live her life and make her own decisions. She would never forget what it felt like to see and experience the world through his senses and body, to literally sit in his chair. And, as she noted, this idea of cherishing a lasting bond with her father seemed entirely compatible with her religious faith, which emphasized their eventual reconnection in an afterlife.

Neimeyer nodded. "Therapy is kind of like an echo chamber in a way. All the things that you need to say to yourself can be said and heard, but also amplified. They seem to have helped you sense and pursue the new directions you want to take in your life."

■ ■ ■

Narrative Metaphors

Central to Neimeyer's work, and a significant part of many constructivist approaches, is to attend carefully to the alternative stories that people might act out, and that sometimes people live. "I am interested in looking at the ways dominant narratives that arise within communities can colonize and constrict the lives of those who are subjected to them. In Joanne's case, one of those narratives had a kind of two-edged-sword aspect to it—as first lady of the church she was accorded respect but also kept within a narrowly defined role. This was a role that was not entirely fitting for her, and one she needed to modify or edit in order to make it more her own. She needed to find a way of being her own preferred self in the church community."

There were, of course, many differences between the therapist and client. Neimeyer, a white male from the dominant culture, needed to connect with Joanne, who was an integral part of the black church. This is another facet of their work together that he finds important—good therapy is culturally responsive therapy, that is, respectful of the unique background of clients. Neimeyer considered this dimension of their work as worth noting because he found himself learning something not about only the content of Joanne's spiritual beliefs, but also about the church community that sustained—and constrained—her. In this he felt like a respectful and curious anthropologist who was being introduced to the belief system and social structure of a society to which he was only a visitor. This position of being "one down" to the client's knowledge of her world rather than a "one up" authority on the right way to live reflected his basic belief in the nature of the therapy relationship: it was basically a relationship between two experts, one of whom was expert on the content of her life, and the other of whom was an expert in fostering the process of reflective change.

Neimeyer's therapy with Joanne reflected other features of his general approach to therapy as well. For one thing, it was technically eclectic but theoretically consistent, incorporating elements of several different models (Gestalt, narrative, feminist, and systemic), all organized under a constructivist, meaning-making umbrella. And for another, it was both intense and emotionally charged, leading to deep engagement between the two of them.

Neimeyer cited this case as an example of the ways that presenting problems occur at the level of meaning rather than behavior alone. "Attempting to modify behavior like panic attacks, focusing exclusively on symptoms that are bleached of meaning, is needlessly concrete and ultimately, I think, stultifying. It also risks establishing a power relationship in which the therapist arrogantly assumes authority and expertise and positions the client as a naive student or learner."

To Neimeyer, therapy is a dialectical process on many levels. It is certainly a collaborative give-and-take between client and therapist perspectives, but also between knowing when to lead and when to follow in order to address efficiently the most important issues that the client is ready to engage. "By going to the root of Joanne's sense of powerlessness and disconnection from her father, we made much more efficient progress in dealing with the anxiety and panic attacks then if we had become concerned only with managing those symptoms."

CHAPTER

25 A Demolition Project

A Case from David Scharff

David Scharff is widely sought as a lecturer and supervisor in the area of Object Relations theory, a contemporary adaptation of psychoanalytic theory that focuses on intimate relationships, both past and present. Among his most influential books are Object Relations Family Therapy, Object Relations Couple Therapy, Object Relations Therapy of Physical and Sexual Trauma, *and* Scharff Notes. *David, and his wife Jill, have worked together as co-therapists and co-writers.*

Scharff was trained as a psychiatrist and received his medical degree from Harvard Medical School. He presently works as the Co-Director of the International Institute of Object Relations Therapy in Chevy Chase, Maryland, where he also maintains a private practice in psychoanalysis and psychotherapy.

The "Ideal Patient"

Don was the kind of patient that any therapist hopes for: he was articulate, gracious, introspective, and curious about himself. He worked hard in individual sessions, scheduled twice per week, plus additional weekly appointments with his wife, Judy. When Don felt some disagreement or resistance, he would carefully and respectfully present his position, but he remained open to continue dialogue.

"I realized," Scharff recalled, "that I idealized him, and that is always dangerous. Partly because of my theoretical background—which holds that an idealized relationship is not a benign affair—I knew to be wary. Nevertheless, I enjoyed having such a gratifying patient."

Scharff is unapologetically and passionately a psychoanalyst, although he includes many other theoretical contributions in his work, which is most often described as Object Relations. "I am always interested in how the patient is seeing me even if he is talking about other things," Scharff explained. "The central guidance system for understanding the role of the therapeutic relationship—known technically as the transference–countertransference interaction—is how I am feeling. I used the training I had in my own therapy and supervision as a way of building a foundation for knowing how to use my own responses to a patient."

Don and Judy had consulted Scharff because their marriage was unsatisfactory. They were neither cruel nor abusive to one another—there was just a marked indifference, a vacuum that had existed between them ever since their children had left home.

Scharff immediately felt an affinity for Don and identified strongly with him. They made solid, consistent progress in their individual sessions, as well as in their meetings with Judy to work on the marital relationship.

The Dream

Several months into their work, Don and Judy began to ask whether they had always misunderstood one another in a way that was just now coming to the surface. After this realization, Don became uncharacteristically quiet in an individual session. "I don't know what I want to talk to you about today," he announced with a shrug.

Scharff nodded. And waited.

"I suppose I could tell you about a piece of a dream," Don said after a period of silence. "I can't remember very much, but if you want. . . ." He stopped and shrugged again.

"Go on," Scharff encouraged him, feeling a bit tantalized by the half-offer of the dream—something Don knew well would interest him.

"Well, in the dream I was teaching in a classroom. It was an old fifties or sixties kind of classroom with small wooden desks and plastic tops. Not like modern classrooms. The students were listening and suddenly there was a loud noise outside the window from a welding torch. I went outside to see if there was something I could do about the noise and found myself on a catwalk on the side of the building. There was a huge construction site adjoining the building. It was a block or so long, wide and very deep. There was a huge crane in it and there were a lot of construction people. It was as though the crane and the construction crew and all of that were one organism operating together. Then there was a shovel from the crane coming toward the building where I was standing on the catwalk. It was taking off huge pieces of the catwalk on the floor above me. There was iron sticking out, and pieces of concrete from the catwalk above. I realized that I was in danger and it could be destroying the building and even the catwalk that I was on. I felt helpless, like there was nothing I could do about it—and then my alarm went off."

Don stopped abruptly and looked up at Scharff expectantly, as if to say, "Okay, you're the expert, so what the hell do you make of that?"

Scharff felt quite excited about the dream and its possible significance for his patient. One of the most challenging, and interesting, aspects of his work is examining the ways that dreams can reveal transference feelings. He works with dreams by encouraging the patient to "associate" to them, that is, to give thoughts that come up in association to the whole dream or its details. To facilitate this, he said, "I wonder what thoughts and feelings you have about the dream?"

Don elaborated about the sense of helplessness he felt, and especially the way the tall crane seemed to represent something important to him. It also struck him as significant that he had been outside the classroom and in some sort of danger that he could not fully grasp. The classroom itself was more like those of his high school than like the modern ones in which he now often taught.

Insight

Scharff listened carefully to Don's associations but could not yet make any direct links to either his current or past life. "What I thought was that this was directly about the therapy, that he was trying to carry out his regular life doing ordinary things while therapy is creating this noise and disturbance that represent both a building project and also a danger. That is to say, I thought that this image of the danger in the construction site might refer to the thoughts of demolition that were going on as part of the building that we were trying to do in therapy, and in which he suddenly found himself frightened."

Scharff kept these possible interpretations to himself, not wanting to rush his patient by forcing him to examine their relationship prematurely. At the time, he thought his own hesitation odd, as he would normally bring such ideas out into the open, especially when the transference theme is so obvious. In retrospect, he realized he felt an inexplicable inhibition about doing his ordinary work of centering understanding on the transference. Finally, he offered mildly and rather indirectly, "I wonder if this dream could refer to our own therapy project together?"

"Well," Don said hesitantly. "I suppose that is a possibility. But I'm not aware of being frightened about what we're doing here."

"There's no fear?"

"Maybe some anxiety," Don agreed, "I mean about what changes would bring."

"What do you mean?"

"Well, Judy and I came here originally to work on our marriage. And then you said I should do some individual work as well. I trust your professional judgement, but if you hadn't made the recommendation I wouldn't be doing this therapy right now."

"You wouldn't be working on yourself," Scharff clarified.

"Right. I only came here to make things better with Judy."

Scharff felt immediately disappointed, although he was careful not to show this in his face. He had come to value his relationship with Don, to enjoy their time together, and now he felt that Don was saying that it meant little to him. He realized that what Don said had the effect of saying that Scharff valued the work more than Don did. "So, you only came to work on your marriage," he repeated while pondering where to go next.

Don nodded. "I've been thinking about the therapy. You've been pushing me to think about the process, am I right?"

Scharff nodded.

"It's kind of like in physics where we've moved from the surface, physical world to metaphysics."

"I'm not sure what you mean," Scharff prompted.

"Well, I was just wondering whether, you know, whether this is all routine for you. Is this just you doing your job? I am wondering if you will even answer that question."

Scharff was surprised how perceptive Don was, how quickly he latched onto the feelings that he had, as yet, not brought out. He thought about the transference and countertransference feelings between them and his own reluctance to interpret that aspect of the dream, even with obvious grounds to do so.

Like most therapists who are puzzling through a problem, Scharff was quiet in order to buy some time for his own thought processes. He thought back to a few weeks earlier, when Don announced out of the blue that he was ready to stop the individual sessions. They had gotten past that impasse when Scharff had interpreted Don's difficulty bringing negative feelings about Scharff into the room, but here they were again. "I realize," Scharff now said, "that we have haven't been focusing on our relationship enough, and that may be the main message in your dream."

Don nodded slowly. "Maybe so."

Scharff waited for him to continue.

"But I still wonder where this is going. I mean, is this what we are supposed to be doing according to the textbooks, or is it actually your judgment that this is what I need right now?"

"I think this is the focus that is called for you right now," Scharff said, taking up the challenge. "And I think that the negative things that you are bringing up in our relationship are also evident in your relationship with Judy. And I also think you are asking if I am really thinking about your specific needs, or whether I'm just cruising along without having your specific needs in mind, because that would be more frightening."

Confrontation

This time Don did not become defensive. He thought for a minute or two. "Yeah, that makes sense. I think I knew that this was part of the dream, which was why I didn't want to bring it up."

Scharff started to get excited. "The dream conveys your fear of things being torn down in here, and rebuilt in a way that you can't predict and so you feel helpless."

"But I really don't feel afraid."

"You did say recently that you were going to quit the therapy, just when things were going well. You have also had a lot of feelings about coming here. You've told me that you really like it, but you think it is such an indulgence that you shouldn't let yourself do it."

"Yes," Don agreed. "I do feel it is an indulgence. Nobody has ever listened to me like this, about these things about my family and siblings. Nobody has ever listened to me say things I'm concerned about, or ashamed of, or afraid about. I really like it."

Don looked thoughtful and hesitated. "But," he continued, "it still feels like an indulgence and I don't think I would be doing this if it wasn't for the need to help us as a couple. If I decided, or Judy decided, that the marriage was over, I don't think I would continue this."

Scharff nodded, understanding the message clearly that Don doesn't have the motivation to continue the therapeutic work, and that he had been asking Scharff to carry that motivation silently for him. "So although you like the sessions, you couldn't do it for yourself."

Don nodded.

"It is not just a matter of doing this as an indulgence. It also has folded into it the fear. You don't actually feel the fear, but you do things that have to do with withdrawing, as though you were afraid. You have these questions for me today, about how I was shifting focus, but you didn't bring them up. You said, 'Oh well, I just had a little dream that I don't understand at all, and it doesn't mean anything, but I can tell it if *you* like.' Before you told me the dream you already had the plan to ask me about how I was working—whether I just work by the book, or did I have you in mind as a unique individual. So you lived something out with me. You told me the dream, which got me to make the statement to you about the relevance of your feelings to the treatment, and that led to the very question that you intended to ask me. Unconsciously, you set me up to do something that embodied just what you were worried about."

Don looked at Scharff for a moment, then looked away. He seemed to be processing things but not yet ready to speak. A minute elapsed, then another. Scharff waited.

"One of the things about this," Don said, "is that it is hard when I learn something about myself that I didn't know before. I feel so stupid for not having known it before."

Scharff nodded, recognizing that the interpretation had hit home, freeing up new material that had been inaccessible previously—a sign of an interpretation that has been useful. "It feels humiliating to you to admit that that there are some things that you should have known all along. I think that further conveys the sense of the dream. The classroom is one that dates back to an old time—that is, your childhood—but you are seeing it as an adult. That classroom relates not just to earlier school time but to earlier in your life and to things that you think you should have learned long ago as a child. Can you say something more about the classroom?"

Scharff was digging for another association to the meaning of the classroom in the dream.

"It didn't relate to high school," Don responded. "I'm sure of that. We had a particular kind of table that was donated by a guy who had given a lot of money to the school. He gave all these tables that were round so that every classroom had the same ones. They would have been the tables in junior high school. I think it pertains not to elementary school, where there would be small desks, but to seventh and eighth grade."

Recognizing the direct link of the dream to a specific time in his life, Scharff probed this further. "Almost as far back as you can remember there is this setting where you have been a learner and a teacher in almost the same way. Now it's being threatened by a blow torch." As he said this he felt the blow torch might be the things that are happening that come out of his mouth. Then he waited a moment for this to sink in before adding: "There is as much demolition as there is hope of construction. But even the construction is in a deep pit, and you don't know what will happen in it or if you are in danger."

Again Don insisted he did not feel like he was in any particular danger.

"Maybe so," Scharff said gently. "But you have acted as though you are." Seeing the quizzical look, he clarified that it was danger that the marriage was falling apart that brought them to therapy in the first place. In the individual therapy, it was the danger of humiliation in learning new things that made him feel he should have known them all along.

Don nodded. "Yes, that is true."

Seeing the session was about to end, Scharff added one further point. "When you feel that Judy has been angry with you about something—even something minor where she felt that you had used her in some way, all she has to do is express some annoyance or partial anger and you feel that the bottom has dropped out of your life. You are so sensitive that the world collapses like that catwalk in the dream, so all the good feelings disappear. Judy's main complaint is that she can't even be annoyed at you without it feeling like doom to you. That special sensitivity works here as well."

"Yes," Don agreed, "I would like to work on that some more."

"Your marriage needs reconstruction but it was in a pit, and you couldn't tell if the catwalk that you were on might represent your narrow perch with your wife. Maybe it represents your marriage itself."

Don looked thoughtful as he stood up. As he walked out of the office, Scharff felt a quiet exhilaration of a breakthrough.

"When somebody like Don," Scharff explained, "buys into the idea that he can really make use of his therapeutic relationship as a laboratory for the way he conducts all relationships in his life, he becomes much more invested in the work we're doing. Then it's available as not just a thing to study in itself, but it is like a global positioning system. We can use it together as a guide to figure out where we are in the work. Then we don't always have to focus in the relationship in every session, but it's always there in the background guiding the work."

Deconstruction

This session, Scharff believes, represents the way that psychodynamic work can reveal issues and themes that had previously been operating like a stealth bomber, under the radar screen. Don was totally unaware of the fears he felt in relationships, both with his wife and his therapist. Yet now he felt freer to own and express his fears without taking refuge in the withdrawal patterns he had exhibited previously.

Scharff noted that Don had learned this interpersonal strategy from the template established in the relationship with his mother. "She wanted her children to be giants among men, and so they had to conform to her idealized view of what the world should be like—and that was pretty frightening. Don wanted to please her, but could never manage to do so in spite of his accomplishments."

Don had observed the way his own father had dealt with his mother through withdrawal. Throughout his childhood, Don witnessed the way his father catered to his demanding mother, pleased her in every way he could, yet remained detached from any real intimacy. And so he had unconsciously chosen a similar coping mechanism in identification with his idealized father.

Now Don faced an ongoing "construction project" in his own marriage, and he was dealing with his wife and with Scharff's therapeutic "demands" much the same way his father had dealt with his mother. Scharff saw his task as to help Don to dig down deeper and open a pit that would allow for greater maneuverability. Rather than a form of demolition, he hoped that Don saw this more as a form of deconstruction. But to facilitate a change in Don's way of seeing the project, he had to expose the underpinnings of personality structure that operated both in the marriage and in the therapy. After all, it was the perception of demolition that was threatening Don's sense of safety.

The sessions continued, although not always with dramatic progress. "There are always a lot of hours that you are just grinding your way through," Scharff said. "You're slogging through it and you're wondering if it is doing anything meaningful. The patient isn't behaving the way you want him to behave, and I am not behaving the way I want to behave. Nothing seems to be happening. Then, once in awhile, there is an hour like this when something happens that really seems to center the treatment and provide a kind of growth. I know it draws on the incremental work of all the sessions that have come before when nothing happens on the surface, but it is sessions like this that feel really good."

■   ■   ■

Lessons

There are two themes that Scharff feels are important in this case. The first is patience; the second is living with uncertainty. Both of these lessons refer to the importance of a therapist learning to tolerate the ambiguity and complexity of this work so that meaning can grow from inside the experience. "You can see that in this hour—At the beginning I was recognizing a transference interpretation but I felt restrained from offering it before Don was ready. That seemingly innocuous puzzle turned out to be the key that unlocked the hour and showed me what Don had been struggling with."

Scharff believes that this case is a particularly good example of how we can learn from inside the shared experience with our patients—far more than we might imagine possible. It is through examining and analyzing the relationships we have with those we help that we are able to uncover and resolve the same processes that have been influencing them since childhood.

CHAPTER

26 To Dare to Tell the Truth

A Case from Terrence Real

Terry Real is a Senior Faculty Member of the Family Institute of Cambridge in Massachusetts and Director of the Gender Relations Program at the Meadows Institute in Arizona. He also works as a social worker and consultant in Newton, Massachusetts. He is the author of several books, I Don't Want to Talk about It: Overcoming the Secret Legacy of Male Depression, How Can I Get through to You?, *and* Closing the Intimacy Gap between Men and Women.

Real has developed a theory called relational recovery therapy that applies family therapy ideas in a way that is particularly responsive to gender differences, and especially men's issues.

Some Basic but Radical Ideas

Before launching into his case, Real first explained the nature of his relational recovery therapy, which he believes is different in significant ways from other helping approaches. As you read the following story it is important to understand the context for his interventions, which may strike you as unusual if not provocative.

Taking sides. Real does not subscribe to the usual convention that therapists should remain neutral and nonjudgmental. Not only is that virtually impossible, it is not all that useful, he contends. Moreover, in the majority of instances, Real not only takes sides with couples, but nine out of ten times he favors the position of the woman.

He pointed out that most therapists would direct couples to respond to one another in the following manner: "What do you think about that, Mrs. Johns?" Or: "Mr. Johns, what do you have to say in response to your wife's observation?" Instead, relational recovery therapy proceeds like this: "Mr. Johns, your wife is perfectly correct. This is what is going to happen if you change; and this is what is going to happen if you do not."

"There is an essential asymmetry to most relationships," Real explained. "It is the women who bring men into couples therapy, not the other way around. And they bring them in to be fixed. What this means is that they want men to be more relational, connected, and interpersonally skilled. This is not a criticism, simply a reality: this is the way we raise men and women differently."

Real admitted that he breaks a cardinal rule of therapy in his work: Thou shalt not take sides, and especially not to "privilege" one gender over the other. He reverses the usual procedure whereby usually first we win the man's trust and then we deal with the difficult truths. In Real's approach, the way he attempts to win the man's trust is by dealing with the difficult truths from the beginning.

Telling the truth. The second order of business that is implicit in the previous point is that Real emphasizes the importance of being totally honest and upfront. He models this in the ways that he confronts couples with the obvious facets of their relationship that they have been ignoring. "I form an alliance with both parties through the truth."

Coming down from grandiosity. Whereas most therapies attempt to help people move up from their sense of shame, Real brings them down from their inflated sense of self-importance. Perhaps not surprisingly from the previous points, he concentrates mostly on helping men to stop "leading" with their grandiosity and instead to deal with their covert issues of shame (he does the opposite with women).

"So," Real summarized, "I want to be clear about the three things that I do that tend to be unique. One, I take sides. Two, I tell the truth—immediately, bluntly, and precisely. And three, I take on issues of grandiosity."

Can't Love Him or Leave Him

Mary and Bill were similar to most couples who come for therapy: they were on the verge of divorce. Mary had already consulted previous therapists without success; this time she was dragging her husband in with her. "As much as I love him," she explained, "and I do love him with all my heart, I find it impossible to live with him."

"What seems to be the problem?" Real asked.

Mary sighed, as if unsure how to list all of them. "Well, let's see. He's irritable with the children. He yells at them a lot. He's impatient. He is controlling—not just with them, but me too. He orders everyone around as if we are his slaves."

"Is that all?" Real joked.

"No," Mary replied, with no hint of a smile. "We all walk around on eggshells because we're afraid he might explode. He has a terrible temper."

Real glanced at Bill for his reaction, but he was sitting there like a machine that had been unplugged. He was eerily still, his face blank, totally disconnected. He sat with the most perfect posture that Real had ever seen, ramrod straight in the chair, hands placed precisely on his knees, head forward, eyes straight ahead. He looked like a marine even though he had never been in the military. In fact, he was a salesman and he had initially greeted Real with the kinetic energy one associates with a fast-talking, skilled professional who is used to convincing people to buy things they don't really need. But now he had gone into complete hibernation, as if he had left the room.

Mary had the scrubbed look of a Midwestern farm girl. Initially, she had seemed rather passive and docile, but once asked about her husband she became quite animated. She talked more about her frustration and helplessness, then finally added: "It's against my religion to say I am mad, but. . . ." She left that thought unfinished, yet made it perfectly clear that she was absolutely furious at Bill for the way he behaved at home.

Real learned that Bill had been taking medication for some time to control his temper, but that it didn't seem to help. He'd also seen an individual therapist for the past few months.

"Have you noticed any difference since then?" Real asked.

Mary nodded. "Yeah, he is doing a little better," she admitted, "but not nearly enough."

"So, you've had just about enough of this and that's why you brought Bill in."

Again she nodded. "I won't say that I'm ready to file for divorce just yet—it's not the way we do things in my family. But I don't know what I'm going to do. I just can't keep living like this."

"When you say, 'like this,'" Real pressed, "what exactly do you mean?"

"Well, the kids are getting older. Our daughter, Kay, is having some problems."

"What sort of problems?"

"She's been overeating and then doing that binge thing. She doesn't have any friends."

"She's isolated."

"Yes," Mary agreed. "She spends all her time alone. The other kids pick on her. And then, as if that isn't hard enough for the poor girl, her father is constantly on her case as well. It's too much. It's just too much!" As she said the last thing, there was fierceness in her voice that startled Real. He looked over at Bill, but he was still sitting there like a stone statue. The only sign that he was alive was the gentle rise and fall of his chest as he breathed.

Kay wasn't Mary's only concern. Their son, Trevor, seemed to be picking up many of his father's traits. He was becoming increasingly uncommunicative, walking around all the time like he had a chip on his shoulder.

"And what do you make of all this?" Real turned and asked Bill.

Bill nodded his head imperceptibly, as if he was the tin man who was trying to reactivate himself after rusting in the rain. Then the rumble of his voice: "She's probably right."

"You agree with Mary's assessment of the situation?" Real was actually quite surprised by this response. Usually, he sees a lot of argument and mutual blame at this stage in the process.

"Well," he said slowly. "She is right about some of the stuff at home. I do have a temper on me," he laughed. "The guys at work tease me about it sometimes. And I am hard on the kids, more than I should be. But I just think if that girl would. . . ."

"You were saying that you agreed with Mary," Real said to get things back on track.

"Look," Bill answered, "I love my wife. I love my family. It's been hard on all of us. I know she's had the brunt of things, but I've been trying."

"You feel you have made some progress," Real clarified.

"I have. And I don't think Mary understands how hard it has been for me, how hard I've been trying. When she threatens me like this, it only makes things worse."

"You don't like it when she tells you the truth about the controlling, abusive ways you treat people?" Real looked for a flinch after this confrontation, but Bill seemed to take it well.

"It isn't just that," Bill protested. "Our sex life stinks. The juice between us has dried up. She used to be affectionate and all, but not any more."

"Oh come on, Bill! How can you say that?" Mary was truly angry, and hurt. "What about last night when I came up to you and I put my arms around you? You just pushed me away because you wanted to watch that game on television."

"But you know how I like to relax. . . ."

"Okay then, what about Monday night? Was that some kind of dream? Was that. . . ."

"Okay, okay, you're right. But still, you've been pushing me away."

"Wait a minute," Real interrupted. "I'm confused. Bill, on the one hand you are agreeing with Mary's assessment that you can be explosive and controlling, and then you are saying that you don't understand why she would withdraw from you and not show you the affection you want."

Bill stared back at Real, giving him the kind of look he might direct toward a balking customer who was not cooperating. This was not going at all like he had hoped. "But I *am* trying," he said, "but I don't think she gives me any credit for what I'm trying to do. This isn't easy, you know." As he said this, he showed real feeling for the first time, losing his stony expression.

The 80/20 Rule

Turning to Mary, Real asked her if she could perhaps provide an example of what she meant by her husband's explosiveness.

"Well," she said after thinking a moment, "last week Kay was in her room. She often goes into her room and shuts the door. I wish she wouldn't spend so much time alone, but anyway, she had grabbed something to eat and was in her room listening to music or something. And then Bill goes in there to check on her and he didn't like it that she had brought food in there. He wants the kids to only eat in the kitchen, you know."

"Another way that he attempts to control everyone," Real said.

"That's right," she answered, like she hadn't thought of it in that way until now. "Anyway, he started banging on Kay's door, insisting that she open up and bring the food outside. I mean, the girl has enough trouble as it is with her eating and now he's on her case when she finally does eat something. So then they started yelling at one another. . . ."

"I was only trying. . . ."

"Let her finish, Bill," Real intervened. He didn't want them to get in a situation where he'd have to defend himself at this time. It was more important to get clear examples of the behavior that was getting in the way.

"So," Mary continued, "then he starts banging on the door and telling Kay to open up the f***ing door or he was going to knock the thing down. That was *his* words, by the way, as I would never use such language." As she said this, a look of fear came into her face, as if she had gone too far.

"Have you ever tried to step in when Bill becomes like this?" Real asked her.

She shook her head and looked down.

"I'm just curious, why not?"

"I'd just be afraid to, I guess," Mary said out loud what she was obviously feeling.

"Has Bill ever turned on you?"

"No," Mary said quickly, looking at Bill, "not like that. But I'm still afraid of him. He just becomes so frightening when he gets like that."

Real looked over at Bill to see how he was taking all this and noted that he seemed calm. "Bill, is there anything about what Mary is reporting that you want to correct, or that is not substantially true."

"Well, I guess I just want to say that I was trying to help Kay. She's been. . . ."

"That's not what I asked you," Real interrupted as gently but firmly as he could.

"It's true that I was angry," Bill admitted. "But the door wasn't really locked. And I didn't start screaming at Kay until she started yelling at me. That's no way to speak to her father."

"Bill," Real responded. "I have an 80/20 no quibble rule."

"What's that?" Bill said, taking the bait.

"If what was said is 80 percent right, that is good enough for our purposes. Now, would you agree that what Mary reported is at least 80 percent accurate, that it captures the main thrust of what happened?"

"Yes, I guess so."

"You guess so?"

"Okay, it is mostly true."

Real nodded, satisfied by the admission. "Do you have any idea how scary you can be, how you terrify your wife and your children?"

Bill looked sheepish. "Well, I guess so, but. . . ."

"You *guess* so. You don't sound very convincing."

"I don't know," Bill said. "It's hard for me to see. They tell me I'm scary and all but I don't feel that way to myself. I just don't see it. But I guess if they tell me that I seem that way that it must be so."

"So," Real reflected, "you're saying that this feels normal to you to be so blustery and intimidating and explosive?"

"Well. . . ."

Before Bill could answer, Mary jumped in. "This pales in comparison to what he grew up with."

Real looked at Bill for confirmation. "Would you be willing to talk about that?" he asked him.

Bill proceeded to talk about how he had been brutalized as a child by his father, who repeatedly humiliated him. He would be made to stand in the middle of the living room in his underwear. It was even worse to watch what his father did to Bill's twin sister. In some ways he felt relief when he had been the victim rather than his sister.

"You are saying that your father was a sadist," Real reflected.

"It wasn't that bad," Bill started to protest.

"Let's be clear about this," Real insisted. "Your father was abusive to both you and your sister, physically, emotionally, and sexually."

Bill nodded.

"And furthermore, he was violent, domineering, and dangerous. He actually took pleasure in hurting you."

Bill nodded again. Tears started falling down his cheeks and then he began to cry in earnest, deep sobs that shook his body. Mary leaned over and squeezed his arm, a gesture that seemed to ignite even deeper weeping. After some minutes, he wiped his sleeve across his face. "I think he even went after my sister mostly to get at me. He knew how much it bothered me."

"What makes you say that?" Real probed.

"Because he'd make me watch what he did to her, terrible things, horrible things, things I can't even talk about. And the whole time he'd be looking at me, checking my reactions."

"And what *were* you feeling then?"

"I just wanted to kill him!" Bill said, with real fury in his voice. For the first time, Real could see the kind of rage welling up in him that Mary found so terrifying to be around.

"What about when you were banging on your daughter's bedroom door?" Real pressed.

"What do you mean?" Bill said, gulping breaths.

"I wondered about how you were feeling toward your daughter when she defied you, whether you wanted to kill her as well?"

Bill slumped in his chair and nodded. He had totally collapsed.

The Truth Will Set You Free

A large part of the work that Real does is educational, teaching his clients about concepts like the toxic legacy of masculinity. He explained to both Mary and Bill that there are many forms of abuse other than those that are most dramatic. "The form of abuse we normally think of we call 'disempowering abuse.' It is about shaming a child, hurting him and making him feel helpless and small. The other form of abuse is about artificially pumping a kid up so that he feels better than others. This is what creates feelings of grandiosity."

Mary and Bill both nodded, indicating they were at least tracking, if not understanding, what Real was saying to them.

"When you are on the receiving end of disempowering abuse, you turn out to be a victim; when you are on the receiving end of false empowerment, that sets you up to be a perpetrator."

"So," Bill responded, "what does all this have to do with me?"

"Good question," Real said. "When your father was doing things to you, when you were on the receiving end of abuse, you were being shamed and injured and humiliated."

Bill nodded that he agreed so far.

"But there's more to it than that," Real continued. "Your father was also communicating to you that when you grew up and were a man yourself, you would get to behave shamelessly the way he had. This is how a man behaves when he becomes angry. The reason why you don't know how scary you are is because your thermostat is busted on this. You grew up in a world and family in which yelling, and screaming, and banging on doors, and giving into rage was considered perfectly appropriate. A part of you thinks that it is okay to be the way you are. But let's be clear about this: it is not!"

"Yeah, well, I know this already."

"No, you don't. The part of you that I am talking to right now knows that it is not okay, but there's another part of you that feels helpless and frustrated, that feels no shame at all about lashing out at others. You feel like your daughter was victimizing you and this gave you permission to hurt her back. And this is shameless."

"Well," Bill protested. "I don't think it's all as bad as you make it out to be."

"No?" Real answered. "Watch this." He then turned to Mary: "Am I exaggerating in any way what is going on in your home?"

Mary immediately shook her head.

"Mary, give me a percentage on a scale of 1 to 10 indicating how much you think Bill's anger is shameless in terms of its effects on the family."

"Ten," Mary answered without hesitation. "If you let me rate it higher, I'd give you a bigger number."

"Bill," Real said, turning back to him, "what's it like to hear Mary say that. Do you think she is making this up?"

"No," he answered. "I don't think that."

As he was speaking, Mary began crying.

"Look, Bill," Real pressed, "I don't know what happened to your father to make him the way he was. And I don't know what happened to the person who abused him when he was a child. But you are on the verge of passing this legacy on to your own son and daughter. How would you like them to grow up and do to their children what was done to you?"

Bill dropped his head. Mary continued crying.

"Would you like this to happen?" Real asked again.

"No," Bill whispered. "I don't want to hurt my kids."

"It must just kill you to see yourself acting like your own father. It must just make you sick."

Bill joined his wife in her tears, both of them crying at this point.

Real waited and watched them both. He had been trying to bring Bill into his shame. "My metaphor," Real explained, "is entering the earth's atmosphere from the coldest reaches of outer space. As you move into the earth's atmosphere, a lot of heat is generated and it is not comfortable. It is like the way a limb feels at first if it is frozen; it feels tremendously painful but you are happy that you feel something at all."

"I do feel so numb all the time," Bill admitted.

Mary cleared her throat and Bill turned to face her. For the first time in the session they were making eye contact with one another. "I just don't know how to love you," Mary said to her husband. "You bug me about being more affectionate, but when I try, or I don't do it right—the way you want it—you get so mad at me. I just wish you could love me. I wish you knew how to love."

Real could feel tears pooling within his own eyes. What a scene this would be if all three of them started crying at the same time! He looked over at Bill and said, "You know, she's right. You really don't know how to love. It's hard to imagine you could know very much about love given the family you came from and what you learned from your own father." Real waited for a moment for this to sink in, then added: "But you could learn to love if you really wanted to."

Real's heart was pounding as he said these words. He felt like he was taking a tremendous risk by confronting Bill in this way, especially when he was already vulnerable. Yet this was a turning point in the development of

Real's ideas about therapy; this is the case in which he learned to dare tell the truth to men about their limitations. He imagined that perhaps if he ever did point out limitations in this honest and direct way that perhaps people would go screaming out of the room, or have some kind of psychotic breakdown, or rip his throat out. But none of these things happened with Bill: he didn't run out of the room, nor did he respond with defensiveness or rage.

Bill sensed that Real was rooting for him. Even though this encounter was nothing like anything he had ever expected would happen in therapy (Weren't therapists supposed to be gentle and supportive and nurturing?), he could still feel the caring that was offered.

From where Real was sitting, it looked like Bill began to melt. All the rigidity went out of him. His face relaxed and his body slumped. In many ways, he looked like a little boy. "I don't mean to be naive or simplistic," Real explained, "but at the moment I told him the truth and offered him the help, he surrendered to it for that moment. I felt a tremendous responsibility to deliver the goods after that, but I thought I could."

Real next talked to Mary about being a bystander and not intervening when she needed to. He drew her out to talk about what this helplessness was like for her. She cried throughout the conversation, sharing her guilt and shame about the damage that had already been inflicted on her children while she had not done nearly enough to stop the abuse.

"It isn't just Bill," she said. "It's not all his fault. I should have found some way to put a stop to it. They're my children too." She then went on to talk about her own family background, which had so ill-prepared her for this sort of situation.

"Yes," Real agreed, deciding that honesty was as important with Mary as with Bill. "You're right. For reasons that are very understandable you let the children swing in the wind with this man, and you are going to have to deal with that."

Mary began sobbing again, moaning her remorse and regrets.

"Look," Real said gently, "you each did the best you could. Mary, what would have happened if you had stood up to Bill? You would have ended up divorced. It is true that you are culpable for the damage inflicted on your children, just as Bill is. There's nothing you can do about what already happened. But now let's deal with it."

Real recalled that this was where he crossed the line from the way he had been trained to a new kind of work that was to become relational recovery work. And it all started with looking in Bill and Mary's eyes and telling them, yes, you did mess up. Big time. Now let's move on.

Stop on a Dime

Real disclosed that he had also been raised in a raging family, an environment in which his grandiosity had evolved as a defense against abuse. "One of the ways I try not to swamp men with shame is I talk about my own recovery with similar issues. The image I use when you grow up with rage is that you become accustomed to level 10. Then, with great heroic effort, you squeeze the knob down to 3 and you think you have done a terrific job. And you have, except that everyone else around you is saying, 'Can you please turn that anger down? I can't stand it.' They are right, because the level you are at is unlivable for anyone else, but it seems like quiet compared to what you grew up with."

Real suggested that Mary and Bill call a family meeting to let their children know about what you are both working on. Next, he negotiated a contract between the two of them, under which any time when Mary felt Bill was crossing the line, she would signal him unobtrusively. "And Bill," Real emphasized, "You may not think you are going too far, but we've already agreed that you can't tell the difference. So you must trust Mary's judgment on this. Are you prepared to do that?"

Bill nodded solemnly.

"Good. It doesn't matter if you think she is exaggerating, or busting your chops, you're still to stop on a dime and take a time-out." They agreed that Bill would immediately stop whatever he was doing and relax somewhere for a 20-minute interval before returning. This was not to be a final solution but rather a transitional step to break the established pattern.

Over time, Mary became more assertive and, not surprisingly, Bill developed more restraint. The effects were immediate on the children, who were also brought into the sessions at one point. During those meetings, Bill was coached on how to be a different father to his son and daughter. And Terry Real learned the power of speaking the truth to his clients as a way to help them confront the dysfunctional legacies of the past.

27 Letters of Faith

A Case from Stephen Madigan

Steven Madigan is a leading narrative therapist and trainer. Madigan works at helping people re-author their lives and develop healthier life stories. He believes that people's problems are actually the result of oppression from the dominant society. Madigan has specialized in applying narrative therapy to the treatment of eating disorders.

Madigan is the Founder and Director of Yaletown Family Therapy in Vancouver and Toronto, Canada, and co-owner of PlanetTherapy, an online professional education program. He is the author of several books, including PRAXIS: Situating Feminism, *and* Discourse and Politics in Narrative Therapies, *and has developed two professional videos on child therapy and family therapy.*

A Hopeless Case

Not too long ago, Madigan received a call from a hospital psychiatrist in his community wondering if he would see a fellow who had been unresponsive to the unit's usual treatments.

"What do you mean by unresponsive?" he asked the referring psychiatrist.

"Well, we've tried just about everything we can think of with this guy. He's been depressed and suicidal, sufficiently so that we placed him on a variety of medications—No luck. Then we tried ECT, about 30 sessions in the past 12 months."

"Thirty shock treatments?" Madigan was surprised that a person struggling hard with depression would be treated in this way. He wondered about the impact the side effects might be having—on the treatment team, the client, and the client's family. He figured the depression had found a way to defeat the whole psychiatric unit.

Madigan gathered a bit more history from the referring physician and learned that Tom, the patient, had been in both group and individual therapy at the hospital for just under a year. The staff had apparently decided that Tom was a "hopeless case" and had given up on him to devote their energies toward others who had better prognoses. Madigan had seen this before.

Initial Thoughts

Tom's 3-pound file arrived before he did, and as always Madigan had no intention of reading the hospital's descriptions/inscriptions about the 66-year-old "chronically depressed patient" before he spoke with Tom (he never did end up reading the file!). Not reading files was a common practice of his, because he found the documented files of "failed" patients were very one-sided and, as a result, never had much good to say. Madigan found himself excited about the referral, as it promised to push his learning.

Tom had endured the conditions of the hospital's relationship with him in full. Madigan remembers wondering how he had managed to survive the ECT, the various medication regimes, and the unfortunate therapeutic rituals of condemnation that occurred when the professional team became frustrated with his "lack of progress." At the point where Tom's therapeutic team was defeated, the word "chronic" finalized the hospital's examination. In Tom's case, the inscribed "condition" was chronic depression. The obvious contradiction was realizing that, on one hand, they condemned him to a life of chronic depression, while at the same time they desired him to "recover" through their technology. He could not, however, please the team, as their technological practices did not work for him. As the hospital's meager description of chronic depression might suggest, Madigan saw Tom as both a "cultural object" and "intellectual product" of the institution.

Madigan realized that within the model of scientific medicine where psychology is situated, the body of the subject is viewed as "the passive tablet on which disorders are inscribed." Madigan was very curious to meet this man who had survived two serious suicide attempts, the hospital team treatment, and the high doses of chemicals and electricity that they had put through his system. He was saddened by the fact that the hospital staff had condemned him to an "identity death" by labeling him as chronically and interminably depressed. This psychiatric sentence led to a number of questions he asked himself:

1. In what ways will I act to further perform and perpetuate Tom's identity as a chronic patient?
2. What effects will my own set of expert opinions reproduce him as a chronic patient?

3. How will I go about soliciting pertinent medical information regarding the long-term effects of ECT, and how might this information affect my relationship with Tom and the hospital?
4. How might I help to deconstruct the hospital's version of Tom (and his wife, Jane) without totalizing all relationships that they have encountered within the hospital?
5. What were the discursive restraints of my own training in psychology, gender, class, and age that will limit my conversation with Tom and Jane?
6. How can I be not respectful of the chronic inscription while remaining most respectful to this couple?
7. Could Tom's body be reclaimed from the fate of chronic depression?
8. What did it mean to this man, and his community, to have a "spoiled" identity?

So many treatments had already been tried without success, and Madigan saw no sense in following their therapeutic logic. From a narrative therapy perspective, he would begin to check out with Tom what it had been like to have others define who he was by way of the psychiatric label. Madigan wanted to find out if the hospital's description was a full description of who he was, and possibly who he might be and/or wish to be. He believed that Tom might have something to say about all the treatments he had received and survived, and perhaps this might provide some alternative meaning to him.

Of similar interest would be how Tom's wife, Jane, felt about the hospital's version of her husband's condition. "One of the first things I wanted to do," Madigan said, "was to ask Tom why he thought the hospital had sent him to me. I wanted to begin to crack away at the whole idea of his identity as chronically depressed—as I believed this was a very shallow description of this man's life."

More Than Depressed

Jane and Tom were a pleasant middle-class couple in their sixties. Both appeared completely focused on the conversation. Tom explained that he was "a little foggy," but given the amount of chemical and electrical treatments he had received in the previous year, it was a wonder that he was coherent at all.

Through a slurred, medicated speech, Tom relayed that he had been feeling depressed since his retirement, one and a half years earlier, and had twice tried to kill himself.

Madigan asked Tom if the word "depressed" was a term of his own, or did it belong to someone else? He relayed that it was a "hospital word," and what he was really feeling was "bored and unaccomplished."

"Tom," Madigan asked, "do you think this bored and unaccomplished sense of yourself is a final description of yourself?"

Tom shrugged. "Maybe not."

"Why do you think this bored and unaccomplished sense of yourself may not be a final description of yourself?"

"It might be the shock treatment, because it makes me slow and I can't remember much. I feel like a rock on the end of a piece of rope."

"Tom, is the hospital's description of you as a chronically depressed person an accurate description of you?"

"I think they helped me get worse," he replied in a slow, deliberate cadence.

"In what ways has the hospital made you feel worse about yourself?"

"Well, being with them a year or so I haven't gotten any better and I think that they are giving up. This is why they sent me to you." He laughed as he said this. "You are the last stop and they weren't much help anyway—most of them are nice, but you know."

"Tom, do you think the hospital staff has hope for you in coming to see me?"

"Well, they told me you helped someone else like me, so my guess is yes."

Good answer, Madigan thought. It showed some hope for the future, some imagined possibility that improvement could take place. "Why do you think that I can help you and they can't?"

"Because I don't think they know what they are doing and I get mad at them for shocking me as much as they did."

This seemed perfectly reasonable, Madigan thought. He needed to walk a fine line because he didn't want to cast blame toward his colleagues at the hospital, yet he also didn't want Tom and Jane necessarily to accept the hospital framing of the problem as some incurable, intractable condition they could do nothing about. Hope was the one thing they needed most. Madigan turned toward Jane. "And are you mad at the people at the hospital as well?"

"Yes I am!" Jane said with real conviction. "And I'm glad we came here to see you."

Yes! Madigan said to himself. An unqualified vote of confidence toward hope and against the chronic label, plus a note of optimism that help was possible.

"And you Tom," Madigan directed the next question, "do you think Jane believes there is hope for you to overcome these feelings of boredom and un-accomplishment?" He was being careful to use Tom's own self-descriptions rather than those supplied by the hospital staff.

Tom nodded his affirmation that he did believe his wife had hope.

"Are there other people in your life who might be pinning their hopes on you beating this boredom?" Madigan wanted to get a sense of the larger support system of which Tom was a part.

"Probably."

"Can you name a few of these hopeful people?"

"There's my kids."

"So they are in your corner?"

"Yes. And Jane too." Tom looked over toward his wife, who squeezed his hand affectionately.

"Don't forget Maggie, your OT," Jane reminded him.

"That's right. Maggie is my occupational therapist," Tom said.

"So," Madigan summarized, "your children, and Jane, and Maggie, they are all hopeful people who believe you can overcome the boredom and unaccomplishment. Do you have any ideas about what these people might remember in you that you have somehow forgotten?"

"I don't know," Tom said slowly and thoughtfully. "The shocks they gave me have made me kind of forgetful. Maybe they could tell you a thing or two. There's a lot I don't remember any more."

"So," Madigan reflected back a crucial point, "there are many parts of who you are as a man, a husband, a father, a friend, an employer, and a worker that you once enjoyed but now don't remember."

"And a gardener too," Tom added.

"Excuse me?" Madigan said.

"He used to love gardening," Jane clarified.

Madigan wanted to bring in other aspects of who Tom was and might be as a person, beyond the meager description as a depressed, retired man. Through the questions he was asking, Madigan was trying to create a richer, fuller description of what had been a narrow psychiatric diagnosis. He wanted to help Tom to remember other aspects of the person he had once been. He was so much more than "chronically depressed," and this more complete picture needed to be fleshed out.

A Letter-Writing Campaign

In the next few sessions, Madigan continued to invite Tom and Jane to talk about their lives in the days before Tom had been "retired and unaccomplished." There were all sorts of experiences and memories that had been part of their lives as parents and grandparents, neighbors and friends. They had been involved in a number of work- and leisure-related activities. And they had all sorts of connections to their larger community. This suggested one approach for Madigan, to bring Tom's community into the sessions since he had so isolated himself since the hospitalization.

"I wonder if you might write a letter to your family and friends," Madigan introduced the idea.

"What sort of letter?" Tom asked, a bit confused by this strange request.

"Well," Madigan explained. "You've both talked about how important many relationships have been in your life, and the ways people you love have known you. But you say you've forgotten these other things partially because of the shock treatment, but also because you have believed what they told you at the hospital that you are chronically depressed." The plan was to invite family and friends to "thicken the plot" of Tom's identity by including facets of his life that had been ignored or forgotten.

The whole idea of writing letters is an integral part of narrative therapy. Back in 1991, while studying in New Zealand and Australia, David Epston and Michael White had personally taught Madigan the tradition of writing therapeutic letters after each session. Their purpose was not only to summarize what had taken place in the session, but "re-storying" the themes, highlighting the victories and appreciating the person's courage in standing up to the problem. Madigan has taken this original idea and expanded it to include ways of helping clients to recruit support and assistance from their larger communities.

"I began writing to the people's community," Madigan explained, "to write back to the person specifically so that we could get a fuller and richer description of the person's life that was not being told by the problems definition of the person. The letters acted to counteract the problems (and the hospital's) description of the person. The letter campaign assists people to be remembered back toward membership systems of love and support from which the problem has dismembered them."

Madigan has launched letter-writing campaigns for clients as young as 6 and as old as 76. He has used them to assist people struggling with an assortment of difficulties that stem from the labels that they have been given as anxiety-prone, bulimic, perfectionistic, and others. The community letter campaign was a way of looking for what narrative therapists call "unique outcomes," or exceptions to the presenting problem.

Sometimes Madigan has encouraged clients to send pictures, poems, collages, tapes, videos, anything that invites a discourse with family and friends about alternative views of oneself other than as disabled or problem persons. "What I want to do is fill in the gaps of the person's idea of themselves, because quite often problems tend to offer up only negative descriptions of persons. Quite often the professional world thickens this idea that clients are only the problems that they are representing. People become somewhat totalized or fossilized within these very destructive and pathological stories. I am attempting to broaden the frame through a person's experience through their community of concern."

For the correspondence constructed on Tom and Jane's behalf, Madigan co-authored the following letter:

Dear Friends of Tom and Jane,

My name is Stephen Madigan and I have been working with Tom and Jane for the last three weeks. As Tom sees it, he has been taken over by a great sense of boredom and feels like he never quite accomplished enough throughout his life as a father, a friend, a husband, a worker and as a neighbor. Tom's feeling of boredom, accompanied by an unsuccessful life, seems to have boxed him into a corner to the point where it has twice convinced him that he is not worthy of living.

Tom, Jane, and I are writing you to ask if you would write a letter on Tom's behalf? We are hoping this might add an alternative description to the story of boredom, the feelings of living an unaccomplished life, and the negative things that hospital staff have said about Tom's future. In the letter perhaps you could relay an experience that you have had with Tom in which you saw him as neither boring nor unaccomplished? Tom, Jane, and I thank you for your help in this matter. Tom wants all of you to know that he is feeling a bit better these past few weeks.

Warm Regards,

Tom, Jane and Stephen

The Wall of Hope

Four weeks after sending out this letter, Tom had received forty-one responses from people supporting him with hope and counter-stories affirming him as someone who was both interesting and accomplished. Tom was beginning to build a "counter-file" to counteract the hospital's file.

Tom could not actually read the letters himself, since the medications and shock treatments had distorted his vision. What he did instead was paper his wall in the hospital with the cards and letters that began to arrive daily. He asked the nurses and other patients on the ward to read them to him. He was so proud of his collection that he began a practice of giving "antidepression" tours to visitors and fellow patients, showing them all the people who had faith in his ability to become interesting and accomplished once again. Tom was not conducting the tours so much out of pride as of hope. He believed that perhaps the letters from his community of concern might act to "inspire other patients on the ward" and to reach out to others so that they too might have hope in themselves.

The therapeutic conversations between Tom, Jane, and Madigan tracked the threads of the institution's discursive practices and destabilized the hard chronic conclusions placed on Tom's body. In taking away expert knowledge from the site of the hospital (and placing the power of description in Tom's community), he was able to enlarge the degree to which alternative other knowledges might be taken up and performed.

About a month after the therapeutic letters arrived, Tom left the hospital, and he never returned to his previous diagnosed state of "chronic depression." Nowadays, Tom volunteers in homeless shelters 2 days a week, helping to inspire others to find hope in their communities. He also works as the "gardener in residence" in his retirement community. Finally, Tom works as a paid consultant on Madigan's website, and in his narrative therapy certificate training courses. Tom teaches practitioners about solutions in standing up to boredom, unaccomplishment, and retirement, and the negative effects of being labeled chronically depressed. Tom is no longer a depressed patient but an informed teacher.

28 You Can't Kill Yourself Until You Pay Your Debt

A Case from Scott Miller

Scott Miller has devoted his career to examining the ways that outcome research can guide therapy practice. Together with his partners Barry Duncan and Mark Hubble at the Institute for the Study of Therapeutic Change, Miller has been influential in altering the ways therapist think about "what works" in treatment. Rather than focusing on the particular techniques that are employed, or theory that is favored, the group has found that positive outcomes are most associated with the client's expectations about and experience of treatment. "It's impossible ever to understand a client," Miller says. "What matters most is that the client feels understood."

In his books, Escape from Babel, Psychotherapy with Impossible Cases, The Heart and Soul of Change, *and* The Heroic Client, *Miller looks at the power of helping relationships and how they may be constructed to best mobilize the resources of clients in their own self-change efforts. He works* pro bono *in a small inner-city clinic, applying the ideas gleaned from his research to economically disadvantaged and other traditionally underserved groups.*

Don't Try to Help

The conversation began with Scott Miller openly admitting that he frequently found doing therapy "a struggle." When asked about his finest hour, he wondered if it wasn't one in which the treatment not only produced a good outcome but also seemed somewhat comprehensible. "So often," he said, "I'm left scratching my head, trying to figure out what happened—why it worked."

So, the best therapy to you is the kind where you don't struggle much?

"Well," he replied thoughtfully, "when I think of a 'finest hour' I imagine some heroic intervention, or perhaps a time when I caught something that nobody had noticed before. But I honestly can't think of anything that fits that description. If anything, it is certainly the exception rather than the rule."

"Surely," we pressed, "there must be some piece of work that stands out to you?"

Still, Miller drew a blank, until he thought back to graduate school, when he was doing an internship at a Veterans Administration hospital. One of the very first cases he had been assigned was a Vietnam veteran who had been in the health care system for a long time.

Nate had struggled with depression ever since he had returned from the war; perhaps the symptoms had been there even before he had gone overseas—nobody was quite sure. He manifested a cyclical depression that was as deep as it was pervasive; much of the time he was actively suicidal.

Given the severity and long-standing nature of the depression, Miller was told to simply monitor the patient. "There's nothing much you can do for him," his supervisor instructed, "nothing much anyone can do for him. So just keep an eye on him. Be as supportive as you can. Tell us when you think he needs to go in the hospital for a while. And for God's sake, don't try and help him!" This last warning was a reminder that, as a student, Miller should not overstep his role, especially when so many other esteemed doctors had worked with this guy previously without measurable impact.

The Greenhorn and the Veteran

"Hi," Miller said, reaching out a hand to greet Nate at their first meeting, "Nice to meet you!" Hands in his pockets, Nate crossed the floor of the office in silence and plopped down in the "client" seat. "Good thing the plan was to stick with reflective listening as much as possible," Miller thought silently to himself, "at least I can do that."

"So you're the new guy, huh?" Nate said, breaking the brief silence.

"Uh huh," Scott responded, unintentionally mimicking the kind and composed figure of Carl Rogers he'd seen in the *Gloria* films.

"First case?" Nate continued, sounding despondent.

"Uhhh. . . ."

"They always give me the greenhorns."

Miller nodded, a little shell-shocked by Nate's comment. "Geez," he thought privately, "was it so obvious that I was a beginner?"

"No one lasts too long with me . . . ," Nate continued, jarring Scott back to the session, "Not in 'Nam . . . and not in therapy."

Before the session, Scott had read the thick file accumulated on Nate over the years. It was loaded with stories about his work as a covert operative behind enemy lines. As far as he could figure from reading the case notes,

Nate had been an assassin, sneaking across enemy lines under cover of darkness and murdering people in their sleep. Some of these targets were political figures or officers, but some had been women and children.

"I'm grateful you're willing to give me the chance," Miller then responded, and continued, "I can't imagine how hard it's been for you since returning."

Now it was Nate's turn to sound like Carl Rogers. "Uh huh," he responded, bowing his head and then looking away. It wasn't a stretch to imagine that Nate was living with a lot of guilt. Or was that just Scott's assumption?

Letting his curiosity get the better of him, he asked, "Is that why you've tried to kill yourself so many times?"

Nate nodded again.

The sessions continued week after week in a similar fashion: long silences and a great deal of listening. The only difference was the darkening of Nate's mood. With each visit, he became more depressed, the stories he told more disturbing.

Following Directions

Encountering this broken man, Miller was surprised to feel something less than compassion. Sure the guy was suffering, terribly so. Privately, Scott found himself wondering if Nate didn't deserve his fate. After all, he had done the most terrible things that a human being could do to others.

To be sure, it was not as if Miller was naive about war. He had grown up in a patriotic family. His father had been a medic in World War II, serving in some of the most horrific of circumstances. Bad things happened. That was the nature of war. Even so, Scott couldn't get the image out of his head of this man sitting before him killing people, often innocent noncombatants, in their sleep.

It didn't help that Nate had been going over and rehashing the same ground for years. A dozen psychiatrists and psychologists had been assigned this very case before, each having minimal impact. "What's the point," Miller wondered "of continuing to talk about this week after week and year after year *and now with a graduate student?*"

"I'm wondering if you've thought about how you would kill yourself," Miller asked at a session a month and a half or so into their relationship. Nate seemed particularly low during the appointment.

"Are you kidding?" Nate responded. "It's all I ever think about."

"So you have a plan?" Scott continued, following the outline of the suicide assessment process he'd learned in school.

"Yes, I do," Nate responded in a quiet voice.

"I'm wondering if you'd be willing to sign a contract with me, agreeing that you won't harm yourself before our next session?"

Looking up, Nate began shaking his head. "Sure," he said, "if that'll make *you* feel better."

The emphasis on the "you" made Scott instantly aware that he wasn't helping Nate. So far, he and his supervisors were simply protecting themselves. But he felt handcuffed by the instructions he'd received.

"Just listen to the guy," they told him. "Be as supportive as you can, given the circumstances."

"That's it?" Scott complained in frustration.

"Look," they told him, "all that's going to happen with this guy is that he's going to end up on the Psych Ward of the hospital. They'll medicate him and keep him on ice until he stabilizes. Then they'll release him again and he'll come back here. We've been through this before. Trust us."

Miller did what he was told.

You're Not Listening

Meanwhile, Miller had been attending a supervision group led by a therapist, Lynn Johnson, who was far more active, directive, and creative than those he encountered at the Veterans Administration. When asked to present a case to the group, he told the story of his work with Nate.

After he was done reciting the details of the case, the group leader said to him: "Well, Scott, the problem with your work is obvious."

"It is? How so?"

"You're not listening to this man."

"Not listening?" Miller sputtered.

"That's right, you're not listening."

"Not listening! But that's all I do, listen. It's all I'm *allowed* to do is listen to the guy! I'm not permitted to do anything else."

"No. You're not listening to him," Johnson insisted.

"What are you talking about?"

"You heard me."

"Yeah, you said I'm not listening. But I am. He says he wants to kill himself. But my job is to stop him from doing that."

"Right," Johnson repeated, "you're not listening."

By this time, Miller was becoming increasingly frustrated, even agitated. Talk about not listening, he was coming to this supervision group for help and all they could tell him was that he wasn't listening. If anyone wasn't listening, it was them.

"How the hell am I supposed to listen to him any different than I am? My supervisors at the hospital tell me I can't do anything to intervene, that all I should do is listen. So that's what I've been doing. Now you tell me that I'm not even doing that."

"Now you're getting it," Johnson agreed.

"But I can't let him kill himself," Scott quickly retorted.

"You're not listening again."

"So, I'm confused, what the hell should I do?" Miller didn't really expect an answer, so he was surprised when he got one.

"You go back to that man and you tell him that if he kills himself he'd be cheating his victims *a second time*."

"Excuse me?" Miller couldn't believe what he'd just heard. That's the craziest thing he'd ever heard of. "Hey look," he started, "I'm just a graduate student. . . ."

Interrupting, Johnson continued, "Don't you get it? This man is trying to atone for his sins, to make restitution by taking his own life."

Miller sat stunned.

Johnson continued, "You go tell that man that his one measly life can in no way repay the debt he owes to humanity. You tell him that."

"Look, Lynn, I know you're trying to be helpful and all. But there's no way I can go back and tell this fellow this. Besides, I'm just supposed to be listening; I'm not supposed to do anything."

Johnson nodded and smiled. "Okay," he said, "who's next?"

Repeating the Lines

In the very next session, Nate went on at great length about his sense of despair and hopelessness. He had nothing to live for and no reason to continue with his pitiful existence. Miller was doing his usual thing, listening (mostly pretending to listen), when his own frustration took over. Against his better judgment, and in direct disobedience of hospital orders, Miller blurted out, "It seems that you are quite serious about committing suicide."

Nate looked at him, as if to say: "Doc, where the hell have you been all these months that I've been telling you this?"

Then, as if the words came out of his mouth from someone else, Miller said, "If you do kill yourself, you'll be cheating your victims *a second time*."

Now it was Nate's turn to be stunned. After a few uncomfortable moments, he recovered, asking Scott to repeat what he'd said.

"I said that if you do kill yourself, you'll be cheating your victims *a second time*."

"I thought that's what you said," Nate responded with anger in his voice.

Scott continued, seemingly on auto-pilot: "Your one life can in no way repay the damage you did to all those people and families you harmed."

And at this point Nate, first looking at him incredulously, abruptly stood up and walked out of the office, not even bothering to close the door.

Miller could feel panic welling up inside him. Now what had he done? What if Nate now went out and did exactly what he had said he would do. And it would all be the fault of his stupid, gullible, inexperienced therapist, who didn't follow orders.

Miller went to confess his blunder to his supervisor.

"But I told you not to try to help this guy," the doctor said in disgust. "I told you that all you were supposed to do was listen to him. I told you not to do anything. You're in trouble, Scott, big trouble."

The hospital staff immediately tried to contact Nate to rectify the damage and apologize for the blunder of their most inexperienced intern. They left messages for him all over, to no avail.

In the meantime, Miller was watched with even closer scrutiny and suspicion. He was directed to bring all of his cases to daily supervision, ensuring that he would never repeat his foolish behavior. It was while under this "house arrest" that he received a phone call several weeks later from Nate, calling to schedule another appointment. That's the good news; the bad news is that Miller's supervisors would not permit him to meet with his patient unless there was a "chaperone" present to monitor the proceedings.

Making Amends

Nate returned punctually at the appointed time, aware that not only his previous therapist would be in the room but also Miller's supervisor. For his part, Miller was feeling so embarrassed and ashamed that he could barely concentrate on the task at hand. Not only had he made a terrible error in judgment, one that he had been specifically warned to avoid, but now his punishment was that he must conduct his business in the present of his "parent."

Miller didn't blame his other supervisor, Lynn Johnson, for getting him in this mess; he realized it was his own doing. In spite of the disastrous outcome, he found the active and directive approach to be quite interesting, if not powerful stuff. In fact, the method is so potent that it either starts a bonfire or burns the whole barn down.

The supervisor began the session by apologizing to Nate on behalf of the hospital and the staff. Before he could finish, Nate interrupted him.

"It's true," he told the supervisor, although he looked directly at Miller as he said the words. "I was so furious when I walked out of the session I could have choked this son of a bitch."

Miller visibly paled, knowing full well that Nate was talking from experience. The guy probably knew a dozen different ways to strangle him, probably without leaving a mark. He found himself glancing in the direction of the exit, relieved at least that he thought he could make it to the door before his supervisor.

"All I could think of to do," Nate continued, "was to get the hell out of here. I just couldn't contain myself."

"I certainly understand that," the supervisor said solicitously. Miller sat quietly, listening. Sure it was humiliating—but he deserved it. At some point, Miller even began thinking that maybe he was in the wrong field and it was time to try something else. He could barely hear what the two of them were talking about until he heard Nate say: "Something started to gnaw at me, though."

At this, Miller perked up a bit. Glancing briefly in his direction and then back to Nate, the supervisor said, "Go on."

"Well, I started to think that maybe he was right." And then, looking directly into Miller's eyes as if the two of them were alone, he continued, "Ever since you said that to me about cheating my victims *a second time,* . . . it started me to thinking. . . . I need to make amends for what I done, to repay the debt that I owe."

Miller's mind was racing. This was incredible! Lynn had been right all along. No one had been listening to Nate.

"So I made some phone calls," Nate said. "And ever since I saw you I've been volunteering to make sandwiches and soup for the Vets who live under the viaduct."

Relieved, Miller smiled.

"It's just . . . I don't know if I can ever repay my debt. I've hurt so many people. But I have to try."

That was all Nate had to say about the matter. He just wanted Miller to know that the words had gotten through to him. Soon thereafter, he left the session, and he never returned.

■   ■   ■

A Lost Art Form

The practice of therapy is often portrayed as a technically complex enterprise, one that involves a number of interrelated factors. Yet when Scott Miller thinks about his finest hours as a practitioner, what comes to mind most readily are those times when he really listened to his clients. When he considers Nate's case, he now realizes it was not the magical incantation, "If you kill yourself, you won't pay back your debt," that made the difference, but the underlying message that "I have really heard and understood your deepest-felt fears."

After recovering from the dual shock of first almost being fired, and then redeemed by the surprise ending that indeed his intervention had made a great difference, Miller went back to Lynn Johnson with a single question: "What is the trick to this?"

"There is no trick," Johnson replied simply.

"What do you mean no trick? Of course there's a trick! I'd been with this guy for months listening to him. You heard a brief summary of the case and you proposed that crazy idea that I should tell him he can't commit suicide until he's paid his debt. Where the hell did *that* come from?"

Johnson shrugged. "When you really, really listen to someone, there is no trick involved whatsoever. All I did was listen to what Nate was saying. Embedded in that is all I need to know."

Reflecting back on Lynn's advice, Miller thinks of this as a seminal moment in his development as a therapist. "Lynn had heard not only Nate's statement that he wanted to atone for his sins, but that he didn't know how to do that. He opened up that door, that possibility, there had to be some other way he could do what he wanted to do besides dying."

Miller paused for a moment, trying to articulate the meaning that this had for him. "When I'm doing therapy," Miller said, "I find myself distracted often. Clients are talking and I am thinking to myself that I might like sushi for dinner tonight. The very idea of being attentive for 6 or 8 hours a day is mind-blowing, much less catching the kind of nuances that Lynn seemed to be able to hear."

Miller still finds that listening is an underappreciated art form that is so rarely practiced except as a precursor to the "real" business of promoting change. Therapists are in love with their techniques and strategic interventions, confronting, waving their fingers back and forth in hypnotic trances. "It's as though all the listening stuff is simply the anesthetic gas before the surgery. And I don't believe that."

A Secret Handshake

Miller mentioned research data that surveyed therapists about their beliefs about what makes the most difference in their work. Invariably, therapists talk about their technical expertise. "I've never been able to figure out what these therapists supposedly do that they think is so wonderful."

This reminded Miller of his days as a graduate student in Salt Lake City. There was a story that circulated about when the Mormons first arrived in the valley and were trying to survive in the harsh environment.

They decided to grow sugar beets as a cash crop and so sent representatives to England to learn the ins and outs of the business. Miller laughed as he imagined that these people thought they could grow sugar beets in the desert the same way they did in England.

"They buy all the machinery they need," he continued the story, "all at great expense. They ship it all back to the valley. They plant sugar beets, and after the first year they go to process the stuff. Pulp comes out, but no sugar. Same thing happens the following year. So they all go back to England and they try to figure out what it was that they missed. The British sell them some more machinery. The Mormons come back and grow a whole other crop. Again pulp comes out the other end. But no sugar. They just can't figure out what is going wrong. As it turned out, the British had purposely left out of the instructions a couple of key steps in the process, because they didn't want the Mormons to compete with them in the sugar market."

"Yes?" we prompted Miller for the point of the story.

"This is the way I have always felt about psychotherapy. Some day someone will open the door and I will be initiated and learn the secret handshake that makes you an effective therapist. But I have never had the confidence that somehow my technical skill or expertise, my fine clinical work, is what makes people change. It is not something that fits for me."

How to Listen

"What would you tell therapists, beginners and experienced practitioners alike, about how to listen accurately and perceptively?"

"Check out what you are doing."

"How do you do that?"

"Just ask the client," Miller said simply. "Say to the client: 'Am I getting this right? Is that what you were saying about this? Is that what you wanted to work on? Does this idea make sense to you?'"

"What about the backlash against Carl Rogers and the charge that listening and understanding are not enough? They are not sufficient conditions for change." We were referring to the not uncommon phenomenon in which people stay in therapy for years, developing insight and great self-awareness, but they don't change a thing about their dysfunctional behavior.

"I would say this claim is absolutely right. Listening isn't enough. Besides, it is not whether you are listening anyway; it's whether the client *thinks* you are."

"Say that again," we pressed, not sure what he meant.

"It is the perception of listening that makes the difference."

This is a crucial point, especially since it is virtually impossible to really understand anyone anyway. The best we can do is to help the person feel understood (and we hope you can see the difference).

29 Learning from Their Finest Hours

A Narrative Analysis of Core Themes

WITH MYF MAPLE

So here we are, at the tail end of a magnificent journey through a vast array of techniques, challenges, trials, and tribulations, as experienced by over two dozen eminent therapists during their finest hours of therapy. From the outset, most of those involved in this project had great difficulty choosing one case that stood out for them over many years of work, yet they could readily identify numerous examples of their worst! For example, Peggy Papp began her story by relating how her finest hour directly followed her worst. Laura Brown told us how she thought that working with Alice could have been her worst lapse of judgment, until later when she realized that her mistake was critical to the successful outcome.

Some of the contributors provide ideas on why it is easier to single out our worst hours: Bradford Keeney suggested this may be because we tend to remember our worst tales of woe, and let the memories of doing the job well fade. David Scharff mentioned that there are loads of hours when you are just grinding through therapy wondering whether you are doing anything useful. Or, as Scott Miller said, his finest hour occurred because the process seemed comprehensible, when so often it is not. Perhaps because most of us come to this field genuinely wanting to help people, categorizing the best hours of our work is incompatible with this intrinsic motivation. It seems an unnecessary distraction. Yet a part of us cannot help but ask: "How am I doing?" Or, better yet, "How are *we* doing together on this quest?"

We are now left the final task of making sense of what emerged during our interviews with prominent theoreticians about their finest hours of work. These are people who have spent two, three, four, even up to six decades reflecting on their work. They have formulated ideas and conceptual frameworks that have helped shape the current standards of practice. What, then, might we learn from their experiences when they operated at their peak levels? What are the lessons and core themes that may be most useful?

Narrative Methodology

Narrative analysis (which is not at all the same as narrative therapy) is a methodology that consists of four main features: (1) helping people to tell their stories as accurately, vividly, realistically, and contextually as possible; (2) collaborating with participants in such a way that their stories include focused themes and plot lines; (3) "re-storying" the narrative to make it more coherent, chronological, meaningful, and accessible; (4) developing practical implications from the narratives that might be helpful in other settings and contexts (Clandinin & Connelly, 2000; Connelly & Clandinin, 1990; Creswell, 2002). Like any good story, attention is given to plot, characters, dialogue, and distinct "scenes" or "acts" that present conflict and resolution.

We felt it important to honor the stories as the therapist/narrator told them to us. While traditional qualitative methodologies of analyzing and coding interviews have the potential to fragment and decontextualize events, narrative analysis respects the manner in which the narrator weaves together and makes sense of elements in their lives, such as their finest hour of therapy. For example, had we chosen to use the popular grounded theory method to analyze these stories, we would have been systematically identifying and coding categories *within* the stories as each was received from the therapist and then used a constant comparative method to determine similarities and differences across stories, with theory development being the desired outcome (Charmaz, 2000). A narrative method purposefully does not break up the data; rather, the focus is on the underlying plotline of the story to reveal the meaning that people ascribe to an event (Gilbert, 2002). Sometimes this may result in appreciating the complexity of a phenomenon rather than merely simplifying it into easily digestible pieces. For example, Steve Lankton asked his client, Cassie, to participate in this project with him. In that chapter, we can see how Cassie and Steve have independently made up theories about why the interventions worked; for Cassie this interaction was life-changing, yet for Lankton it was unremarkable therapy. He was just doing his job.

Each of us independently weaves together the events we experience in our lives in a manner that helps us to make sense out of these occurrences. However, no two of us do this in the same way, as we have our own collections of experience that shape the meaning that we attribute to events. In reviewing the transcripts, remembrances, and written narratives of these conversations, each of us felt drawn to different facets of the "data" even if we found consensus in some common themes.

Here we have looked at the underlying thread that weaves these instances of therapy together to see what shaped these interactions into examples of therapy at its best. We described our methodology and process in

Chapter 1, in which we interviewed therapists and asked them to tell us a story that best illustrates their work. The interviews were then transcribed and "restoried" or rewritten into narrative prose. The therapist was then asked to review and edit the chapter where needed. Analysis on this final work then began by reading and rereading each chapter to uncover the main plot that joins the events described together into a meaningful encounter, rather than reading merely for the content of what happened or unrelated events. The focus during this process was on why certain events were threaded together in a particular way, in order to make meaning out of what happened in therapy on that occasion. Our aim was to read the text in order to answer the primary question: What is it that the narrator is really trying to tell us?

For example, what was it about working with Mary and Bill that made this session pivotal for Terry Real to further develop relational recovery therapy? What meaning did Real attach to this therapy? Or, as Michael Mahoney reflects on working with Karen, he reports being confronted and stretched during this therapy. What is it about this story that facilitated such profound insight for him?

Analyzing qualitative data is an inherently subjective experience. Each of us takes particular parts from the stories to which we can most easily relate. To help overcome this challenge, the three of us reached agreement about the core plots and lessons learned that are discussed below.

So What Can We Learn?

Counseling 101 texts tell us to "be there" for the client, to be empathic and use reflective listening skills. What we see and hear in the contributors' stories is that—and more. There is certainly a strong theme of the power inherent in being there for a client—being present as fully and completely as possible. As Scott Miller says, "It is impossible ever to really understand a client. In fact, we can never really understand ourselves. What matters most is that the client feels understood." It is this understanding of the client that provides a positive outcome in an unusual situation, in John Krumboltz's chapter about the man who believed himself to have been captured by aliens.

Yet the stories of one's finest hour go far beyond presence alone. For example, Alvin Mahrer's remarkable recount of his "out of body" experience with Melanie—his first time of being totally there—it was this session that made him contemplate the depth of the human spirit and encouraged him to delve deeper with clients in the future. Other stories involve risk taking (Lazarus, Miller, Pittman, Real), making mistakes (Brown), getting outside of one's comfort zone and not knowing the way ahead (Cummings, Mahoney, Madigan, Papp), and learning from the experiences (Ellis, Johnson, Jordan, Scharff). These and other plotlines are summarized in Table 1.

Many of the stories document the very limited times in a therapist's career when the long-term outcome is known. So often, clients walk out the door

TABLE 1   A Summary of Principal Plotlines

Main Plotline	Contributors
Commitment to theoretical framework	Brown, Cummings, Doherty, Gray, Keeney, Love, Madigan, Mahrer, Neimeyer, Pittman, Wheeler
Being challenged	Carlson, Ellis, Johnson, Kottler, Krumboltz, Lankton, Lazarus, Mahoney, Miller, Papp, Scharff, Stuart, Yapko
New beginnings	Jordan, Glasser, Real
Knowing the outcome	Cummings, Jordan, Lankton, Lazarus, Love, Mahoney, Mahrer, Yapko
Reciprocal influence of client and therapist	Brown, Carlson, Ellis, Glasser, Johnson, Jordan, Kottler, Lazarus, Mahoney, Mahrer, Scharff

and we never hear from them again; the stories remain unfinished, without endings. The therapist is so often left wondering what changes really took place and how long they lasted. Perhaps one reason these particular stories stand out in the contributors' memories is because they recall how the story ended, most often happily.

Others recall their finest hours because they felt themselves to be especially helpful. In Kottler's story of helping people on the street, he testifies that there has never been a time when he felt more useful. He knows he made a difference and he knows this resulted from something specific that he was in a position to do with someone in need. Likewise, Nick Cummings recalled his case because he most likely saved his client's life, quite literally. He recalls his "courage to bust all the rules and do extreme therapy with this young man." Still others mentioned these particular sessions because of the risks they took or the experimentation that occurred. Scott Miller related how as a young clinician he put his career on the line by disregarding the unequivocal direction of his supervisors to do more than just listen to his client. William Glasser described how he disarmed Jake at great risk to himself. In Gordon Wheeler's case, he remembered Joe so well because he had worked with him over a 14-year time span.

Each of these chapters contains captivating stories. It is easy to imagine being a fly on the wall, experiencing the awkward moments, the triumphs, and the tragedies that have provided each of the therapists with an example of their finest hour. Each story is unique. The methods and theoretical frameworks used to get to the end point differ enormously. Robert Neimeyer worked with Joanne in establishing a continuing bond with her father in order to overcome her anxiety. John Krumboltz hypnotized Bill to confront his fears stemming from alien abduction. At times these techniques are applied deliberately (Cummings, Doherty, Keeney); at other times the therapist flounders for new ideas and directions (Jordan, Madigan, Papp).

Themes and Stories

Some of the chapters show examples of prominent theoretical frameworks in use. Other theoreticians talk about being inventive, *really* listening to the client, knowing they were useful, and knowing the long-term outcome. Yet others show us the exciting embryonic cells of innovative new genres.

The cases presented by several therapists (Brown, Cummings, Doherty, Gray, Keeney, Love, Madigan, Mahrer, Neimeyer, Pittman, Wheeler) resonate their commitment to their theoretical frameworks and emphasize how these are applied successfully in the counseling room. Even though each clinician is grounded in fundamentally different theoretical orientations, in practice clients achieve real results from each of these varying methods. We are shown, through the reporting of these clients' journeys, changes in behaviors and lives, even when there had been prior intervention with little or no result.

For Laura Brown, it was her commitment to a feminist framework that made this case a success story for her. She trusted her intuition with this client, refusing to "make her sexual." Alice needed to test her therapist and then learn to trust her before they could move on. Even though at the time Brown thought she had made a lapse in judgment, it was the showing of real emotion and honesty that moved the therapy forward.

The starting point for John Gray is a fundamental belief that each of us has an abundance of personal resources. His recollection of therapy with Trina is summarized by the statement, "we always have what we need most; we are often just looking in the wrong direction." For William Doherty, it is the recognition of the broader familial influences on an individual's health and well-being as crucial to the long-term success and understanding that at times his job is just to stay out of the way. "I asked no questions," Doherty said. "I made no reflective comments. I did no paraphrasing. It was just so out there beautifully that I just bore witness to it."

For Bradford Keeney, his case stands out because of its short duration (and because it was recent). While not certain how to define fine therapy, Keeney used his eclectic mix of skills to draw on a person's strengths. In this case, Melanie's mothering skills were the focus in finding ground to reconnect with her husband. In Frank Pittman's chapter, we read about success over generations in one family and the recognition that even though he cannot personally be there for as many clients as he would like to be, his books can act as guides. He professes his strong belief in being a "professional uncle" who is direct and honest with his clients—unafraid of danger, taking risks, and taking a stand.

Being Challenged

A number of contributors (Carlson, Ellis, Johnson, Kottler, Krumboltz, Lankton, Lazarus, Mahoney, Miller, Papp, Scharff, Stuart, Yapko) talked about the dual struggle of being present for their clients—celebrating their compassion and caring—yet also feeling challenged by the process. It is an uncomfortable place for most of us to delve into the unknown. Most of us enjoy the security of knowing the ways in which we like to live and work. However, such security is often challenged. These chapters provide insight into an uncomfortable place—where we are floundering for new ideas, new ways in which to work, or simply allowing another person to affect us.

Consider Michael Mahoney's reflections on how he was stretched and challenged by his client—defining "fine therapy is fundamentally an authentic encounter between therapist and client." Or using the very refined technique of "nagging"—which by Arnold Lazarus's own admission is not even remotely close to his preferred theory. However, it certainly had the desired outcome! Clive got out, met new people, and was on the road to recovery; Lazarus reflects, "Clive is such a lovely human being, that all I had to do was offer him a little common sense." Most directly, it is Albert Ellis's belief that his therapy is great therapy because it "actively and directly attacks people's tendencies to avoid accepting themselves and others." Regardless of the technique, the value of caring about, and being challenged by another person, whether you are the client or the therapist, is an educational experience.

A New Framework

A third core theme that emerged was related to how a "finest hour" was a seminal event in a theoretician's life work (Real, Jordan, Glasser). The third group of chapters are those in which a new or emerging technique was defined—a significant and exciting moment for client, counselor, and the wider profession. In taking the chaotic challenge of not knowing which way to proceed, and having that glimmer on the side of consciousness that marks the birth of a new idea, a new way of working emerged. Thus, we witnessed Judy Jordan realizing the foundations of her relational-cultural approach. Cindy presented a challenging area for Jordan—the first time she had to work with sexual abuse. Her interaction with her client helped Jordan crystallize her views about the ways therapists often distance and objectify their personal reactions and experiences rather than utilize them as opportunities to help people feel heard and understood.

William Glasser provided an account of the development of his choice theory and reality therapy, moving away from passive psychoanalytic techniques to a far more directive style. "A good counselor," Glasser said, "should be active, and this was the session when this became most clear to me." He related how he saw therapy not so much as discrete sessions, but rather many, many slow incremental relationship steps that lead finally to a new beginning.

Another example is when Terry Real broke the "cardinal rule" of couples work by "taking sides," most often with women who bring in their husbands for therapy. He admitted that his approach is unique in three ways: that he aligns with one partner, that he bluntly tells the truth, and that he addresses issues of grandiosity. This case was a turning point for Real in that he learned the power of telling men the truth about their limitations in an honest and direct way—the birth of relational recovery therapy.

Knowing Outcomes

As we mentioned before, stories need endings, or at least illusions of closure, in order for us to remember them fondly. Yet recognizing when we are doing excellent therapy appears to be determined (in part) by knowing the long-term outcome. It was the phone call to Nick Cummings 20 years after his sessions with Dan, his finding out that Dan was still healthy, that cemented the memory of their work together. When Mandy e-mailed Richard Stuart 30 years after he had thought she had passed away, that was when he learned that she was happily married and doing well. In Stephen Lankton's chapter, it was seeing his previous client on television that sparked a recollection of the significance of the case. Finally, Jon Carlson recalled his case most clearly, in part, because of the gift mug he received with the inscription, "Only you would believe that elephants really can fly."

Many of the therapists said that great therapy is about the long-term outcomes, rather than the short-term benefits, that we see, observe (and experience) with our clients. As we mentioned, however, the long-term outcomes of our daily work are so rarely known. Perhaps, then, one lesson to be learned is that we should devise alternative ways of measuring the impact of our interventions, being reflective on both our lousy sessions and our good ones.

If we measure hills rather than mountains, we may have a more effective way in which to determine the quality of our therapy. In a previous study of therapist imperfections and experiences of failure (Kottler & Blau, 1989), Arnold Lazarus talked about the ways that he assesses his work in order to prevent discouragement and morbid views of apparently negative outcomes. Using a football analogy, rather than seeing his job as "scoring touchdowns" with his clients, his role is more to help them attain "first downs," that is, to move the ball down the field 10 yards or so. With this more realistic, more modest set of expectations, he searches for whatever progress can be found.

So often, we may quickly devalue ourselves when something goes wrong in an individual session while being rarely inclined to allow ourselves praise. Whatever choices we make, whatever interventions we introduce, whatever things we say or do, we may feel flooded with alternatives that might have been better. There is that little voice inside our heads, constantly nagging and asking things like: "What did you do *that* for?" "How can you have been so stupid to have missed that?" "Why didn't you do what you did before in these situations? You had to get fancy, huh?"

Certainly it is the instances of everyday therapy that lay the groundwork for the best work that we do. Just as our clients are more than the sum of their parts, so too is the therapy we engage in on an hourly, daily, weekly, and yearly basis. If we know that we have been there for our clients, truly listened to what they are saying, challenged them, and allowed them to challenge us, then we have abided by the same principles that these therapists have taught us in the pages of this book.

Reciprocal Influence

One of the interesting and salient messages in this book is the impact the client has on the therapist that is demonstrated in so many chapters. Clearly, the influence that takes place in therapy is a reciprocal process, in which the therapist may be affected just as significantly as the client, for better or worse (Kottler, 2004). We are working hard to change our clients, but they are working just as diligently to change us in line with their preferred ideals. Moreover, there are so many serendipitous and unforeseen events that take place during the encounter—some that result from the intimacy in the relationship, some stemming from the potent issues that emerge, some from our own unresolved issues, and others simply the logical result of the collaborative process between participants going as deeply as possible into their innermost thoughts and feelings.

Developing an understanding that therapy is about the relationship between the participants, we can readily observe the two-sided growth and learning that evolves. Glasser made this very point when he said—surprisingly for someone known for reality therapy—that our work is 99 percent about the relationship and 1 percent related to anything else we do.

Most often the therapist is the one with the skills to help offer options to a client, to act as a guide through the forest at a time when there appears to be no path. Michael Yapko has told us that he believes that "the power of the future is that it has not happened yet, it's open to creating bigger and better things than have existed before. So the best thing that you can do to come to terms with a crummy past is to create a really great future out of it."

Some Personal Reflections

Jeffrey Kottler

Just as I have felt in our two previous collaborations, *Bad Therapy* (Kottler & Carlson, 2002) and *The Mummy at the Dining Room Table* (Kottler & Carlson, 2003), I feel so humbled when I talk to these prominent theoreticians. I am simply amazed not only by how articulate the contributors are about their work, but also how confident they feel in the frameworks they employ. Maybe that is because I am a flake—or, more generously, a chameleon, a pragmatist—but for me almost every session I teach or counsel or supervise seems like nothing I've done before.

I remember learning long ago that if ever we were to attain respectability in our profession, to be accepted *as scientists,* we were going to have to develop methods that were both valid and reliable. Consistency was taught to me as a key feature of great therapy. And indeed, many of the contributors selected sessions that were excellent precisely because they were the best representative of the ideas they hold most sacred.

I envy the contributors (and other practitioners) who have settled into a theoretical model they have developed (or adopted). Jon Carlson and I have had this discussion many times because of his passionate devotion to Adlerian ideas, which he can quote chapter and verse. But I am still very much a work in progress. Or, more critically, I am indeed a flake—easily influenced and altered by what I am exposed to next.

After each interview we conducted, I found myself thinking, "Yes! This is indeed the best way to do therapy. I want to be just like this when I finally grow up. These are *exactly* the principles and practices that are best used to do good work. It's time for me to make some changes in the ways I work with people."

There was one point while writing this book that I was feeling stuck with a client I was seeing. This was a man who was having a secret affair, which we worked to end so that he could devote himself more fully to his floundering marriage. I consulted with several of the contributors to this book and, perhaps not surprisingly, each one told me something different. In some cases, their guidance and advice was exactly the opposite of what the last expert had told me. I am used to this paradox in our field—that one's finest hour as a therapist can be conducted in some many (apparently) discrepant ways (my own belief is that we are really all doing the same things). But I still have such respect for the colleagues I consulted that I found myself (almost) on the verge of actually doing what they told me to do with this client. Just as the words formed in my mouth, I realized in a flash that this was not the sort of intervention I could do (or at least could apply with confidence and reasonable skill). It was then I realized that I was so hungry to trust others' opinions about the way things should work that I forgot to trust my own wisdom.

And so it was with each interview we conducted. I resolved almost each time the conversation ended that I was going to get more training in *that* particular approach, since clearly my own methods were sadly outdated. Of course, this commitment lasted just until the very next interview, when another distinguished contributor presented his or her own views about therapy (which, of course, directly contradicted what the previous one had said).

In some ways, I guess I am saying that I am more confused than ever about what good therapy is all about. For decades now I've been searching for, and writing about, what constitutes great therapy, regardless of theoretical allegiances or ideology. I watch someone like Jon Carlson work with a client by doing one thing, and Frank Pittman do something very different. Papp and Brown and Keeney appear to work in such radically varied ways that it gives me a headache. It just doesn't seem possible that we can help people by doing so many things that *appear* to be so different.

I picture going to see a doctor because I have pain in my abdomen. She tells me that that I have a ruptured appendix and that it needs to be removed immediately. Then I seek another consultation and this physician says it is only indigestion and prescribes some medication. A third doctor says it is actually deferred, radiating pain that is actually located in my lower back; he prescribes some exercises. And still a fourth doctor tells me the pain is all in my head and I should just forget about it. I know this sounds ridiculous, but that seems exactly what the experience of talking to these eminent scholars and practitioners every week has been like. Each time we are done, I shake my head and think: "*Now* what do I do?"

But of course, there is another version of this story. This process of doing a narrative analysis has helped immensely to sort out the complexity of what great therapy is all about. In fact, what all these great therapists do is not as different as we might imagine. They might use different concepts and language to describe their work. They might focus on different features of a case. They might have very different personalities, value systems, interpersonal styles, and favored beliefs. But they also do some things that are very, very similar and congruent.

So, what stands out most for me in this regard? Every single one of these theoreticians is filled with love. They feel intense love for the people who come to them for help (although many would never use that term). This goes way beyond mere empathy, or concern, or compassion—I really believe that what drives their work is the tremendous caring and love that they feel for other people. Second, almost all the contributors feel intense love for their work as practitioners. I find this most amazing of all, I suppose because I got so burned out doing clinical work myself. I came to dread session after session after session, and so had to stop my practice for a number of years. Yet professionals like Carlson or Pittman see forty, fifty, or more clients each week, have been doing this their whole professional lives, and report that they still love what they are doing (and I believe them!).

Another theme that stands out for me, related to the first one, is the power of relationship. I have been surprised again, just as I was in our previous books, about how many of our contributors value and cherish their relationships with clients. Even theorists who are known primarily for their rather specific techniques and interventions (Ellis, Lazarus, Glasser) talk about their relationships with clients as the key feature of their work. I guess I shouldn't be surprised by this at all, considering that it is so much a part of everything I know and understand about how change takes place, but still it was interesting and powerful to feel affirmed in my own beliefs that relationships are where the action takes place. Related to this awareness is also the surprising discovery that many of our contributors have moved far beyond the ideas they are most known for. This is what gives me the most hope and encouragement: maybe I'm not a flake after all—just a work in progress who is as changed by my clients and students as they are influenced by me.

Myf Maple

I am a social worker who has been out of active clinical practice for a number of years to concentrate on doing research in narrative analysis. I volunteered for this project because I enjoy the process of finding meaning in stories.

The first thing that I felt in going through the narratives (and the stories presented in the previous books) was relief. It was so good to know that even the most well-known therapists have moments of not knowing which way to turn! It was so refreshing to know that behind the textbooks and practice videos, there are such awkward moments.

I have a very strong memory of talking to a mother and daughter while working in an oncology unit. The mother had just had her voice box removed due to cancer caused by smoking. The daughter had paged me to come and see her mother, who had just been discovered smoking a cigarette through the hole in her throat. The tension in the room was incredible!

I was concerned that all-out warfare was imminent. I had no idea how to engage either the mother or the daughter, nor to make sense about how someone who is dying from cigarettes would actually and literally stick one in a hole in her throat. We had been working together for a number of weeks, yet all that previous work and relationship went out the window. I was floundering and scared. How on earth was I going to diffuse the anger, and try to reconnect with both mother and daughter so we could even begin a helpful discussion?

Then it came to me: the daughter and I had had many previous candid discussions about similar interests. So I launched into a chat about trekking in the mountains, a shared passion. Within 5 minutes or so of dreaming about faraway places, the daughter relaxed and I had found the place to start to discuss the much more sensitive reasons that I was there. I did not use any method or technique I had ever learned in my training, certainly not to avoid the one reason why I had been called to the scene in the first place. But it worked!

When I read Arnold Lazarus's chapter about how he used "nagging," it really hit home. Sometimes, good therapy has nothing to do with using a preferred theory, but rather is about making a connection in whatever way one can, even an unorthodox one. I know that Jeffrey Kottler mentioned something similar when he talked about his own surprise that the contributors are so much more innovative, flexible, and integrative than he ever imagined.

The second impact I felt from reading these stories is that they really made me miss doing therapy on a regular basis; I felt my passion renewed. For so long I have told myself that working at the next level, in research, where your work can affect many rather than one, is what I want to do. Yet reading the wide range of interesting cases in this book has made me rethink this. Having that personal connection with people, and knowing that you have had a positive impact on their lives, is unique to counseling individuals, couples, and families. After time out of practice, I had begun to wonder whether I would have the skills to reenter the field. This book has given me greater confidence and inspiration.

As I see it, one of the main messages that we all bring to this field is a deep caring for others. It is this quality that makes therapy work, regardless of one's theoretical orientation. Thus, my skills may be a bit rusty, but my caring is very much present when I return.

Jon Carlson

Of all the hundreds of hours of therapy I have read about, the hundreds of hours I have supervised, the hundreds I have viewed, and the thousands I have been involved with as the therapist, I found it both humbling and mind-boggling to think that we were so honored to collect the very best hours of the very best practitioners on this planet. I felt honored to be in their presence and to be able to receive these deeply personal accounts of their struggles in helping others. The emotion and excitement when we were listening to their insights, stories, and creativity was like it was when we were children waiting for the time to open our birthday or Christmas presents. I ponder, how did I manage to get into such a place? How is it that these icons of psychotherapy have been so honest and open with us? Many of the contributors are dear friends of mine with whom I have shared passionate discussions over beers or meals. I am just shocked by their trust. As one example, when John Gray and I finished his interview, I said that after the story has been written up it would be sent to him for final approval. He said "I trust you, Jon, don't worry about it." I know for my part I deeply appreciate and respect what they have done with their careers and hope that others realize their contributions. In general, I am looking for what they have to offer, not what I can critique. These people did not reach their places of status by luck or trickery but have genuine gifts.

As each interview approached I tried to imagine what good therapy might be like for each of the experts. I have read their work, witnessed their sessions in action, and studied their theories. I thought I knew and understood their ideas better than most; after decades of teaching and writing about their theories, as well as producing their demonstration videos, I figured I had a clear handle on their core beliefs and practices. I expected few surprises.

I was quite shocked to discover the extent of the contributors' differences, even in defining what good and bad therapy are all about. Some were very scientific, while others thought therapy was good because of the miraculous change in the client. Some thought it was good because it was brief, while others were struck by their own changes, others with the client's resilience, and several by the longstanding impact of their involvement without any follow-up. Yet almost everyone decided that the outcome was indeed critical—if the client does not get better, or feel better, or behave better, then the treatment was not very useful.

That is not to say that process is not as important as outcome, because I believe it is. I was pleasantly surprised to see that the experts' cases seemed to be consistent with the latest research findings (Lambert, 2003). Trauma and client resilience seemed a common theme. The therapists were able to help the clients to understand and accept that they possessed the resources that could change their lives. This seems to fit recent psychotherapy outcome research, which indicates that the client's resources are accountable for 40 percent of all change. The therapist's validation and acceptance of the clients created strong relationship bonds that often lasted over years. This is consistent with research that indicated that 30 percent of all change is attributed to the relationship. Most of the therapists talked with confidence and were able to instill hope in their clients, which according to research accounts for 15 percent of change. Finally, many innovative strategies and techniques were used by the experts. The range of strategies and techniques was great—anywhere from saying nothing to telling someone what to do. Techniques and strategies account for 15 percent of change in psychotherapy. Although the collection of finest hours was varied, they seem to match these recent research findings. The single common factor that stood out to me (as well as to Jeffrey Kottler) was that each expert loves people. They value the human experience and were able to find hope and possibility for the hopeless and impossible. They were able to create relationships of safety in which clients could take risks and become like the *Man of La Mancha* and "dream the impossible dream." It really stood out to me that the contributors felt that people mattered to them much more than things or even ideas. They consistently supported and attended to their clients, and less so to the facts or presenting (often overwhelming) problems. They saw their roles as freeing the client to become what the client wanted to be and not trying to be gods or goddesses to shape others' futures.

I was very impressed by the humility of most of the experts, and this did not strike me at all as false modesty. Rather than dwelling on what magicians they might be, most expressed some regret that they could not have done more.

As I listened to each case I was able to grow and learn something more about people and treatment. I became much more confident in my own work with clients. I was less interested in doing therapy "correctly" and more interested in helping. I did not have to be perfect or do it by the book. Instead of following the book, or any given template, I needed to be myself, show compassion and caring for the client, enjoy the relationship, see my clients' assets, and use my intuition. Therapy has become more fun for me and I think for my clients.

I guess what I am saying is that doing this project has been just like the practice of therapy. Although we were not able to find the one right, best, or good way to do therapy, we have highlighted some of the many paths possible to reach desirable outcomes. How or when that shining hour comes is still a mystery, and perhaps that is the way it should be.

I was very surprised when I chose as my own finest hour a woman and family that I still see every week. I was additionally surprised when I realized how many years I have spent working with them without financial compensation or material reward. I hear of others who have these life-long cases, but usually it is to pay for the addition on their home or their children's college tuition. I was also surprised that my choice may have showcased my ineptitude more than a shining therapeutic masterpiece. I guess I relearned that the real changes that therapists look for and prize seem to be the ones that rest more in our souls and the new levels of compassion that our clients help us to develop.

In closing, what we would like to say to you, the reader, whether you are a therapist, a helper or healer, a student of the field, or an interested observer of the profession, is that we hope your finest hours are yet to come. We hope you have shared our exhilaration and fascination with all the ways it is possible to do good *for* others, and *with* others.

REFERENCES

Charmaz, K. (2000). Grounded theory: Objectivist and constructivist methods. In N. Denzin & Y. Lincoln (Eds.), *Handbook of qualitative research* (2nd ed.). Thousand Oaks, CA: Sage.

Clandinin, D. J., & Connelly, F. M. (2000). *Narrative inquiry: Experience and story in qualitative research*. San Francisco: Jossey-Bass.

Connelly, F. M., & Clandinin, D. J. (1990). Stories of experience and narrative inquiry. *Educational Researcher, 19*(5), 2–14.

Creswell, J. W. (2002). *Educational research.* Upper Saddle River, NJ: Prentice-Hall.

Gilbert, K. (2002). Taking a narrative approach to grief research: Finding meaning in stories. *Death Studies 26*(3), 223–239.

Kottler, J. A. (2004). *On being a therapist* (3rd ed.). San Francisco: Jossey-Bass.

Kottler, J. A., & Blau, D. S. (1989). *The imperfect therapist: Learning from failure in psychotherapy.* San Francisco: Jossey-Bass.

Kottler, J. A., & Carlson, J. (2002). *Bad therapy: Master therapists share their worst failures.* New York: Brunner Routledge.

Kottler, J. A., & Carlson, J. (2003). *The mummy at the dining room table: Eminent therapists share their most unusual cases and what they teach us about human behavior.* San Francisco: Jossey-Bass.

Lambert, M. J. (2003). Psychotherapy outcome research: Implications for integrative and eclectic therapists. In J. C. Norcross & M. R. Goldfried (Eds.), *Handbook of psychotherapy integration.* New York: Oxford University Press.